ESG Investing

for dummies®

A Wiley Brand

ESG Investing

by Brendan Bradley

A Wiley Brand

ESG Investing For Dummies®

Published by: **John Wiley & Sons, Inc.,** 111 River Street, Hoboken, NJ 07030-5774, www.wiley.com

Copyright © 2021 by John Wiley & Sons, Inc., Hoboken, New Jersey

Published simultaneously in Canada

For general information on our other products and services, please contact our Customer Care Department within the U.S. at 877-762-2974, outside the U.S. at 317-572-3993, or fax 317-572-4002. For technical support, please visit https://hub.wiley.com/community/support/dummies.

Wiley publishes in a variety of print and electronic formats and by print-on-demand. Some material included with standard print versions of this book may not be included in e-books or in print-on-demand. If this book refers to media such as a CD or DVD that is not included in the version you purchased, you may download this material at http://booksupport.wiley.com. For more information about Wiley products, visit www.wiley.com.

Library of Congress Control Number: 2021931609

ISBN 978-1-119-77109-8 (pbk); ISBN 978-1-119-77110-4 (ebk); ISBN 978-1-119-77111-1 (ebk);

Manufactured in the United States of America

SKY10025036_021721

Contents at a Glance

Table of Contents

Introduction

Welcome to the ESG community! Thanks for picking up this book, in which I explain the ins and outs of ESG investing. As you may know, ESG stands for environmental, social, and governance, and perhaps the reason for your interest is the growing evidence that ESG factors can be integrated into investment analysis and portfolio construction to offer investors long-term performance advantages. Also, ESG criteria are used by socially conscious investors to screen investments and assess a company's impact on the world. You want to know that the companies you're investing in are "doing the right thing" or "doing no harm" as well as producing a positive return on investment.

With growing action from governments, companies, and investors to consider environmental and societal impacts, it seems inevitable that ESG considerations will be included in all of our investment decisions at some point in the future. Given that companies with high ESG ratings exhibit a lower cost of capital, less volatile earnings, and lower market risk than companies with low ESG ratings, sustainability should be our new standard for investing. Furthermore, all collective investment funds may be compelled to consider ESG criteria in their investments, alongside traditional financial factors.

However, be aware that there are many challenges to surmount before you reach the "promised land." There is still a lack of common sustainability criteria, standardization of disclosure requirements, and therefore ESG ratings that can be questioned from a multitude of different rating providers. In short, the available data and the methodology behind ESG criteria for investment products is still opaque, and investors should carefully monitor what's "under the hood" and not be victims of "greenwashing."

About This Book

In writing this book, my primary aim is to educate potential ESG investors about the opportunities, but not to forget the potential risks. Many ESG-related books have been written, but the landscape has changed so much in just the last year that I felt there was a need to update investors, and also to be wary of the hype and not get caught up in the fear of missing out. So I focus in certain chapters on the developments around improvements in disclosure, leading to better data quality and more informed ratings of given companies, which in turn leads to better investment products. While the asset management industry is focused on voluntarily reaching these goals, given the "wall of investment" flowing into this space, there will also be increasing regulatory requirements to mandate behavior.

The idea here is to provide a pragmatic look at the most important aspects of ESG investing and highlight that this approach to responsible investment can help companies provide strong returns while helping to make the world a better place.

A quick note: Sidebars (shaded boxes of text) dig into the details of a given topic, but they aren't crucial to understanding it. Feel free to read them or skip them. You can also pass over the text accompanied by the Technical Stuff icon. The text accompanied by this icon offers some interesting but non-essential information about ESG investing.

One last thing: Within this book, you may note that some web addresses break across two lines of text. If you're reading this book in print and want to visit one of these web pages, simply type in the web address exactly as it appears in the text, pretending the line break doesn't exist. If you're reading this as an e-book, you've got it easy — just click the web address to go directly to the web page.

Foolish Assumptions

I wrote this book so that all investors can understand it, but I assumed a specific type of audience. I considered the following readers:

>> Financial service professionals who want to educate themselves about ESG and sustainability, instead of bluffing their way through

>> Active investors who are considering increasing their asset allocation toward ESG criteria

>> Asset owners who are relatively new to the concept and need to understand the nuances

>> Company executives who recognize the need to "up their game" to improve their ESG score and ensure that their company is deemed suitable for ESG indexes and portfolios

>> Professional service providers, such as accountants, consultants, and lawyers, who are trying to define their places in the ESG ecosystem

>> Regulators, politicians, and other industry participants who are charged with safeguarding the investment community

The general assumption is that you'll have some experience with and understanding of traditional investment, but you can build your ESG understanding as you progress through this book or dive into certain chapters that are more specific to your role or interest.

Icons Used in This Book

Like all *For Dummies* books, this book features icons to help you navigate the information. Here's what they mean.

This icon highlights especially helpful advice about getting started with ESG investing.

If you take away anything from this book, it should be the information marked with this icon.

This icon points out situations and actions to avoid in the world of ESG investing.

This icon flags information that delves a little deeper than usual into a particular ESG investing topic.

Beyond the Book

In addition to what you're reading right now, this book also comes with a free access-anywhere Cheat Sheet that provides a mini-glossary of important ESG terms and an overview of the key topics that are driving ESG investing. To get this Cheat Sheet, simply go to www.dummies.com and search for "ESG Investing For Dummies Cheat Sheet" in the Search box.

Where to Go from Here

You don't have to read this book in strict chapter-driven order. Each chapter is self-contained, so you can jump around as much as you like. Flip to the table of contents and the index if you're looking for a specific topic. If you want to find out more about ESG and keep up to date on the latest developments, you should check out the following objective websites:

>> **Principles for Responsible Investment:** www.unpri.org/sustainability-issues

>> **United Nation Sustainable Development Goals:** www.un.org/sustainabledevelopment/sustainable-development-goals/

>> **Sustainability Accounting Standards Board:** www.sasb.org/standards-overview/materiality-map/

>> **Global Reporting Initiative:** www.globalreporting.org/how-to-use-the-gri-standards/

>> **Task Force on Climate-related Financial Disclosures:** www.fsb-tcfd.org/about/

>> **ESG Clarity:** www.esgclarity.com/

1

Getting to Know ESG

Discover how ESG investing isn't to be confused with socially responsible, ethical, or impact investing.

Understand what has driven the evolution and major growth in ESG investing in recent years.

Run through the reasons why ESG is important, what the criteria for ESG ratings and metrics are, and what a company needs to do to enhance its ESG score.

Investigate the key material indicators and risks for each aspect of ESG: environmental, social, and governance.

Identify concerns around "greenwashing," given the surge in ESG investments.

Chapter **1**

Entering the World of ESG Investing

The acronym ESG has undoubtedly become one of the hottest topics in investment management in recent years. Google searches for the term "ESG investing" have grown exponentially in the last three years, so it's certainly caught people's attention! (Don't believe me? Just look at Figure 1-1.) As a result, executive management has a range of new stewardship topics to contend with, now that global warming issues have created 'E'nvironmental concerns, and the COVID-19 pandemic has further highlighted 'S'ocial issues. (Corporate 'G'overnance issues have always been closely monitored by the investment community.)

But what's all the fuss about? Is ESG investing a passing fad or a long-term trend that will dominate investment management for the foreseeable future? This chapter looks at the fundamentals behind ESG investing, highlights some of the key drivers behind it, and identifies some of the goals and standards that have been established.

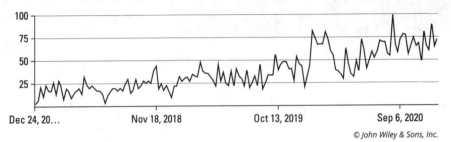

FIGURE 1-1: Google Trends chart — a search for "ESG Investing" over the last three years.

Surveying the Current ESG Landscape

Broadly defined as the analysis of a company's environmental, social, and governance practices, ESG first grabbed the financial world's attention following a 2005 United Nations Global Compact report, which claimed that incorporating ESG factors into capital markets would make it possible to "do well by doing good." Since then, the significance of ESG issues has experienced a meteoric rise. The Principles for Responsible Investment (PRI) network of investors, which was introduced in 2006, has grown from 63 asset manager and owner signatories with US$6.5 trillion in assets under management to more than 3,000 signatories with over US$103 trillion in assets under management. Driven by increased stakeholder attention to corporate environmental impacts and investors realizing that strong ESG performance can safeguard a company's success, ESG is no longer a niche investment concept.

REMEMBER

As the world is changing, there is a greater requirement to understand what risks or opportunities a company faces from ESG issues that may determine its long-term prospects. The COVID-19 pandemic has highlighted the need to consider these factors even further, hence the recent surge in investments in this space. Even within this century, the context in which businesses operate has changed radically. Businesses have generally profited from economic growth, globalization, increased consumption, and fossil fuels, and have strengthened and developed their role as the major providers of goods, jobs, and infrastructure worldwide. Consequently, their contribution to essential sustainability issues, such as climate change, biodiversity, social diversity, and inclusion, has also grown. Concurrently, the rise of technology has allowed stakeholders, as well as shareholders, to challenge businesses on how they behave.

Consequently, transparent measurement and disclosure of sustainability performance is now deemed to be an essential part of effective business practices, and a necessity for maintaining trust in business as a force for good. Corporate reporting is a means by which stakeholders, including investors, can identify and measure companies' performance, just as companies themselves use reporting internally to inform decision-making. Financial reporting has developed as a result of internationally recognized accounting standards that bring transparency, accountability, and competence to financial markets around the world. Therefore, while sustainability disclosure is inevitably more complex than financial reporting, internationally recognized sustainability standards will be the basis for calculating relevant ESG ratings.

Exploring What ESG Is (and Isn't)

In recent years, the term "ESG" has generally become synonymous with socially responsible investment. However, ESG should be seen as more of a risk management framework for evaluating companies and not as a stand-alone investment strategy. ESG measures the sustainability and societal impact of an investment in a company. These criteria help better determine the future financial performance of companies. Likewise, impact investing is more about the type of investments a manager is targeting, while ESG factors are part of an assessment process to apply non-financial factors to a manager's analysis in identifying material risks and growth opportunities. Also, impact investing seeks to make a measurable, positive, environmental, or social effect with the investments that a fund manager purchases, whereas ESG is a "means to an end," serving to identify non-financial risks that may have a material impact on an asset's value.

Moreover, ESG is often incorrectly commingled with terms such as *corporate sustainability* and *corporate social responsibility* (CSR). While some overlap exists, these terms aren't interchangeable:

>> *Corporate sustainability* is an umbrella term used to describe the long-term creation of stakeholder value by encompassing opportunities and managing risks resulting from economic, environmental, and social developments. To many companies, corporate sustainability is about "doing good" and doesn't require any set conditions.

>> *Corporate social responsibility* is an embedded management concept where companies incorporate the concerns of key stakeholders into their operations and activities. In comparison, ESG assesses a company's ESG practices, together with more traditional financial measures.

Finally, ESG is also commonly intermingled with ethical investing. However, taking an ESG approach is effectively a precursor to the point of investing. It provides a framework that allows you to consider 'E,' 'S,' and 'G' issues facing a company and to score them either individually or collectively to identify where they sit relative to each other. This leads investors to consider stocks that may be "best-in-class" from an ESG score perspective or exclude them entirely because, for example, their environmental score doesn't reflect their values. Ethical investing involves selecting investments based on ethical or moral principles. Such investors typically avoid "sin stocks," such as those related to gambling, alcohol, or firearms, which can be implemented via an ESG exclusions strategy (where sin stocks are explicitly excluded from a portfolio).

TIP

You may be used to gauging financial ratios when investing in stocks, from the relative price-to-earnings (P/E) ratio to EBITDA margins. (Yes, I'm talking about earnings before interest, taxes, depreciation, and amortization — good thing there's an acronym to use.) All of those ratios are still relevant, but now you can view the same stocks through an additional lens. The sustainability evaluation of ratings firms is normally blended into a single ESG score, similar to the stock recommendations offered by investment banks and brokers. Just as mainstream research analysts calculate different recommendation valuations for the same companies, using largely the same information, so ESG analysts also differ on their recommended scores. Check out Chapter 2 for an introduction to ESG ratings.

The following sections look at the different components of ESG, including financially material indicators, how those indicators can differ according to industry sector, and how various ESG strategies can be applied across these factors. These elements can be analyzed in the *ESG Cube*, which represents the intersections between these factors.

Defining the breadth of ESG

Unlike common financial ratios, there aren't a common set of ratios that neatly define what a good 'E,' 'S,' or 'G' score looks like. And whether you should aggregate the three siblings together or you should consider each one individually depends on your determination of what issues you believe are most relevant from an ESG perspective. Indeed, some of the factors may be more material to some stocks than others. For example, the environmental risks associated with a bank will be less material than those facing a mining company, while such risks may be counterbalanced by more concerns over governance with a bank. Also, to what degree should you be concerned, and what data or methodology will you use to gauge that concern? As you can see, ESG analysis brings an entirely new set of indicators that you need to consider, which can result in a complex analysis that isn't reasonable for a layperson to calculate.

Of course, investment managers are offering to take all of that hassle away from you and present you with products that incorporate the myriad of factors in different ways. And as the investment world has moved toward passive investment, a number of these products will be index driven. To ensure that you're familiar with these new products, and that they closely track the performance of established benchmarks, many of the new products will be ESG variations of traditional indexes, such as the S&P 500 or FTSE 100 indexes. So, they represent what you "know and love" with just a few exclusions here, some different weightings there, or a bias or tilt toward or away from given stocks. This should be easy for most investors to comprehend.

Then there is the version for sophisticated investors, including large asset owners such as pension funds and family offices, where that approach won't pass the "smell test" given the level of fees they are paying for investment management. They expect a much more active management approach, with full consideration of the complex interdependencies that can be analyzed in this process. One way to visualize the approach that an asset manager could take is to consider a matrix, or a three-dimensional cube. An asset owner considers at least three dimensions to be important:

>> What are the key industry sectors that exhibit the greatest ESG risks or opportunities?

>> Which ESG execution strategy approach should you employ to benefit from this data?

>> What are the material ESG components that affect a company's financial performance?

Welcome to the concept of the *ESG Cube*, which represents the intersections between these factors. Figure 1-2 illustrates the cube, using three axes: Industry Sectors on the X-axis, ESG Strategies on the Y-axis, and Material Indicators on the Z-axis.

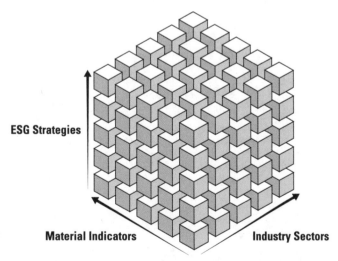

FIGURE 1-2:
ESG Cube with intersections between factors.

© John Wiley & Sons, Inc.

Each of these dimensions can be further categorized, as you find out in the following sections.

Industry sectors

Figure 1-3 expands on the concept by adding the industry sectors utilized in the Sustainability Accounting Standards Board (SASB) Materiality Map:

» Healthcare

» Financials

» Technology and communications

» Non-renewable resources

» Transportation

» Services

» Resource transformation

» Consumption

» Renewable resources and alternative energy

» Infrastructure

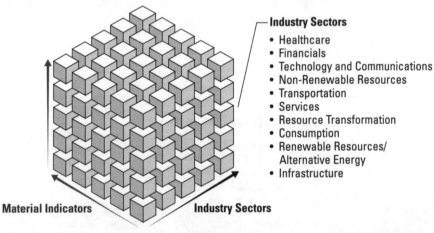

FIGURE 1-3:
Industry sectors per the SASB's Materiality Map.

Material Indicators   **Industry Sectors**

Industry Sectors
- Healthcare
- Financials
- Technology and Communications
- Non-Renewable Resources
- Transportation
- Services
- Resource Transformation
- Consumption
- Renewable Resources/ Alternative Energy
- Infrastructure

© John Wiley & Sons, Inc.

ESG strategies

The most common ESG integration strategies that asset managers tend to employ on behalf of their clients are outlined in Figure 1-4:

- **» Screening:** Excluding or including stocks based on exposure to certain factors

- **» Best-in-class:** Selecting stocks based on high ESG scores

- **» Stock rating:** Using an ESG performance rating system

- **» Value integration:** Integrating ESG issues into stock valuations

- **» Thematic:** Focusing portfolios on certain themes

- **» Engagement:** Maintaining an ongoing dialogue on ESG issues

- **» Alignment:** Affiliating with social or environmental goals

- **» Activism:** Using voting capacity to engage companies

- **» Systematic:** Employing quantitative or data-driven factors

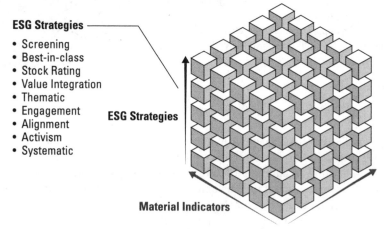

ESG Strategies
- Screening
- Best-in-class
- Stock Rating
- Value Integration
- Thematic
- Engagement
- Alignment
- Activism
- Systematic

ESG Strategies

Material Indicators

© John Wiley & Sons, Inc.

FIGURE 1-4: Popular ESG investment strategies.

Material indicators

Figure 1-5 shows the details of the cube's third dimension, where the SASB has identified, per industry sector, the likely financially material ESG issues. These are just indicators, and investors can choose their own material issues that are relevant to their values. They are as follows:

- **» Environment:** Greenhouse gas emissions and biodiversity impacts

- **» Social capital:** Human rights/community relations and data security and privacy

- **» Human capital:** Diversity/inclusion and fair labor practices

>> **Business model and innovation:** Life cycle impacts of products and product packaging

>> **Leadership and governance:** Supply chain management and accident/safety management

Material Indicators

- GHG Emissions
- Biodiversity Impacts
- Human Rights/ Community Relations
- Data Security/Privacy
- Diversity/Inclusion
- Fair Labor Practices
- Life cycle Impacts of Products
- Product Packaging
- Supply Chain Management
- Accident/Safety Management

ESG Strategies

Material Indicators

FIGURE 1-5: Material indicators per the SASB's Materiality Map.

REMEMBER

ESG strategies, applicable by type of client or sustainability preference, can be visualized relative to given industry sectors. For example, you might have a client seeking an alignment strategy (ESG Strategies on the Y-axis), focused on a social or environmental goals solution (Material Indicators on the Z-axis) within the transportation sector (Industry Sectors on the X-axis). If specific companies from the transportation sector are overlaid on top of this approach, a Best-in-Class filter could also be applied to identify the right addition to a portfolio.

Comparing SRI, ethical, and impact investing to ESG

Having identified that strictly speaking, ESG isn't actually an investing style, but a consideration of relevant ESG issues to manage risk, it's worth considering how ESG ratings can be used in various sectors of the social investment arena. This starts with social investing as an umbrella term that assumes the provision of finance to achieve a combination of economic, social, and environmental goals. Some of the more specialized approaches are described here, with each one increasingly representing a more tangible approach to investment (see Chapter 7 for more details):

» Sustainable and Responsible Investing (SRI) uses relevant ESG criteria to choose companies for investment, typically based on a negative screening approach to exclude companies that produce or sell harmful substances, like tobacco, and those that engage in harmful activities, such as polluting or violating human rights. SRI doesn't necessarily include positive screening to include companies that engage in beneficial activities, such as using sustainable practices, or producing clean technologies. There are attempts to establish standards and indexes in areas like climate change and human rights to further facilitate such investments.

» In ethical investing, investments are selected or excluded according to the individual investors' personal beliefs and values. Similar to SRI, ethical investing may exclude investments in certain industries (such as firearms) and is connected with the movement to divest from fossil fuel companies. The key difference with SRI is that ethical investing tends to be more issue-based and produces a more personalized result, whereas SRI normally uses one all-encompassing set of parameters to select investments.

» Impact investing goes a step further by intentionally looking to produce both financial return and positive social or environmental impacts that are actively measured, so it's much harder to apply ESG factors. Impact investors attempt to generate specific, positive impacts using financial instruments, and then require the companies to report evidence that the impacts have really been produced. It's distinct from SRI in that it seeks positive impacts associated with areas such as renewable energy, sustainable agriculture, water management, and clean technology. Many of the independent companies or funds in such areas may not have specific ESG ratings. Moreover, measuring the actual social and environmental impact is difficult, and a standardized measurement system (the Impact Reporting and Investment Standards, or IRIS) has been developed to facilitate measurement and produce comparable impact performance data, rather than using ESG criteria. IRIS (https://iris.thegiin.org/about/) is a free, publicly available resource that is managed by the Global Impact Investing Network (GIIN) for measuring, managing, and optimizing impact.

REMEMBER

Socially responsible investments can be used to represent the political and social environment of the day. Therefore, it's important for investors to recognize that if a given social value falls out of favor, their investment may also suffer. Considering such investments through an ESG lens may guard against some of these issues. Similarly, investors should carefully read any fund prospectuses to ensure that the philosophies being employed are in line with their values.

REMEMBER

COVID-19 has helped illustrate the growing importance of social issues, many of which have been further exacerbated by the pandemic, while others that weren't already a priority have appeared on the radar. Some of these include occupational health and safety, responsible purchasing practices, supply chain issues, and digital rights, including privacy. Looking beyond the pandemic, further social issues that have been highlighted include human rights, mental health, and access to healthcare.

Determining whether ESG delivers good investment performance

ESG integration is consistent with a manager's fiduciary duty to take into account all relevant information and material risks. It should be remembered that ESG integration isn't just a negative screen in the investment process that limits one's investment universe. Therefore, because it includes a more thorough application of traditional financial analysis, it isn't constrained by reduced diversification and can include companies with poor ESG ratings if they are believed to be "mending their ways."

Along these lines, nearly all large institutional investors are using ESG data in some capacity. More specifically, the PRI members have pledged to incorporate ESG issues into investment decision-making processes. For example, BlackRock, the world's largest asset manager, has announced that sustainability, including a company's ESG performance, will be BlackRock's new standard for investing. In addition, one of the key reasons that firms undertake ESG analysis is to assess risk. However, such ESG analysis is also a way of uncovering investing opportunities by spotting companies that are improving their 'E,' 'S,' or 'G' profiles before the broader market does.

REMEMBER

So, although the ESG trend was well underway before the COVID-19 crisis in 2020, it has served as the first main confirmation that ESG-informed investing doesn't come at a cost to performance and can be a guide to future-proof investments while boosting returns. This has proven the resilience of ESG investing and provided a significant boost to sustainability while the world is establishing how to "build back better." Nevertheless, some investors rightly highlight the concept of "ESG momentum," produced by the sheer weight of money that has flown into "good" companies that are expected to become the champions of the future. Performance data can be inconsistent and period-dependent, but there is also evidence that over the long term, ESG has outperformed relative to the broader market.

WARNING

On the other hand, some investors question whether ESG stocks exhibit true alpha and contend that the stock market returns from technology stocks in recent times have fueled ESG performance, given that the typical ESG mutual fund has at least 20 percent of its assets in technology stocks. If the technology bubble bursts (perhaps due to anti-trust enforcement), and as investors move toward value stocks (which should be ESG-friendly as well!) and away from growth stocks, where will the alpha or additional performance for ESG strategies come from? Just be aware of the potential for a speculative bubble in ESG investing.

Understanding ESG's Impact on the Environment, Society, and Governance

Having left 2020 behind us, with most of us feeling bruised and battered, the poster child continues to be climate change in the environmental corner, but COVID-19 will stay front and center in the social corner for longer than some people think. Meanwhile, heading into 2021 with a questionable Brexit deal for some and the continuing pandemic fallout, supply chain management is holding its own in the middle of the ring for governance (or rather, stewardship). The requirement to make sense of ESG has never been greater; the following sections can help.

Meeting environmental and global warming targets

Many challenges face the environment, but the clear focus is on climate change and the move toward net-zero emissions by 2050. This means that all man-made greenhouse gas (GHG) emissions must decline dramatically (need for decarbonization), and what we can't stop emitting needs to be removed from the atmosphere through reduction measures. Thus, reducing the Earth's net climate balance to zero and stabilizing global temperatures is a key goal. While there is an increasing focus on issues such as biodiversity and water management, from an investment point of view, the performance of the energy sector has been relatively poor in recent years, and the COVID-19 pandemic has exacerbated that trend due to lower GDP-related demand and investors continuing to exclude fossil fuel stocks from their portfolios.

While there was an expectation that the pandemic might divert focus away from climate change targets, it seems to have accelerated structural changes in the energy sector, which will present opportunities for policy reform and renewable energy. Meanwhile, new players will participate in the transition to the low-carbon economy because there is now a greater awareness of the risks and opportunities linked to proactively addressing climate issues. Starting in January 2021, with a supportive Democratic government in place in the United States continuing to back a major green deal in Europe to help fund the energy transition, and the COP26 (United Nations Climate Change Conference) taking place in Britain in 2021, the fight against global warming seems to be heating up!

Therefore, on one hand, you have the largest asset manager in the world, Black-Rock's CEO Larry Fink, releasing a statement to other CEOs emphasizing that climate risk is investment risk, and there is a need for consistent and comparable data. On the other hand, there is expectation for a surge in clean energy policies and investment, putting the energy system on track to achieve the sustainable energy objectives in full, including those established in the Paris Agreement. However, the global energy companies' transition to renewable energy will require a major investment of time and money, so monitoring their ESG credentials in the interim period is necessary. See Chapter 3 for more information on the environmental factor in ESG.

Providing solutions to social challenges

The global COVID-19 pandemic has shone a spotlight on the social aspects of ESG, with social issues rising from third place to first in the list of investors' ESG priorities in 2020. While the pandemic has obliged some companies to temporarily deprioritize ESG efforts, investors still believe a strong ESG strategy has a positive impact on share price and flexibility. The additional impact of social movements, such as Black Lives Matter and Me Too, has compelled executive boards to incorporate social risks front and center within new standards for corporate governance structures. Human rights, community relations, customer welfare, and employee health, safety, and well-being have all been moved up the prioritization line.

Furthermore, in addition to boardroom diversity, the attention of companies and investors will move toward diversity across companies, from executive management to the overall workforce. Policies on equal pay, equal opportunity, and corporate culture will also come under closer inspection as the idea of corporate social responsibility morphs into the new concept of corporate purpose, with greater emphasis on all stakeholders as well as shareholders.

WARNING

However, while disclosures on ESG factors are becoming more standardized and widespread in general, social aspects are still seen as the most difficult element to analyze and integrate from an ESG perspective. Chapter 4 introduces you to the social factor of ESG.

Meeting corporate governance requirements

While corporate governance practices have always been a key valuation factor for companies, for fixed income as much as equities, governance has also received a lot of attention during the COVID-19 pandemic — not only for how corporate boards are ensuring the health and safety of their employees and business partners, but also their wider reach into their supply chain management and how they are coping. At a time when their employees may be on government-supported job retention schemes, attention is also being paid to how management is playing its part in executive compensation plans.

The old days of shareholder resolutions serving as an appliance to identify and inspect governance issues — leading to reform in company practices and the acceptance of standards (for example, annual director elections, board gender diversity, and so on) — have changed to a more proactive stance, where asset managers are more engaged and lead policy initiatives and change within some organizations. This greater engagement has led to joint approaches on corporate access, from analysts on the ESG team to traditional financial analysts. Proposals for enhanced ESG disclosures from companies in their sustainability reports will also allow asset managers and owners to further incorporate ESG risk assessments into their investment decisions.

Investors are also pushing for executive pay to be tied to ESG initiatives, so that boards will be compelled to achieve social and other key targets, rather than paying "lip service" to ESG integration. Already, it's clear that governance is much more about stewardship (see Chapter 18), assuming a given level of accountability as well as responsibility to generate sustainable benefits, rather than hiding behind the preordained rules that have been handed down through the organization. Some would argue that ESG could be transformed into ESS (Environment, Social, and Stewardship) to recognize the role of stewardship in this process. Regardless, there should be a seamless link between stewardship and wider ESG integration, with investors systematically assessing companies based on ESG risks.

Flip to Chapter 5 for the full scoop on the governance factor in ESG.

Using International Standards to Determine ESG Objectives

The global regulatory ecosystem is moving fast, with many countries upholding ESG requirements in regulations. A recent study suggests that in the last decade, governments have enacted over 500 new measures globally to advocate ESG issues. Numerous market participants feel that regulatory developments are a key driver in the uptake of ESG investing. While many voluntary disclosure bodies have contributed to an increase in the availability of ESG data by pushing for greater disclosure and creating frameworks and standards, and therefore the success of the ESG explosion in recent years, the sense is that we're at the point where we need further mandatory disclosure requirements.

However, a group of five sustainability standard-setters has declared their own intent to collaborate better, appearing to accept the complaints of "reporting overload" with the "competing initiatives" concerns. It was felt that the plethora of entities was holding up progress and encouraging jurisdictional fragmentation.

However, this statement of intent comes at a time when the European Union (EU) has set in motion a large-scale legislative program to make ESG concerns a central piece of regulation in the financial services industry, which will further increase disclosure requirements. Ultimately, the market should put a common, standardized disclosure mechanism in place, whereby material reporting will be unearthed that provides more informed input to the ESG rating models, which should lead to greater consistency on ESG scores.

WARNING

Although companies report a lot more sustainability information than in the past, much of the disclosure is aimed at a broader set of stakeholders, which limits its usefulness to investors. They are more interested in a subset of sustainability issues representing key business drivers for value creation, such as the industry-specific factors identified by the Sustainability Accounting Standards Board (SASB). Corporate sustainability reporting has generally lacked an investor focus, encouraging companies to primarily report information on broader ESG factors, which affects the ratings that data providers have been able to produce. The majority of ESG risks that investors want to see are more industry-specific factors.

The following sections emphasize the increasing shift to regulatory oversight on sustainability as well as the roles played and foresight shown by the United Nations and the disclosure reporting standard-setters in building the agenda that has contributed to the success of ESG.

Leading the charge: European legislation on ESG

In Europe, the EU Commission has introduced new disclosure requirements related to sustainable investments. The Sustainable Finance Disclosure Regulation (SFDR) requires all financial market participants in the EU to disclose on ESG issues, with additional requirements for products that promote ESG characteristics or that have sustainable investment objectives. This regulation aims to limit the risk of greenwashing by financial market participants while increasing transparency, which allows investors to better understand how ESG and sustainability influence their investments.

Parallel to this, the EU Commission has also introduced the Taxonomy Regulation, which establishes an EU-wide taxonomy (akin to a dictionary) of economic activities that can be viewed as environmentally sustainable, using reference to six environmental objectives. This will enable investors and clients to identify environmentally sustainable investments, while bringing greater clarity for asset managers.

The regulation was implemented around three pillars: the elimination of greenwashing (see Chapter 6), regulatory neutrality, and a level playing field for all investors. Added to this, the EU Commission has agreed to introduce new standards on climate change through the launch of two climate benchmarks: the EU Climate Transition benchmark and the EU Paris-aligned benchmark. The regulatory environment is clearly driving institutional investors toward a substantial change in ESG practices, but that might help them get ahead of regulation or mandatory reporting in other jurisdictions.

Ahead of its time: The United Nations

REMEMBER

Going back to much earlier days, one has to applaud the foresight of the United Nations and their influence on the development of sustainable investing in this century. In all, the United Nations have provided a significant contribution to supporting investors' drive to sustainable impact:

>> Starting early in the century, the formation of the United Nations Global Compact is a non-binding pact to encourage businesses worldwide to adopt sustainable and socially responsible policies and report on their implementation. See www.unglobalcompact.org/.

>> The Principles for Responsible Investment (PRI) initiative then corralled together a network of international investors to work to put the six principles into practice. The principles were developed by the investment community and signaled the view that ESG issues affect the performance of investment portfolios and therefore should be given suitable consideration by investors in order to fulfill their fiduciary duty. This allows investors to incorporate ESG issues into their decision-making and ownership practices and so better align their objectives with those of society at large. See www.unpri.org/.

>> The Sustainable Development Goals (SDGs) came next, in 2015. The SDGs have enabled institutional investors to transition from a "cause no harm" investment approach to one that focuses on driving long-term value through investments that support long-term development impact. Some investors feel that the ESG framework offers less direction for investors than the SDGs, given the standardization and language for areas of impact, which offer more opportunity for investors to track and compare progress. See https://sdgs.un.org/goals.

Staying focused: The Sustainability Accounting Standards Board

The main standard-setter that has focused on helping businesses identify, manage, and report on the sustainability topics that are financially material to their investors is the Sustainability Accounting Standards Board (SASB). Their reporting standards also differ by industry, which enables investors and companies to compare company performance within an industry. Moreover, they are discussing with the International Financial Reporting Standards (IFRS) Foundation and merging with the International Integrated Reporting Council (IIRC) to form the Value Reporting Foundation (VRF) to focus on the global alignment of a corporate reporting system (see Chapter 15).

Given the IFRS Foundation's credibility related to financial reporting, that can only add weight to establishing further validity around sustainability disclosure standards for capital markets. The IFRS, in conjunction with the SASB, the CDP, the Climate Disclosure Standards Board (CDSB), the Global Reporting Initiative (GRI; see the next section), and the IIRC, should be able to provide a disclosure standard/framework that enables companies to disclose information that is useful to investors and other stakeholders. In turn this will further enhance the core data that the rating agencies need to develop their ESG scores.

Visit www.sasb.org/ for more information.

Building a framework: The Global Reporting Initiative

The Global Reporting Initiative (GRI) is one of the predominant independent standards organizations helping businesses and other organizations communicate their impacts on issues such as climate change, human rights, and corruption. As one of the first entities involved, they provide a framework that addresses broad social, environmental, and economic performance on how an organization is reporting to stakeholders, providing a guide to their approach to "proving" impact.

A key element for investors is their set of tools for integrating SDGs into sustainability reporting. Moreover, they are a key player in the collaboration between five sustainability, ESG, reporting framework, and standard-setting organizations that are attempting to create a more comprehensive corporate reporting platform. Given the IFRS Foundation's proposal to also work with these entities, this could level the playing field to help investors and businesses deliver long-term value that benefits not only capital market participants but the world in general. Again, this should provide more clarity to the information that ESG rating agencies require to provide material scores.

Check out www.globalreporting.org/ for more information.

Chapter **2**

Back to the Future: Understanding the Evolution and Growth of ESG Investing

The current hype around ESG (Environmental, Social, and Governance) investing would suggest that this is another overnight success story come true, as assets under management increase at pace. However, as with many overnight success stories, ESG investing was a slow burn for many years until the global awareness of ESG issues peaked in more recent times. This chapter follows the evolution from socially responsible investing to today's broader sustainable development goals, and it highlights some of the major factors influencing this investment progression, including the traits of an ESG company, the ratings and metrics associated with those traits, and the associated asset owner's ESG policy for investing in an ESG theme.

Studying the Evolution of Investing in ESG

According to the Global Impact Investing Network (GIIN), the number of asset managers offering ESG strategies has grown by more than 400 percent in the past 20 years. The initial surge of ESG investing during this period can be credited to a United Nations Global Compact report in 2005, which stated that integrating ESG into capital markets resulted in more sustainable markets as well as better outcomes for society. Governments and regulators are now demanding that companies consider the wider ESG implications of their business activities by introducing or strengthening stewardship codes. But what has been the full evolution of this approach and what catalysts have been important for its development? The following sections discuss the highlights in the history of ESG investing.

Investing through the ages: From SRI to ESG

Responsible investing has evolved from the original faith-based approach of avoiding "sin stocks" that profited from alcohol, gambling, and sex-related industries to today's broader view of how to integrate ESG components into the asset management mix. The incorporation of firms that promote positive environmental and societal traits within a solid corporate governance framework, while delivering comparable or better investment performance, is the growing mantra of the investment management industry.

The 20th century

The genesis of responsible investing was to promote the allocation of capital to firms that "did no harm." This developed into investing in companies that didn't profit from war or regimes with poor human rights records, until the focus on ESG principles that we know today emerged later in the century:

>> 1900s and before: Socially responsible investing (SRI) originated among religious groups over 100 years ago. Methodists and Quakers established faith-based investing guidelines for their followers, and other religious orders soon adopted similar investing guidelines for their brethren.

>> 1930s: The Great Depression produced numerous corporate scandals, so investors turned their attention to governance issues. Consequently, the 'S' in SRI was no longer the major focus, and a broader view of responsible investing was born.

>> 1960s: The rise of civil rights and anti-war demonstrations prompted investors to consider shareholder advocacy (to have their voices heard on issues that were important to them) when influencing corporate behavior. For example, Vietnam War protestors urged university endowment funds to exclude defense contractors in their investment policies.

>> 1980s: The Chernobyl nuclear power plant accident, Bhopal gas leak, and Exxon Valdez oil spill raised further concerns about corporate responsibility, and the related threats of climate change and ozone depletion.

>> 1987: The Brundtland Commission (Our Common Future) report recognized that human resource development in the form of poverty reduction, gender equity, and wealth redistribution was crucial to formulating strategies for environmental conservation. It introduced the most widely accepted definition of "sustainable development" — that is, "development which meets the needs of current generations without compromising the ability of future generations to meet their own needs."

>> 1992: The United Nations' Earth Summit, which took place in Rio de Janeiro, marked the largest environmental conference ever held, with 172 governments in attendance. The Summit's message — "nothing less than a transformation of our attitudes and behavior would bring about the necessary changes to preserve the planet" — was transmitted around the world. Also, the United Nations Framework Convention on Climate Change (UNFCCC) and the UN Convention on Biodiversity were both signed.

>> 1993: Investors began to exert pressure on fund managers to avoid investing in South African companies due to that country's apartheid policy.

>> 1997: The Global Reporting Initiative (GRI; see Chapters 1 and 15) was founded, with the aim to create the first accountability mechanism ensuring that companies adhere to responsible environmental conduct principles. This was later broadened to include social, economic, and governance issues.

The 21st century

With the arrival of the 21st century, the world's focus on responsible investing has fully incorporated issues around global warming, diversity and inclusion, and associated corporate governance principles in what people know as ESG:

>> 2000: Norway's Government Pension Fund and the largest pension fund in the United States, CalPERS (the California Public Employees' Retirement System), committed to 100 percent integration of sustainability principles over 15 years.

>> 2006: The Principles for Responsible Investment (PRI; see Chapter 1), a set of six investment principles encouraging ESG matters to be incorporated into investment practice, were launched by the United Nations. The principles were developed "by investors for investors." They are voluntary principles but have attracted more than 3,000 signatories from over 60 countries, representing over US$100 trillion.

- » 2009: The Global Impact Investing Network (GIIN), a not-for-profit organization devoted to increasing the effectiveness of impact investing, was launched.

- » 2011: The Sustainability Accounting Standards Board (SASB; see Chapters 1 and 15), a non-profit organization, was founded to develop sustainability accounting standards.

- » 2012: A new edition of International Finance Corporation's (IFC's) Sustainability Framework, which includes the Environmental and Social Performance Standards defining responsibilities for managing environmental and social risks, was published.

- » 2015: The United Nations (UN) Sustainable Development Goals (SDGs) were established. They serve as a blueprint for significantly changing the world by ending global poverty, safeguarding the planet, and ensuring prosperity for all by 2030. Also, 195 countries adopted the first-ever universal, legally binding global climate deal with the Paris Agreement (a much more extensive follow-up to the original Kyoto Protocol in 1997). For more information on the SDGs, see Chapters 1 and 15.

- » 2016: The Global Reporting Initiative (GRI) converted its reporting guidance to the first global standards for sustainability reporting, featuring a modular, interrelated structure representing global best practices for reporting on economic, environmental, and social impacts. See Chapter 1 for details.

- » 2017: In a new European Union (EU) Pensions Directive, member states have an obligation to "allow Institutions for Occupational Retirement Provisions (IORPs) EU pensions to take into account the potential long-term impact of investment decisions on ESG factors."

- » 2017: The Task Force on Climate-Related Financial Disclosures (TCFD) published its recommendations on climate disclosures. They were based around four thematic areas that represent core elements of how organizations operate: governance, strategy, risk management, and metrics and targets. These thematic areas are designed to interlink and inform one another. (For more information, see www.tcfdhub.org/recommendations/.)

- » 2019: This year marks the tenth-year anniversary of the United Nation's Sustainable Stock Exchange initiative, which is committed to promoting debate about ESG issues among issuing companies and investors. Most global stock exchanges are part of the initiative.

- » 2020: The final report on EU taxonomy was published (developed by the Technical Expert Group [TEG] on Sustainable Finance), which contains recommendations on the overarching design of the taxonomy, and guidance on how companies and financial institutions can make disclosures using the taxonomy to improve the coverage of disclosed data. See Chapter 1 for more information.

>> 2020: The COVID-19 crisis provoked a shift in investor perception of social factors, which have a critical and constructive impact on long-term value creation and risk mitigation. The Black Lives Matter demonstrations also highlighted interconnections in the way companies approach social issues, including treatment of employees and inequalities, in their long-term sustainability strategy. These events, allied to ongoing environmental issues, will be a game changer for ESG investing.

Go green: The changing global environment

REMEMBER

Many investors consider that the global environmental future is the highest-priority ESG issue facing investors. Problems such as greenhouse gas–induced climate change, pollution, deforestation, biodiversity, and water pollution have serious and sometimes unclear implications. To understand global environmental change in the last 50 years or more, you need to focus on the connections between environmental systems, predominantly the atmosphere, biosphere, geosphere, and hydrosphere, and human systems, which include cultural, economic, political, and social systems. These systems interact where human actions create environmental change, directly altering aspects of the environment, and where environmental changes directly impact human values.

As you may know, the major contributors to the buildup of greenhouse gases include the burning of fossil fuels for heating and energy creation and the use of chlorofluorocarbons (CFCs) as aerosols and coolants. Air pollutants include carbon monoxide, lead, sulfur dioxide, and nitrogen dioxide, which are all by-products of industrial and energy-creation processes. Moreover, stratospheric holes in the ozone layer are considered to be a direct result of the buildup of CFCs in the upper atmosphere.

Therefore, to tackle climate change and decarbonize the global economy, there's a need to generate political action, social change, and financial support. The COVID-19 pandemic has shown that, faced with an imminent humanitarian crisis, a huge amount of political action can be implemented very quickly. Also, societies have changed their behaviors in a matter of weeks, and there's been a great deal of financial backing to support these measures. The scale and pace of change for environmental concerns hasn't been anywhere near comparable, but the pandemic may be a catalyst for further environmental action, with a greater emphasis on climate change after the crisis.

TIP

It's now the final decade to address the UN's Sustainable Development Goals (SDGs), which set targets in 2015 for the world to become safer and more sustainable by 2030, based on the principle of "leaving no one behind." To realize these impressive goals, policymakers and businesses must share the responsibility to mitigate and adapt to the risks of the climate emergency. This is further supported by the business case for environmental change as companies that manage sustainability risks and opportunities tend to have stronger cash flows, lower borrowing costs, and higher valuations over time. Visit `www.un.org/development/ desa/disabilities/envision2030.html` for details on the SDGs, and see Chapter 3 for more about the environmental aspect of ESG investing.

On trend: Changing investor demographics

REMEMBER

In short, demographics are the characteristics of populations that change over time. This makeup includes age, gender, race, birth and death rates, education levels, income levels, and average family sizes. The world is constantly changing, and many of these shifts have the potential to shape how society is organized at a fundamental level. Demographic and social changes form the undercurrents for many economic, cultural, and business decisions and significantly influence how the world evolves.

The biggest shifts in demographics that the world faces today include the following:

» **Aging population:** The global population is aging rapidly (and living longer) in more developed economies as fertility rates decline, while in developing countries the population continues to increase.

» **Baby boomers, millennials, and Generations Z and X:** Millennials, those between the ages of 23 and 38, account for over a third of the global population and are starting to receive a multitrillion dollar wealth transfer from their parents, the baby boomers, as they pass on their inheritance to the next generations. Both this group and those slightly older, Generation X, who have deeper pockets, and those younger than them, Generation Z, with fewer funds but a keen interest in sustainable investing, will drive investment flows in the future.

» **Future workforce:** As the population continues to age in developed economies, fewer people are available to sustain the working population. With a declining working population, modifying a workforce's skill set may be key to keeping economies buoyant. As automation increases, workers must develop more advanced skills to stay competitive. The New Economy will have to ensure that automation supports a shrinking workforce, without limiting job and wage growth.

» **Immigration increase:** Immigration has been further increasing since the beginning of the 21st century. Key migration factors range from political turmoil and conflict to the continuing quest for a better quality of life.

>> **Consumer spending:** In developed economies, an aging population is gradually shifting the purchasing power to older households. Global consumer spending from those over 60 years of age has nearly doubled from 2010 to 2020.

>> **Education reform:** By 2100, over 50 percent of the world will be living in India, China, or Africa. Future education and training must be based on skills relevant to the modern workforce and shifting global demographics in these regions.

>> **Rapid urbanization:** Population concentration in certain countries supports the case for rapid urbanization and is an overarching trend to consider, given that this principle originated in developed economies in the 20th century, with people transitioning from agricultural work to factory and service jobs.

REMEMBER

While the pace of development and the scope of consequences are difficult to quantify, demographic change is now taking center stage as one of the major global megatrends that have the greatest economic, social, and political impact. Strong social change movements are also influenced by demographic changes. As a result, these trends will offer unique challenges and opportunities for businesses, societies, and investors and will therefore influence investment flows.

Crunch the numbers: Evolving data and analytics

The rapid growth in ESG investment strategies has been underpinned by the increasing availability of corporate sustainability metrics. Investors have embraced this information and integrated it into financial analyses and decisions. In addition, new technology, including artificial intelligence (AI) approaches, has allowed investors to run more enhanced analysis.

Investors are progressively applying non-financial factors as part of their analysis process to recognize material risks and growth opportunities. ESG metrics aren't generally part of mandatory financial reporting, though companies are gradually including disclosures in their annual reports or in stand-alone sustainability reports. Also, institutions such as the Sustainable Accounting Standards Board (SASB) and the Global Reporting Initiative (GRI) are forming standards and defining *materiality* (a means of identifying which factors matter most for a specific company, from a wide and complex universe of sustainability indicators) to simplify incorporation of these factors into the investment process.

WARNING

While the quality of these metrics is improving, many still question the reliability, consistency, and utility of such data. Agreeing on the broad principles of ESG is one thing, but having a standardized view of how one company ranks relative to another is a key component in comparing performance of companies and portfolios as ESG investing develops. The most important concerns include filling in gaps in the data, adding new metrics, and improving dependability, which improves comparability across companies. I discuss rankings and metrics in more detail later in this chapter.

The practice of reflecting ESG issues has evolved considerably from its origins in the negative or exclusionary screening of listed equities based on moral values. Some providers still focus on negative screening, where they exclude firms or sectors from investment portfolios, often on ethical or religious grounds (for example, tobacco, alcohol, ammunition, and gaming). Another common use case is limiting exposure to poor labor conditions, corruption, or other issues in the supply chain. A variety of methods are now being used that consider concerns for both purely investment-motivated and more values-motivated investors across asset classes. For example, ESG screens that identify what investors consider to be the worst-performing or "best in class" companies, in terms of their ESG score within a specific sector, are frequently applied. Yet providers don't agree on which factors are most important, and much less data is available to help identify positive opportunities for sustainable investment. I discuss the ratings bias in more detail later in this chapter.

REMEMBER

Composite ESG scores, where the individual elements of 'E,' 'S,' and 'G' are aggregated into one total score, can risk further reducing an investor's understanding of a company and its real-world impact. A comparison of some major providers of ESG scores shows relative correlations of only 30 to 40 percent, depending on the period you're looking at, which is rather low! This issue arises as different ratings agencies use different methodologies to arrive at both their individual and composite scores, including different metrics and weightings, so disparities will naturally exist. However, traditional investors don't only look at a balance sheet when analyzing a company, and therefore they shouldn't rely on a mixture of ESG scores, which they don't really understand, to create a false sense of confidence. They need to focus on the quality and comparability of ESG information provided by corporate issuers, and determine how best to integrate various ESG factors into their investment selection process. Many active management investors have also begun to apply their own research perspectives on this scoring issue, leading to yet another set of results. See Chapter 14 for more about the integration of ESG performance in the investment process.

So, while consistency across ESG scores is needed, you also need heterogeneity of methodologies so that investors can decide what is more compelling for their ESG-related objectives. Moreover, in 2020 the EU Technical Expert Group (TEG) on Sustainable Finance published a taxonomy report for sustainable finance that aims to improve the coverage of disclosed data. Perhaps there will be a convergence of ratings, as seen in the credit ratings space since the 1960s, with agencies in that area keen to apply their current domain expertise to an ESG offering. There is also an increasing demand for real-time reporting around ESG issues to understand immediately what ESG-related risks investors have in their portfolios.

REMEMBER

Clearly there is an ongoing race to provide a "single point of truth" platform for ESG data. An increasing number of providers are producing thousands of metrics and scores, either within their platforms or over an application programming interface (API). This further supports the use of AI, as it enables continuous, real-time, big data ESG harvesting and analytics. This should lead to the creation of stronger ESG investment signals, through sustainable ratings, that facilitate the creation of more forward-looking analysis rather than largely backward-looking corporate disclosure. The result could be the realization of transparent performance attribution analysis that correctly determines the premium on ESG investments. Whichever way, greater data quality and integrity are required.

TIP

You can visit www.researchaffiliates.com/en_us/publications/articles/ what-a-difference-an-esg-ratings-provider-makes.html to review how different service providers apply their ratings. The physical scores or rankings offered by service providers are proprietary, but more of the ratings agencies are now providing indicative scores on their websites without the requirement to be a subscriber. One example is www.sustainalytics.com/esg-ratings/.

Exploring the "Personality" of an ESG Company

In principle, many companies would argue that they are ESG-compliant because they have paid lip service to some of the major environmental, social, and governance issues that are the flavor of the month. However, ticking the box and engaging in a true analysis of the ESG factors that your company faces, and what they can do to mitigate those factors, are two very different issues. Moreover, some firms deliberately undertake greenwashing (see Chapter 6) to mislead stakeholders as to their real ESG credentials. This section highlights what the true characteristics of an ESG-focused company should be and how companies define the material factors to their issues to achieve such characteristics.

Determining material ESG factors

Materiality is a concept within accounting that relates to the significance of an amount or discrepancy. The purpose of an audit of financial statements is to enable an auditor to state an opinion on whether the financial statements are prepared, in all material respects, in conformity with an identified financial reporting framework.

REMEMBER

Likewise, financially material ESG factors represent a significant impact, either positive or negative, on a company's business model, such as revenue growth, margins, and risk. The material factors differ from one sector to another, including supply chain management, environmental policy, worker health and safety, and corporate governance. For sustainability to translate into financial performance, it must have an influence on either the amount of cash flow generated or the cost of external financing to the company.

Many firms consider ESG factors such as renewable energy, community relations, and political contributions to be material indicators that they are being good corporate citizens and following an ESG strategy. However, there is a difference between "doing good" and "doing well." From an investment perspective, these factors may not be financially material to the company's bottom line, so they don't score highly in terms of investment-grade aspects that will impact their share price. Therefore, a company needs to consider which ESG issues present real financial risk or opportunity. This analysis should include stakeholder engagement to agree on the priority issues that need to be addressed. For example, an airline company could focus on energy efficiency, customer satisfaction, and executive compensation as core ESG factors that make a difference, but there isn't always consensus as to what constitutes financially material ESG factors.

WARNING

It's not surprising that a critical part of ESG scoring is determined by material factors that affect a company's financial performance, but data providers typically take their own view on materiality issues. This proprietary approach doesn't allow full transparency, and any differences add to the difficulty that asset owners and managers face in selecting an ESG data provider (find out more details later in this chapter).

Performing a materiality analysis

A *materiality analysis* is a method used to pinpoint and prioritize the issues that are most important to an organization's value chain and its stakeholders. After identifying these issues, they are typically analyzed using two different lenses. For direct environmental issues or working with sustainable suppliers, the organization needs to evaluate the capacity for each issue to positively or negatively impact growth, cost, or trust. They then need to determine how important each issue is to their stakeholders. The final result gives a picture of which issues should be prioritized according to their importance to the company's success and stakeholders' expectations.

The analysis required can also improve a company's business strategy, as it forces the company to analyze business risks and opportunities and understand where they are creating or reducing value for society. In providing the process of how to measure different financial, social, and environmental performances, this analysis can spot trends and help anticipate emerging issues. In turn, it can allow companies to focus their efforts on how they allocate resources and develop new products or services to stay ahead of the competition. Therefore, a materiality analysis can create its own business case on why and how a company should report ESG data, and it can be used for communications with individual stakeholder groups like investors, partners, customers, or employees. This also increases the chances of satisfying stakeholders' demands.

WARNING

However, companies voluntarily self-report information that they consider materially relevant. Moreover, companies also tend to overreport areas of positive impact and underreport areas of negative impact. As such, for investors performing cross-company or cross-industry comparisons, it can be difficult to find or develop consistent data sets or methodologies that allow a true assessment of materiality (see Chapter 12 for more information). Further moves toward mandatory reporting, and clarity on what should be reported and how, should improve this issue in the future.

Applying weights to materiality measures

After you've determined that material issues should either impact a company's business significantly or be important to their stakeholders, or both, it's important to determine the relative weight that needs to be applied to those issues, which are driven by the respective impact across the value chain. Most service providers for ESG scores refrain from giving transparent, quantitative guidance for the mathematical calculation of materiality. While provision is suggested for the use of benchmarks to calculate materiality, they don't recommend specific benchmarks or formulas.

For traditional accounting materiality, single-rule methods and variable-size methods have been used to determine weighting. Single-rule methods can include the effect on a given percentage of pretax income, total assets equity, or total revenue. Sliding-scale or variable-size methods apply given percentages to different levels of gross profit. In general, companies use blended methods to combine some or all methods by using appropriate weighting for each element.

REMEMBER

Within ESG there are currently no industry norms or globally recognized practices for evaluating and measuring materiality weighting. Moreover, each ESG data provider has developed a method to aggregate and weigh materiality for its summary scores, but these are proprietary judgments made by each provider. Indeed, analyzing the different methodologies used by leading ESG providers highlights the challenge that investors face. There are distinct differences in the way they collect and analyze ESG data, resulting in low correlations between their aggregation metrics; this increases the difficulty in extracting weights given to material issues.

Furthermore, not all weightings have the same importance to every industry (see Chapter 14 for more information). Some providers use levels of data disclosure as a proxy for the relative weight of materiality issues for each industry. This data highlights which sectors contribute most, and their proportion of the contribution to the total is used as a proxy for the level of materiality for that sector. For example, greater disclosure on carbon emissions data suggests that they are more material to companies in that sector. In addition, if given companies in a sector aren't reporting relevant metrics, they may be arbitrarily assigned a score of zero to encourage disclosure and transparency.

REMEMBER

Size matters! Given that larger market capitalization companies have more social media hits than smaller companies, some providers have applied a greater weighting on a small company's material issues as they are likely to have a greater adverse effect. Likewise, every business is impacted by global macro trends and events (such as the coronavirus pandemic) that shape the world and businesses within it. It's important to monitor those trends to assess their impact on a company's material issues.

Understanding Why ESG Is Important

If it wasn't clear already, ESG and sustainability issues are counted as important long-term factors, and they are the focus for ever-increasing amounts of research to identify them as catalysts for long-term corporate and investment performance. This has encouraged advisors, consultants, investment platform providers, and ratings agencies to develop tools to identify asset managers with the ability to pinpoint those factors and companies and to highlight the advantages in this rapidly increasing market.

There have been major advances in the understanding of how ESG factors may impact performance. The growth in academic and other research is providing evidence to underpin that belief. For the world's major asset owners and other stewards of capital, how a company classifies and oversees its operational and reputational risks as well as the economic and commercial opportunities from ESG issues is a fundamental gauge of the quality of its board of directors and the overall business. Investors are now seamlessly integrating an assessment of ESG quality with financial analysis to form a holistic view of an enterprise's risk and the potential to deliver long-term earnings growth and therefore value. This section highlights some of the issues that are driving the need for ESG investing.

Global sustainability challenges

The year 2020 marked the start of the "decade of delivery" for the 17 Sustainable Development Goals (SDGs; see Chapter 1 for more information). In light of the impact of the COVID-19 pandemic, these words may have more resonance than they did previously for most people, and there is more awareness of the sustainable development issues that impact us all. Indeed, the international community could use the pandemic as a way to get back on track to achieve the SDGs and accelerate progress during this decade to deliver sustainable development. More recently, many countries have carried out Voluntary National Reviews (VNRs) of their implementation of the 2030 Agenda, and companies are reviewing their ESG agendas in tandem.

REMEMBER

The science is clear: As greenhouse gas emissions have decreased during the pandemic, there has been a greater focus on the target to continue decreasing emissions by 3.5 percent per year between 2020 and 2030 so that the average temperature on the planet stays well below 2 degrees Celsius by the end of the century. Meanwhile, businesses are paying much more attention to the scarcity of resources than climate change or related natural disasters. While both factors directly affect businesses, and one often causes the other, businesses may feel that they can more proactively tackle resource scarcity with core business practices, such as supply chain management, whereas climate change is a factor over which they have less control. With an estimated addition of 2 billion people by 2050, global demand for resources will drive the need for improvements in infrastructure associated with a growing population. Either way, these factors help explain further why companies and investors are keen to embrace ESG principles. Moreover, businesses are responsible for much of the greenhouse gas emissions that contribute to climate change, so they must adapt in order to help address climate change issues.

The interest of millennial investors in ESG

Millennials, those youngsters born between 1981 and 1996, are part of the generation entering their prime earning years. Numerous surveys have indicated that the vast majority of high net worth (HNW) millennials consider a company's ESG track record before investing, or alternatively they want to tailor their investments to their personal values. This reflects a need for their money to not just earn a decent return but to contribute to the social good and how it impacts society and the planet at large.

Why is that important? Millennials are a large demographic, representing about 25 percent of the world's population and a greater percentage of the workforce now and into the future. Moreover, this group is due to inherit a large amount of wealth as their parents, the baby boomers, pass on their considerable nest eggs.

Furthermore, surveys have suggested that wealth management firms typically lose more than 70 percent of assets when they are transferred from one generation to the next. Subsequently, asset managers that offer millennials ESG investment options will be well positioned to attract new assets as well as retain beneficiary millennial clients.

REMEMBER

So, millennials will require more active involvement in their investments, as they need to feel they are controlling their own destiny, and consequently they will have more activist tendencies. They are interested in ensuring that their financial return is linked to positive, or at least not unduly negative, environmental and social impact. In summary, while ESG investing will be used to create a competitive advantage, asset managers have to adopt socially responsible practices to continue gaining business in the investment industry.

More systematic, quantitative, objective, and financially relevant approaches

As the significance of the ESG market has grown, the financial industry has evolved the definitions of which ESG factors are relevant and how they can be applied to the performance of a company. Using this more informed data from companies, combined with enhanced ESG research and analytics capabilities, the industry is producing more systematic, quantitative, impartial, and financially applicable approaches to highlight the core ESG factors.

In turn, this has generated more research that advocates a better understanding of ESG investing and resultant data points to feed the new AI approaches to filter unstructured data through Natural Language Processing (NLP) and Machine Learning (ML) to drive predictive analytics (find more information on this later in this chapter). There are tens of thousands of company issuers and hundreds of thousands of equity and fixed-income securities — combined with an increasing array of ESG ratings and metrics — to be considered when identifying the risks and opportunities within a portfolio.

Surveying Specific ESG Ratings and Metrics

REMEMBER

ESG ratings are used to evaluate how far companies have integrated and applied ESG factors into the management of their business, and these evaluations are then used as part of the investment process when deciding what securities to buy. Different industry providers have developed different approaches to how they score ratings for their solutions, but they all need to fundamentally consider the following issues:

>> Identify the most material ESG risks and opportunities that a company and its industry are facing. (I cover materiality earlier in this chapter.)

>> Quantify how exposed a company is to those key risks and opportunities.

>> Determine how well a company is managing the key risks and opportunities.

>> Conclude what the overall picture for a company is and how it compares to similar companies within its sector or geographical region.

This allows an objective consideration of any negative externalities that companies in an industry may face, and highlights potential, unforeseen costs apparent in the mid to long term. Equally, understanding negative externalities should help emphasize ESG factors that present opportunities for companies in the mid to long term. This section highlights the metrics around ESG and hones in on some of the "good, bad, and ugly" issues relating to how data is applied. Chapter 14 has even more information on ratings and metrics.

Data quality, ratings bias, and standardization

ESG ratings are still evolving. Keep in mind that they rely on limited and sometimes misleading disclosures by companies, which themselves are learning the ropes as to how they should report their ESG exposure. So, as with traditional securities analysis, the analysis of any data can be subjective because the selection and weighting of data points is qualitative. Historically, investors have questioned the inherent bias that has been displayed by ratings agencies or the recommendations of securities analysts, and ESG ratings will face similar scrutiny as they develop further. ESG data providers generally develop their own sourcing, research, and scoring methodologies.

WARNING

Therefore, individual ESG ratings aren't comparable across providers, due to a lack of standardization of the objective criteria required. As a result, the rating for a single company can vary widely across different providers. Moreover, there are differences in how providers obtain and purchase raw data that's released by the company or publicly disclosed. Data providers also use statistical models to generate approximations for unreported data. These models are based on norms and tendencies from comparable companies and established benchmarks. As such, investors are integrating convictions from the data provider into their investment procedures.

To be fair to the data providers, some of the differences in methodology are also due to the different priorities of their customers — the asset managers and asset owners that subscribe to their services — who have different investment objectives. This exacerbates the difficulties in standardizing an approach.

Issues with ESG scoring

ESG data providers perform a significant part of the investment procedure by collecting and assessing information about companies' ESG practices and scoring them appropriately. The expansion of these ratings systems has helped to encourage the growth of ESG investing by providing asset owners and managers with an alternative to managing such widespread due diligence themselves. There are more than 100 ESG data providers, which include well-known suppliers such as Bloomberg, FTSE, MSCI, Sustainalytics, Refinitiv, and Vigeo Eiris, as well as focused data providers such as S&P's Trucost (providing carbon and "brown revenue" data) and ISS (corporate governance, climate, and responsible investing solutions). Investors increasingly view material ESG factors as being essential drivers of a company's capacity to produce sustainable long-term performance. In turn, ESG data is growing in importance for investors' ability to assign capital effectively.

WARNING

Despite the significant contributions that data providers have achieved in evolving ESG investing, asset owners and managers should understand the intrinsic limitations of this data, as much as the challenges of relying on any one data provider.

Quality data has always been the lifeblood of investment analysis. While "quality" can be expressed in different ways, most investors agree that consistency and comparability in the accessibility of data among companies are critical elements of an operational data set. However, the current environment imposes barriers to realizing such quality when a company's ESG data practices are rather ad hoc. Associations and regulators don't always require companies to report on all of their ESG data; therefore, they can decide which ESG factors are material to their business performance and what information to reveal to investors. As such, asset owners and investment managers can be left to find their own solutions to these challenges, which can create an additional stream of inconsistent, non-comparable, and less material information.

WARNING

These opposing methodologies have repercussions for investors. In selecting a given provider, investors are, in effect, associating themselves with that company's ESG investment ethos in terms of data acquisition, materiality, aggregation, and weighting. This selection is further complicated by the lack of transparency into those practices. Most data providers regard their policies as proprietary information. By depending on an ESG data provider's score, asset owners are accepting the assessments of that provider without a full appreciation of how the provider determined those ratings.

ESG momentum importance

In addition to considering current ESG ratings, investors looking for positive alpha generation within an ESG framework can seek changes in ESG ratings. This is known as ESG momentum, and various studies have shown that using this strategy helps outperform the established benchmarks. Positive ESG rating momentum is defined as when a company's ESG rating has improved by more than 10 percent on the previous year. On the contrary, negative ESG rating momentum occurs when a company's ESG rating has fallen by more than 10 percent on the previous year, and neutral momentum occurs when the rating remains unchanged or within the −10 to +10 percent range.

The principle behind an ESG momentum strategy is that future stock performance is connected to a change in the ESG quality of the company and potentially a reduction in future liabilities. Various studies have shown that buying more stocks with improving ESG ratings can lead to investment outperformance. The premise of this idea is that companies with lower ESG scores have more improvement potential and should therefore be included in a fund's investment universe, although this does introduce timing issues on when the optimal time is to invest in such stocks. However, this is no different from the challenges facing active fund managers within a traditional investment approach.

WARNING

The contrary opinion is that investors should view companies that embrace new, improved ESG policies with skepticism, and ought to focus on companies with a proven ESG record. Moreover, changes in the methodology of a data provider could create false momentum signals. To counter this, investors need to consider using multiple data providers to blend the momentum score. This helps reduce variations and gives a clearer picture of ESG momentum.

Applying artificial intelligence and data science to ESG analysis

Several investors mention the lack of high-quality information as the biggest challenge in adopting ESG principles. Industry bodies are developing international standards and guidance for ESG disclosure, but in the absence of standards, the burden lies with individual companies and investors to ensure quality ESG disclosures and to confirm the sustainability of vendors, suppliers, customers, and counterparties. But how do you verify it?

TECHNICAL STUFF

For most companies, ESG verification implies asking such partners to abide by the vendor code of conduct. However, artificial intelligence could play a central role in collecting, verifying, and analyzing ESG performance by using techniques from *Natural Language Processing* (NLP; programmatically mining information from text), *graph analytics* (understanding how different entities influence each other's

ESG), and *Machine Learning* (ML; predicting how ESG factors will influence investment performance in given conditions). Moreover, ML could be used to generate missing values for companies that have incomplete reporting by using the known rating of an established ESG company and defining the similarities between the companies and their industry sector.

REMEMBER

It's clear that without solving their fundamental data problem, companies won't have an accurate understanding of their own ESG metrics (garbage in, garbage out). However, as the industry evolves toward a standardized set of metrics and reporting formats, investors will deploy AI to verify evidence of materiality, evaluate investment risk, and forecast investment return. Eventually, ML will produce automatic investment decisions integrating ESG factors, just as it does in traditional investing. Therefore, the investment professionals who understand how to leverage AI resources to contextualize and produce ESG data will be best positioned as ESG data standardizes.

Defining an ESG Policy

Developing a responsible investment policy doesn't need to be a burdensome task. The methodology applied to "policy writing" needs to be inclusive to confirm representation of all relevant and material viewpoints. You could use existing channels of communication with stakeholders and integrate their input on the contents of your policy. Such approaches to an ESG policy should be informed by the internal review process, appointment of external service providers, stakeholder soundings, and so on. Within the planning stage, it's crucial to ensure that ownership of the policy and outcomes is driven by the highest possible management within the organization. In addition, cultural fit and organizational governance buy-in are essential elements in effective policy-making. Planning can also be supported by following wider industry guidance on ESG integration — there is no need to reinvent the wheel when there is so much best practice and peer analysis that can be followed.

This section provides a "whistle-stop" overview of some of the key factors to incorporate. Flip to Chapter 13 for details on building an ESG strategy.

Familiarize yourself with ESG and asset owner–specific legislation

Local jurisdictional law may require pension funds and other investors to have a statement of investment principles, or their fiduciary duty may oblige trustees to consider any ethical or ESG issues that are financially material. Similarly, other jurisdictions explicitly require diversity and inclusion to be considered as material ESG factors in their investment analysis and decision-making. In short, given the growing acceptance of responsible investment practices, most pension funds already subscribe to various methods of ESG investing. In many countries, the corporate governance and stewardship codes can also provide valuable insight when developing an ESG policy, which should consider the performance of investment portfolios to varying degrees across companies, sectors, regions, and asset classes.

TIP

Furthermore, many of the points suggested here for money managers will be similar for individual companies implementing their own ESG policies.

Undertake a peer review

It may sound obvious, but investigating how your peers have communicated their ESG policies can be invaluable. This is because given policies may be more applicable to given industry sectors or geographical locations, while there may be specific elements that could be followed or excluded, depending on the specifics of your company.

Review your statement of investment beliefs and core investment principles

REMEMBER

This is an appropriate time to identify and review the core beliefs and principles that are central to your organization. Your ESG policy should be informed by these beliefs and your strategic investment approach. It's also appropriate to identify and reflect on your organization's culture and values so that they are adequately represented in the resulting policy. Note that without well-defined core principles, trustee and fiduciary oversight and accountability mechanisms are very difficult to implement.

Specify responsible investment guidelines

Recognize the responsible investment practices that leverage your organization's investment process and philosophy, and consider how your policy will relate to both internally and externally managed assets. Moreover, analyze jurisdictional specificities and legal aspects that could affect the guidelines.

There should be minimum ESG standards that your organization expects investee companies to follow. These standards may initially constitute a high-level statement on ESG goals but should ultimately include specific details on how companies need to manage particular issues and adhere to established standards. Differing guidelines and procedures may vary across different asset classes, including listed equities, bonds, private equity, real estate, hedge funds, and commodities. Specific guidelines could be devised for the asset classes that you regularly invest in, while the policy could be more generally applied to emerging asset classes. External investment managers should be expected to have their own ESG policy in place or agree to adopt the asset owner's policy. Ultimately, guidelines on manager selection and monitoring could include ESG expectations in the Request For Proposal (RFP) and requirements on reporting of ESG issues.

Outline responsible investment procedures

This part of the policy should outline which ESG approaches your organization will implement. These approaches could include positive and negative screening, ESG integration, themed investing, and active ownership. Further elaboration on specific sustainability themes or what you'll abstain from investing in should be outlined, along with the thinking behind those approaches. Additional information on impact investing could be incorporated here. Last but not least, there should be clear guidelines on how ESG issues will be integrated into the investment analysis and processes across different asset classes.

Include engagement and active ownership approaches

Depending on the stance of your organization, it may be appropriate to include proxy voting and engagement guidelines in your ESG policy. This should include some general guidelines on what ownership activities you'll use or prioritize. These activities could include annual general meeting (AGM) participation and proxy voting, ongoing engagement with the investee companies, addressing specific issues around raising shareholder resolutions, and requesting a seat on the board.

This section could also be used to clarify responsibilities — for example, whether ESG integration will be covered in-house or by external managers. Likewise, will active ownership activities be administered by internal staff or outsourced? Just as important, who will supervise the range of activities undertaken by different actors within this approach?

Spell out reporting requirements

REMEMBER

In today's environment, it would seem a best practice to report on your ESG activities to both beneficiaries and more publicly (if only on an aggregated basis across various clients). However, the guidelines outlined earlier should clarify how, when, and to whom reporting will be made, as well as the associated level of publicity. There should certainly be clarity around expectation in terms of reporting from portfolio managers, external engagement, and proxy voting. Finally, review processes should be put in place to ensure that objectives are being met and that analysis of the Key Performance Indicators is undertaken to measure whether ESG expectation outcomes are being met.

Chapter **3**

Give Me an 'E'! Defining the Environmental Sector in ESG

Investors are becoming increasingly aware of the financial impact of environmental issues on companies in their portfolios. These investors are paying greater attention to issues such as climate change, water usage, energy efficiency, pollution, resource scarcity, and environmental hazards so that they can increase awareness of relevant issues and influence disclosure. The negative impact for companies failing to manage environmental risks includes increasing costs (for example, the need to clean up oil spills), reputational damage due to pollution incidents, and litigation costs.

Integrating environmental factors into a company's strategy can present opportunities — for example, using resources efficiently can decrease costs and offering innovative solutions can create a competitive edge. These environmental factors measure a company's impact on living and non-living natural systems, including the air, land, water, and entire ecosystems. These factors also indicate how a company employs best management practices to avoid environmental risks and capitalize on opportunities that generate shareholder value.

This chapter outlines how companies manage their natural resource usage both directly and indirectly through their value chain. It also describes how analysis of these factors allows investors to determine whether the companies are meeting their environmental stewardship targets or managing the risks involved. Numerous environmental issues can be relevant to different companies in diverse sectors of the economy, but this chapter focuses on the material issues that both companies and investors need to consider, as such issues may have the greatest impact on both return on investment and sustainability.

Outlining a Company's Use of Natural Resources

The environmental sector of ESG reflects on how a company considers its stewardship obligations in terms of protecting the natural environment. The 'E' in ESG considers the company's use of natural resources and the effect its operations have on the environment, in terms of direct operations and throughout its supply chains. Therefore, a company's environmental disclosures provide an insight into its efforts to reduce material risks and opportunities for stakeholders. Those companies that fail to anticipate the effects of their practices on the environment may face financial risk. Failing to act or protect against environmental "accidents" can lead to sanctions, prosecution, and reputational damage, which reduces shareholder value.

In the following sections, I describe the different environmental factors that companies need to consider when investing.

CO_2 or GHG? Climate change and carbon emissions

The key environmental target that most nations have targeted is net-zero emissions by 2050, which indicates that all man-made greenhouse gas (GHG) emissions must be removed from the atmosphere through reduction measures that reduce the earth's net climate balance. This should primarily be achieved through a rapid reduction in carbon emissions, but where zero carbon can't be achieved, offsetting through carbon credits (a permit that allows the holder to emit a certain amount of CO_2 or GHG) seems to be the preferred approach. However, the risk of relying on carbon credit offsets rather than rapid decarbonization is that companies can maintain emissions at a steady level, using carbon credits to reach net zero, which negates the need to actually reduce their own emissions.

To meet the internationally agreed-upon target of confining the rise in global average temperatures to well below 2 degrees Celsius above pre-industrial levels, science suggests that most fossil fuel reserves need to remain in the ground. The emergence of carbon pricing and decreasing technology costs implies that low-carbon energy sources will be more attractive and the demand for fossil fuels will fade, leading to the demise of the companies that explore, mine, and burn them. Moreover, any fall in oil prices decreases the incentive for producers to drill for many fossil fuel assets. This has led to an even steeper fall in the price of carbon credits, or Certified Emission Reduction (CER) units.

These developments have led to the divestment of many fossil fuel stocks by asset managers, from both a sustainability and investment performance perspective, and have prompted further analysis of the relative carbon footprint of individual stocks and a call for pension funds to disclose their aggregate carbon footprint. However, some ESG investors argue that simply selling a stock to investors who don't care about climate change will have zero impact on the overall climate program. A more positive approach would be to encourage engagement with management of fossil fuel companies to encourage a shift away from current production approaches and move more toward the development of a renewable energy infrastructure. In addition, divesting particular energy and utility stocks may create divergence away from benchmark investment performance.

WARNING These approaches require an assessment of a company's carbon (greenhouse gas or GHG emissions) strategy, exposure, and long-term approach to decarbonizing their business. A range of low-carbon benchmarks have been developed to help investors track their investments in relation to their carbon exposure or potential risk. Asset owners are increasingly concerned that hydrocarbon-based assets will become "stranded" over time due to climate change concerns. (In this context, *stranded* refers to assets that turn out to be worthless due to the transition to a low-carbon economy.) The stranded assets concept was pioneered by the UK-based non-governmental organization (NGO) Carbon Tracker (CT), which provides research and analysis on this issue (`https://carbontracker.org/terms/stranded-assets/`). The CT approach focuses on the valuation of companies, which includes projections of the future value of their coal, oil, and gas inventories. The stranded asset concept is worrying asset owners as they question what happens to assets that are worth less than their projected value due to changes linked to energy transition that spans the typical lifetime of pension scheme assets, which can be 40-plus years. Therefore, investors need to be fully aware of initiatives that require companies to report on the repercussions of the future value of their assets on their business model, and what impact that may have on the value of their investments.

TIP

Moreover, financial regulators have recognized the significance of scenario analysis for measuring climate risk through the inclusion of scenario analysis in the Financial Stability Board's Task Force on Climate-related Financial Disclosures (TCFD) recommendations. Visit www.tcfdhub.org/scenario-analysis/ for more information on how the TCFD has developed a framework to help companies and other organizations more effectively disclose climate-related risks and how scenario analysis is used to explore alternatives that may significantly alter the basis for "business as usual" assumptions.

Clean and green: Energy efficiency

Energy efficiency is most often associated with clean technology companies where green energy businesses are looking to decrease hydrocarbon-sourced energy consumption by displacing it with clean energy sources, or to integrate systems to improve energy usage. Because of the numerous alternatives to working toward and investing in energy efficiency, it's challenging to classify and define companies based on fields or themes, as some of the world's historic hydrocarbon energy companies are investing heavily in transitioning away from coal, oil, and gas.

TIP

The definitions of how firms are categorized and compared by industry and sector by established data/index providers such as Morgan Stanley Capital International (MSCI) or Financial Times Stock Exchange (FTSE) Russell can be useful for investors. Visit www.msci.com/gics and www.ftserussell.com/data/industry-classification-benchmark-icb.

The International Energy Agency (IEA; visit www.iea.org/) is the global authority for energy efficiency data, analysis, and policy advice. They help governments realize the huge potential of energy efficiency, guiding them on growing, implementing, and quantifying the impacts of policies to alleviate climate change, improve energy security, and develop economies while delivering environmental and social benefits. They track global policy progress in over 200 countries, regions, and states, and global investment in energy efficiency as published in the *World Energy Investment* report. As of 2016, energy efficiency investment represented 13.6 percent of the US$1.7 trillion invested across the entire energy market.

Such investments are directed into different fields, with approximately 58 percent focused on buildings, 26 percent allocated to transport, and 16 percent assigned to industry. The types of services or infrastructure projects benefitting from alternative fuels and renewable energy include generation, transmission, and distribution of electricity from renewable sources such as wind, solar, geothermal, biomass, wave, and tidal (more information on these investment themes is found in Chapter 10).

A crisis awaits: Conservation of water

The world is facing a global water crisis! However, while the world has increasingly recognized the significance of environmental sustainability, there is less focus on the forthcoming water crisis. This lack of urgency can be attributed to the fact that the water crisis isn't seen as a global crisis — in the way that climate change is seen as a shared and global problem — but rather a group of local ones. Moreover, observers fail to differentiate between the interdependent facets of the water crisis — namely, water access, pollution, and scarcity.

REMEMBER

However, there are some positive signs that organizations, such as the United Nations, are better defining and evaluating impact companies in the water and sanitation sectors. To move further forward, global cooperation among distinct stakeholders is required to appreciate that water issues in one area impact economies in other areas, especially where they contribute to disruptive conflict, and companies can't ignore local problems when they impact global supply chains. Public-private partnerships are required to address these issues, but they need access to precise data and information; otherwise, the wider economy will suffer from resource reduction and a company's results will be vulnerable to stakeholder criticism caused by a negative reputation.

Water is in focus in Europe, where the vast majority of investors see it as a concern, but perhaps this is driven by the establishment of the European Union (EU) Water Framework Directive. In addition, the World Economic Forum (WEF) has cited water as a driver of global risk, for everything from conflict to health crises and mass migration. And note that water security is one of the United Nations' Sustainable Development Goals (see Chapter 1). Therefore, water is considered a multi-impact investment because it affects the microclimate, food supply, industrial chain, health, productivity, and the environment overall. This confirms that water is fundamentally linked to other impact themes and has wide applicability to business and the investment community. Water management, technology, distribution, and conservation are some of the issues that organizations face, following years of poor water and waste management practices.

There is increasing pressure for water-themed investments given the huge number of people who lack access to securely managed sanitation and drinking water services. Meanwhile, water-related perils are responsible for 90 percent of natural disasters. However, most firms still lack a water-efficiency policy, and even fewer of them have set targets for water efficiency. The only bright spot is that the momentum appears to be building and institutional investors have noticed, as water now ranks among their top three ESG concerns. Stock index providers are designing more sustainable indexes that explicitly cover water and sanitation companies, while analysis of some of the major global indexes by Ceres (www. ceres.org/) found that 50 percent of component companies face medium to high water risks.

There is no Planet B: Air and water pollution

Pollutant emissions are a major risk for both air and water supplies. Healthy ecosystems rely on a complex web of elements that interact, directly or indirectly, with each other. Damage to any of these elements can create a chain reaction, endangering all kinds of environments due to the air and water pollution created. An unintended benefit of the COVID-19 pandemic is the slowdown in global economic activity, which has led to reduced air and water pollution. However, when the U.S. Environmental Protection Agency (EPA) suspended enforcement of environmental laws during the outbreak, stating that polluting the air or water will be allowable as long as the violations are "caused by" the pandemic, there may be unintended drawbacks as well.

Human behavior has been stressed as the major cause of air pollution, especially in cities. Beijing's smog cloud has been "clear" for many years, but there have been important developments in air- and water-quality metrics more recently due to social and government attention. Nonetheless, air pollution has caused damage to crops, forests, and waterways. Moreover, the effect of air pollution leads to the formation of acid rain, which harms trees, soils, rivers, and wildlife.

Similarly, human behavior is also to blame for the major cause of water pollution: microplastics. Primary microplastics are tiny particles found in cosmetics or as microfibers shed from clothing and other textiles, such as fishing nets. These microplastics have been specifically produced for commercial use, while secondary microplastics result from the breakdown of larger plastic items, such as water bottles. These microplastics find their way into our rivers, from where they become a major source of plastic waste flowing into the oceans. Estimates suggest that over 1,000 rivers are accountable for 80 percent of global annual emissions, which range between 0.8 and 2.7 million metric tons per year, with small urban rivers being among the most polluted.

These are examples where, to reduce the problems of air and water pollution, companies should be more aware of their impact in these environmental areas. Transition risks can include new regulatory restrictions that increase costs for the most polluting factories, or the withdrawal of licenses to operate due to pollution or poor environmental standards.

REMEMBER

In addition, World Bank data suggests that most countries have explicit regulations on water and sanitation companies, yet not all countries accept or follow basic conditions defined by the World Health Organization. Consequently, several companies that are obligated to offer sustainable water and sanitation services embrace voluntary certifications to achieve their sustainable and responsible goals. However, this isn't true for the entire industry, particularly in emerging markets and developing countries, where greater adoption is required. For example, Asia (excluding Japan) produces over ten times more water pollutants than the rest of the world combined! Companies may implement procedures that offer access to water but at an increased cost to customers, including low-income groups. As a result, when evaluating industries in this field, it's essential to clarify whether companies observe national and international principles. For example, companies that score highly on the Carbon Disclosure Project (CDP), which runs a global disclosure system for investors, companies, cities, states, and regions to manage their environmental impacts, can be found here: `www.cdp.net/en/companies/companies-scores`.

Live and let live: Biodiversity

The effects of human action on the natural world are deeply harmful, and as our population increases and the search for economic growth continues, the threat will only increase. Damage to ecosystems across the world, and the resulting loss of biodiversity, has collected fewer headlines than other sustainability challenges, even though the biodiversity crisis is a direct risk to humankind.

Part of the problem is that it's difficult to quantify due to the heterogeneity of ecosystems, making the correct response difficult to identify. Clearly, biodiversity loss is directly related to the climate emergency, and more companies, governments, and the public are recognizing this. For example, the protection of the ecosystems found in natural forests is a key solution to mitigating global warming. Extinction rates are multiple times higher than the historic rate, and approximately 1 million species are at threat out of a total of 8 million plant and animal species on earth. However, companies have consistently struggled to evaluate how their activities affect biodiversity, partly due to the exceptional complexity of the living systems that their value chains interact with.

Investments in biodiversity contribute directly to the full range of UN Sustainable Development Goals (SDGs). Conserving biodiversity and ecosystems preserves the ability of our planet to sustain our prosperity. Biodiversity finance combines conventional capital with financial incentives to fund sustainable biodiversity management. It can include private and public financial resources, and investments in commercial businesses that create positive biodiversity outcomes. However, most funding originates from public funds, including domestic public budgets, biodiversity-positive agricultural subsidies, and international transfers of public funds, and these activities haven't been well communicated on a national scale. Moreover, without specific information on recipient-country expenditures and priorities, development partners have been unwilling to promise support to reach biodiversity management goals and objectives. Investors tend to lump the associated risks in with industries such as mining.

Therefore, investors are demanding more information on biodiversity to ensure any risks are well managed. Meanwhile, increasing awareness that assets can become stranded through biodiversity loss is escalating the response. For example, biodiversity issues on agricultural land diminish its capacity to grow crops and can lead to the land becoming stranded. Financial organizations need to support the growth of methodologies to gauge biodiversity loss, conservation, and enhancement. More data is required to quantify biodiversity risks to enable integration into valuation tools. Investors should allocate assets toward companies that work in environmentally sustainable ways and create biodiversity-positive technologies while embedding biodiversity protection. And companies need to further disclose the impact of their economic activities on biodiversity.

Some tools are currently being developed that compare how companies respond to material biodiversity risk, which should help investors understand how companies are mitigating "known unknown" risks, as well as compare how they balance economic returns with sustainable benefits. Many hope that such indicators will realize for biodiversity loss what the tools highlighting CO_2 emission levels achieved for climate change (I cover CO_2 earlier in this chapter). These indicators will need to identify any correlation between biodiversity and the success of the economy and allow investors to place an economic value on biodiversity.

The COVID-19 pandemic should accelerate the focus on sustainable investing in general and biodiversity more specifically. Still, the pandemic shows that when biodiversity is destroyed, the system that supports human life is also affected, as the loss of biodiversity provides an opportunity for pathogens to pass between animals and people more freely. However, the risk is that policymakers and companies spend too much time focused on the fallout from the pandemic, including increasing debts, balance sheet damage, and weaker profits, such that other biodiversity issues remain in the background.

See the forest for the trees: Deforestation

The EPA defines deforestation as the "permanent removal of standing forests." However, such removal can occur for different reasons and has a variety of destructive consequences. Reports suggest that 80 percent of deforestation results from extensive cattle ranching and logging for materials and development. It has been happening for thousands of years, primarily since humans evolved from hunter-gatherer to agricultural-based societies and needed larger swathes of land to facilitate farming and housing. Modern requirements have converted this into an epidemic, leading to the loss of animal and plant species, due to their loss of habitat, as well as the following issues:

- » Healthy forests act as carbon sinks by absorbing carbon dioxide. Therefore, cutting down forests releases carbon into the atmosphere and reduces their ability to act as carbon sinks in future.

- » Trees also help manage the level of water in the atmosphere by regulating the water cycle. In deforested areas, there is less water in the air that is returned to the soil, resulting in dryer soil and an inability to grow crops. Furthermore, trees help the land retain water and topsoil, providing rich nutrients to sustain additional forest life, without which the soil erodes and washes away, causing farmers to move on and perpetuate the cycle.

- » The barren land left behind due to these unsustainable agricultural routines is more susceptible to flooding, especially in coastal regions. This also has an effect on seagrass meadows, a group of marine flowering plants, which are one of the world's most productive ecosystems. They constitute an important CO_2 sink, which is responsible for about 15 percent of the total carbon storage in the ocean.

- » As large amounts of forest are cleared away, indigenous communities, which rely on the forests to maintain their way of life, are also under threat. The governments of countries with native rainforests generally attempt to evict the indigenous tribes before the clearing occurs.

REMEMBER

Four main commodity supply chains — beef, soy, palm oil, and pulp and paper — are predominantly sourced from regions with high deforestation risk. The production of these commodities is worth hundreds of billions of dollars annually across the tropical forest regions of Latin America, Southeast Asia, and Sub-Saharan Africa. Within these four commodities, analysts suggest that 50 to 80 percent of current production is linked to past deforestation. The extent of production related to deforestation can differ by location, but avoiding further deforestation, while supporting restoration and rehabilitation, will require changes from all producers. Furthermore, a report on climate change and land released by the Intergovernmental Panel on Climate Change showed that 11 percent of greenhouse gas emissions are caused by poor forestry and land-use management, including commodity-driven deforestation.

In 2019, institutional investors representing US$16.2 trillion in assets under management and coordinated by two organizations — Principles for Responsible Investment (PRI) and Ceres — demanded that companies take urgent action due to the destructive fires in the Amazon, which were partly due to the accelerating rate of deforestation in Brazil and Bolivia. They argued that deforestation and loss of biodiversity not only are environmental problems but also have major negative economic consequences that need more effective management of agricultural supply chains. In addition, large corporations have been wary of the reputational risk if their supply chains are linked to these issues and have pledged to exclude deforestation from their supply chains. Meanwhile, pension funds are considering divesting holdings in transnational commodity traders operating in such countries. As a result, it's likely that they will need to shift to deforestation-free methods in the future.

Don't throw your future away: Waste management

The traditional model of waste management is changing. Collection methods, waste-to-energy solutions, and innovations are all essential elements directing us to a circular economy model (an economic system aimed at eliminating waste and the continual use of resources). Focus on waste is impacting all companies that produce products, and they all need to consider how they take greater ownership of the waste they produce throughout their production cycle. As populations have grown and urbanization has increased, the work of waste management companies has become increasingly vital. The market size of global waste management is anticipated to grow at a compound annual rate of 5.5 percent from 2020 to 2027, becoming a US$2.34 billion marketplace (go to www.alliedmarketresearch.com/ waste-management-market for more information). The market can be broken down into municipal, industrial, and hazardous wastes, where collection and disposal services are provided. The collection services include areas such as storage, handling, and sorting, while disposal services focus on landfills and recycling.

REMEMBER

The key mantra of waste management companies should be to take care of the environment by managing and reducing waste (some refer to this as the 3Rs: the reduce, reuse, and recycle approach). Their main objective, assuming a sustainability focus, is to reduce and reuse waste materials wherever possible, thereby avoiding further waste, minimizing pollution, and endorsing recycling. Ideally, they should encourage waste-to-energy development by converting waste to energy when it's not recyclable. Finally, they need to ensure and promote proper solid waste management, especially when removing and safely managing toxic or environmentally harmful materials like solvents and industrial waste.

However, the continuing introduction of new legislation and regulation will drive new policies that will demand new technologies and products, particularly in helping to achieve net-zero carbon emissions and to protect biodiversity. Governments have played a key role in many OECD (Organization for Economic Co-operation and Development) countries by providing support for waste management investments, including grants, loans, and tax exemptions that support investments made by businesses and specialized producers. But major investments in a range of new technologies will be required, such as chemical recycling and turning residual waste into fuels and chemicals, while new systems of data collection will be needed to monitor the fulfillment of obligations.

Studying the Effects of a Company's Operations on the Environment

Businesses don't operate in a vacuum. In a global economy reliant on cross-border trade, convoluted supply chains, and diverse workforces, companies are constantly challenged by environmental issues as well as product safety and relationships with regulators and local communities. Therefore, managing these factors is simply part of maintaining a competitive advantage in today's economy.

A company needs to use best management practices to avoid environmental risks and capitalize on opportunities that produce long-term shareholder value. Where companies earn excess profits by externalizing the cost of environmental and social issues upon the communities in which they operate, investors risk paying the price when this is corrected, and costs are internalized to the company's financial statement. In recent years, shareholders have experienced considerable losses following the negative environmental impacts of oil spills, mine explosions, and unsafe products. While there isn't just one solution to circumvent such catastrophes, identifying material environmental impacts and mechanisms to reduce these can help mitigate risks and even identify new opportunities.

The following sections discuss two working areas of a company's impact on the environment: direct operations and supply chains.

Direct operations

Evaluation of environmental issues can reduce costs by, for example, minimizing operating expenses (such as raw-material costs or the real costs of water and carbon). Therefore, when analyzing the comparative resource efficiency of companies within given sectors, investors should look for correlation between resource efficiency and financial performance. Studies suggest that companies with more developed sustainability strategies will outperform their peers. One approach is to integrate environmental policies into their operations strategy and functions, incorporating operations such as product design, technology choice, and quality management. Companies that don't acknowledge the consequences of environmental problems on the operations function may not succeed in the future in a competitive market, so this element of operations strategy needs to be aligned with the corporate strategy.

Large companies are transferring sustainability from the bottom line to the top line. They are becoming more sustainable and implementing changes tied to their direct operational control. For example, strengthening distinctive competence in terms of operations objectives contributes toward a competitive advantage. The environmental properties that an organization can control determine whether a particular activity, product, or service creates emissions, waste, or land contamination. Other issues that a company may be able to influence include the environmental performance or extended life of product design, minimizing the use of material resources and energy in packaging, and improving the biodiversity of land use.

Therefore, organizations should ensure that environmental inspections are undertaken on a regular basis to mitigate factors that could impact the company. While larger companies have more resources for such activities, it's equally important for small and medium-sized businesses to consider the influence of external factors on operations, as they may be more vulnerable to such issues. Moreover, this helps organizations take advantage of opportunities before their competitors, tackle issues before they become substantial problems, and support plans to meet shifting demands.

Supply chains

Companies can't always control indirect environmental factors, such as those in the supply chain, but they can influence suppliers and users to reduce, minimize, or eliminate the impacts that are caused. Sustainable procurement is firmly on the agenda, and companies don't want to be linked to suppliers with questionable business models, as this generates negative media coverage. Many firms have implemented a supplier code of conduct that requires suppliers to follow the core principles of the UN Global Compact (see Chapter 1) within the areas of human rights, labor standards, environment, and anti-corruption. Suppliers are obligated to impose similar principles on their suppliers.

In many industries, the vast majority of issues around sustainability are external and related to providers across the supply chain. In particular, for companies in some industry sectors, suppliers' operations are responsible for over two-thirds of a company's total CO_2 emissions. Large, multinational companies are the ones looking to improve on this the most, as they realize the importance and weight that supply chains have, and their priority is in finding ways to hold their suppliers accountable. Many have begun to apply a risk-based approach, where they focus efforts on areas with the greatest impact, recognizing that supplier subdivision is an ongoing process. Potential suppliers are prescreened on a number of factors, such as country, sector, and reputational risks, including compliance with sanctions. Based on the prescreening, high-risk suppliers are further assessed, which then determines whether additional engagement is pursued to advance sustainability performance. This can include developing a company's technological systems, scoring suppliers, making public targets, or considering an inter-industry collaboration.

However, one of the clearest barriers is the struggle to monitor complex supply chains and find the know-how to assess suppliers' sustainability, particularly when there's a lack of support from top management or government agencies. The companies that have applied sustainability scores, using a supplier scorecard, can distinguish and choose between suppliers with comparable quality and cost while estimating how eco-friendly the suppliers are. Firms using public targets will claim that they'll only work with suppliers that use low-carbon technologies or have waste reduction programs. Moreover, some companies request suppliers to set their own reduction targets and urge them to, for example, deploy renewable energies or start providing biodegradable or recycled packaging materials. Finally, through industry collaboration, where a collaborative network is formed with suppliers, intermediates, or civil society, companies can help improve the broader industry.

Whatever the approach, suppliers must be encouraged to share their sustainability challenges so that both sides generate better solutions together.

REMEMBER

Defining "Green" for a Company

Reports suggest that from 2007 to 2009, eco-friendly product launches increased by more than 500 percent. More recent surveys have found that two-thirds of senior management see sustainability as a revenue driver, and half anticipate that green initiatives will present a competitive advantage. This striking change in the corporate mindset over the last ten years reflects a developing consciousness that environmental responsibility can contribute to growth and differentiation.

Supporters of green companies argue that it's more efficient to go green than to continue adding toxic chemicals to the atmosphere and the environment overall. However, challengers dispute the environmental claims of some "green companies" as exaggerations and have raised allegations of greenwashing (see Chapter 6 for further information), where a company is claiming to be green when its practice suggests it is not.

To appreciate the advantages of a green business, you need to understand what the term means. If a company makes a determined attempt to decrease its negative environmental impact, it can rightly claim to be "going green." Typical measures include starting recycling and reusing procedural programs, as well as buying green products and services. Most countries have laws that order environmental compliance to varying degrees. For some companies, going green can indicate anticipating future regulation and getting ahead of the curve. The EPA launched an Action Agenda in 2020 with wide-ranging plans to decrease carbon emissions, promote sustainability, and provide enticements for being ahead of the "green curve." (Go to www.epa.gov/sites/production/files/2016-07/documents/ej_2020_factsheet_6-22-16.pdf for details.)

In the following sections, I define what the term "green" means for a company: managing externalities and following the 3Rs (reduce, reuse, and recycle).

Internalizing (or managing) externalities

It will come as no surprise that, while generating wealth for investors, economic activity also creates externalities or impacts. The majority of externalities are negative! They also have associated costs that aren't entirely covered by the entity that creates them. In particular, a negative externality assumes an indirect cost to the public that causes harm to people in the surrounding area; one example would be toxic gases that are released from chemical firms or mines. Rather than the company paying for the cleanup, the public or local government has to bear the indirect cost to clean up the problem.

Internalizing, or managing, the externality means shifting the burden from external to internal. This is generally achieved through taxes, which are levied when the externality reaches a certain point and a "penalty" is imposed, thereby discouraging these activities. Conversely, government can provide subsidies to stimulate activities that address the problem, such as limiting the effect of externalities on the community.

However, because regulators don't always have full information on the externality, it's difficult to impose the right penalty or subsidy. Moreover, historically, externalities have continued because of the lack of information needed to recognize them adequately. Therefore, as externalities become more transparent, they should be easier to internalize, creating the link between ESG factors and financial returns. Policy changes will require companies to reflect the cost of externalities in their business models. This generates a risk to future returns for investors, but is it acceptable for them to "turn a blind eye" to such activities? Investors are now aware of the potential cost of litigation for failing to protect their investments against environmental risk and have been placed in the spotlight for not building such risk considerations into their investment decision-making.

The 3Rs: Reduce, reuse, and recycle

The 3Rs that refer to the three basic skills taught in schools — reading, (w)riting and 'rithmetic — will be familiar to children and adults alike. However, the 3Rs of sustainable living — reduce, reuse, recycle — are probably more familiar to our children than adults as they are already better educated on the amount of waste we throw away!

With the cost of goods and materials rising, using resources efficiently and reducing business waste makes sense financially and for the environment. Moreover, the cost of sending waste to landfills is increasing, as are the restrictions on what can be sent. Increasingly, penalties are levied if waste isn't handled appropriately or the right paperwork hasn't been completed before it leaves your premises. Using the 3Rs also helps minimize the amount of space needed for landfill sites.

TIP

Some index providers have launched indexes focused on companies that reduce, reuse, or recycle. One example of this is the Solactive ISS ESG Beyond Plastic Waste Index, which includes companies focused on plastic waste. Investment in such products is intended to alleviate the waste problems caused by production of plastics (for more information, visit www.solactive.com/beyond-plastic-waste/).

Reduce

Reduce the amount of waste you produce. Reducing waste in the first place is the preferred method of waste management, as you're immediately protecting the environment. You can reduce waste by doing the following:

» Purchasing durable, long-lasting goods

» Seeking products and packaging that are toxic free

» Redesigning products to use fewer raw materials in production, or to aid in recycling

Reuse

In a world with so many disposable items, the idea of cleaning an item and using it again is alien to most people. When purchasing a new item, look for a product that can be used repeatedly rather than used once and thrown away, or buy or rent secondhand items. The items you reuse may end up being waste, but by reusing them, you're reducing the overall amount of waste produced. Here are some examples of what you can do:

» Refill bottles and reuse boxes.

» Purchase refillable items and durable coffee mugs.

» Use cloth napkins or towels.

Recycle

Recycling prevents the emissions of many greenhouse gases and water pollutants, saves energy, and generates less solid waste. Also, when products are made using recovered rather than original materials, less energy is used during manufacturing, fewer pollutants are emitted, and pollution caused by the extraction and processing of original materials is reduced. In summary, recycling does the following:

>> Prevents emissions of many greenhouse gases and water pollutants

>> Saves energy and stimulates the development of greener technologies

>> Reduces the need for new landfills and incinerators

Detailing a Company's Performance as a Steward of the Physical Environment

The term *environmental stewardship* has been used to describe activities such as reducing harmful activities or pollution, purchasing more sustainable products, and replanting trees and limiting harvests. Stewardship itself embodies the responsible planning and management of resources and can be applied to the environment and nature, economics, or property. Such actions can also be differentiated, from local to global efforts, or in rural and urban contexts. Many environmental issues are seen on a global scale, which suggests that local actions can't meet those challenges; however, engaging in local stewardship actions and initiatives can be the catalyst to ensure involvement in promoting broader sustainability issues. Business initiatives that improve environmental impact are increasing in number, but there is a growing consensus that transformations need to take larger steps than those that are currently underway.

WARNING

Many businesses don't fully understand the driving forces that promote environmental sustainability in the context of their own operations. Without understanding these forces, they are likely to sub-optimize their transformation initiatives and fail to realize the expected value. More work is required to establish clear definitions as well as a framework in different contexts to effectively support material activities.

Environmental stewardship is considered a growth area, with business leaders taking action to apply environmental sustainability principles. They need to create insights that allow them to better understand the driving forces behind their actions and better align initiatives to achieve business value. The actions in the following sections can help.

Managing operations to reduce emissions and promote sustainability

Most firms understand that by building a business model that reduces reliance on fossil fuels, they should benefit from opportunities that the new ways of doing business create. And in doing this, they expect to lower operational costs, improve resilience in their energy supply, and attract more investors who are concerned about carbon risk.

Greenhouse gases (GHG) can be reduced considerably in manufacturing, where they control the operations, and even in supply chain processes such as distribution and retail. Indeed, some companies are intending to support the generation of more renewable energy than they need to make the surplus available to the markets and communities in which they operate. This would help some companies reach their target of becoming carbon-positive in their factories and site operations by 2030.

Eco-design programs are being developed to reformulate products to use fewer but higher-performing ingredients, particularly in the use of their most GHG-intensive products. Interestingly, most of the GHG footprint for many products occurs when people use them at home. Therefore, innovation and research and development (R&D) are also focused on delivering the products while considering the climate change challenge. Tackling these issues requires transformational changes to broader systems in which firms operate, and so government policy will need to dictate the right context for change and business action so that all sectors can work in collaboration on given projects and initiatives. (I discuss GHG in more detail earlier in this chapter.)

Collaborating with others to create solutions for environmental issues

WARNING

Unfortunately, business collaboration has been the greatest contradiction within corporate sustainability. Numerous efforts by companies to collaborate on the most complex issues facing civilization, such as climate change, resource exhaustion, and biodiversity loss, have been unsuccessful mainly due to self-interest, lack of a shared purpose, and an absence of trust. Companies have embraced sustainability, and many have effective ongoing programs in areas they can tackle on their own — for example, rationalizing manufacturing processes or decreasing their fleet emissions. However, when tackling collaborative answers to systemic problems, little progress has been made.

Collaborative governance is often stressed as the answer to different environmental problems. However, cooperation around environmental issues in a complex world is difficult to achieve as different players want different things, diverse environmental issues are related to each other in dissimilar ways, and given groups have differing amounts of influence on certain questions. So, can collaboration lead to a better environment?

Research shows that the capacity to resolve environmental problems is in part associated with the way such networks are structured and in the patterns of collaboration between players. For example, where there is a risk of one player free-riding on the efforts of others, the conflict may be improved by linking such players with a third entity to form a triangular cooperation, in the hope that peer pressure will resolve the issue. It can also make a difference based on whether the problem is temporary or more permanent. When it's temporary, it can be more successful where the network chooses a coordinator or leader to hold it together. The Environmental Collaboration and Conflict Resolution (ECCR) is a process whereby neutral, third-party facilitators work with agencies and stakeholders using collaboration, negotiation, structured dialogue, mediation, and other approaches to prevent, manage, and resolve environmental conflicts.

REMEMBER

This decade will determine whether civilization can develop a more socially and ecologically sustainable society. A vital part of that target requires a better understanding of how cooperation can be improved and become more effective, both among private stakeholders and public institutions. Continued leadership from businesses, governments, cities, and regions is required to maintain leadership in areas such as deforestation; business commitments to act; science-based targets and zero pledges; policy reform to level the playing fields; and financial disclosure to allow markets to correctly price risk and capital to flow to more sustainable investments.

Chapter **4**

Give Me an 'S'! Investigating the Social Aspects of ESG

What does the 'S' in ESG mean? Is it Sustainable? Or Stakeholder? Actually, the "Social" factor suffers from the middle child syndrome! There is a sense of exclusion as the 'E' (see Chapter 3) is the poster child that everybody talks about and the 'G' (see Chapter 5) is the dependable sibling that has the fundamental traits that everybody relies on. Therefore, while the focus on the ESG family has grown in recent years, the wider market still struggles to agree about what aspects the 'S' should take in company evaluation and integration into investment decisions.

Companies have made real progress in disclosure on their environmental impact and governance standards, while their social impact and performance measurement is, relatively speaking, the poor stepchild! This can be explained by the urgency surrounding climate change issues and the enhanced governance control even before the 2008 financial crash, both of which have kept 'S' in the shadows.

However, every child gets their chance to shine! In a COVID-19 setting, 'S' has been hauled into the spotlight (not quite kicking and screaming!) and will attract much greater attention from investors than previously. The speed, extent, and intensity of the crisis is without parallel in our lifetime, and factors relating to 'S' are now among the most urgent issues for companies globally. Entire sectors of the economy are facing a bleak and uncertain future. Therefore, a company's reputation will be a function of how they engage with and relate the 'S' to their stakeholders in a clear and transparent way.

Investors have found 'S' to be the most difficult to analyze, measure, and integrate into investment strategies. The qualitative nature of social performance and the wide range of related issues contribute toward the difficulty of building consensus in the industry. Therefore, it has often been seen as an interface between the 'E' and 'G,' while the lack of data and consistency in social reporting from companies has added a further layer of complexity.

WARNING

But getting what you wished for should come with a risk warning! Regulators, government, customers, and employees will scrutinize the corporate story and their social credentials more closely. Issues such as health and safety, human rights, labor standards, diversity, inclusion, and data privacy have gained more prominence. Companies need to take this opportunity to communicate their social activity and progress to all stakeholders. This new emphasis will also bring more scrutiny on third-party rating agencies, reporting frameworks, and standards.

Rating agencies, in particular, have been questioned about the lack of correlation between their respective ratings. 'E' and 'G' issues, which are more easily defined, have a recognized track record of market data and are often associated with strong regulation. Given that social issues are less tangible, with less mature data, there are challenges to showing how they impact a company's performance. To confuse matters further, these issues are estimated differently in different countries. Therefore, it's important to have clear definitions and measurements for what represents good social practices and performance to decide what weighting each factor has so that investors can compare different companies and adopt uniform reporting on social issues.

This chapter outlines the primary social activities and indicators that companies consider within their social programs. It also considers how to evaluate these factors, determines how to define and measure them, and discusses how specific social indicators could be weighted, both within the 'S' element itself and in the broader ESG universe.

Identifying Factors in a Company's Social Performance

The broad definition of social indicators is that they are essentially statistical measures that express social trends and conditions impacting human well-being. They can represent how a company acts in a social context by evaluating its impact on the life quality of its employees and the local communities in which it operates. Common examples include the rates of accidents and fatalities, poverty, inequality, employment or unemployment rates, supply chain labor standards, life expectancy, and educational attainment.

Objective social indicators represent facts independent of personal evaluations, whereas subjective social indicators measure perceptions, self-reports, and evaluations of social conditions. Examples of subjective indicators include trust, confidence, life satisfaction, well-being, and perceived security. The following sections outline specific social indicators that form the basis for the 'S' in ESG and elaborate on how they are used to determine the social rating of a company.

Customer satisfaction

REMEMBER

Customer satisfaction can be seen as a task that is both simple and complex to achieve. In general, companies create value by providing the products and services their customers need and aim to build long-lasting relationships by maintaining trust and loyalty. Moreover, to achieve long-term success, companies must operate with high standards and deliver fair outcomes to the customer. If things go wrong, they should act and respond quickly to customer feedback to improve their communication, processes, and services. Complaints should be examined and reported to governance forums, while senior management should be measured against customer satisfaction performance. Meanwhile, related staff training should emphasize the importance of recording complaints in order to improve practices, procedures, and systems. Conduct principles need to be embedded into the way products are developed and sold, with strong risk management controls in place to meet customers' expectations and regulatory requirements. Companies that fail to meet those targets are less likely to maintain revenue and profitability.

This summary should be seen as the basic expectations that society has of a company that is delivering customer satisfaction. But investors can monitor other indicators to ensure that the company is preserving those principles:

>> Put customer feedback at the center of decision-making in order to identify issues and prioritize change more effectively.

>> Consider customers' needs in offering products, review the suitability of recommended products, and monitor sales quality and how salespeople are incentivized.

>> Use customer panels and user labs throughout the design process to adapt products.

>> Test during the design and development process to ensure a clearly identifiable need in the market, and maintain consistent standards when providing advice and recommendations to customers, including regulations.

>> Implement a globally consistent methodology to measure the riskiness of products, which is customized for local regulatory requirements, with a detailed customer risk-profiling methodology, while observing local regulations.

>> Monitor for fraudulent activities, as they are a risk and concern to customers; therefore, commitment to impact reduction is required, including fraud prevention systems and communications to raise awareness.

>> Introduce procedures for potentially vulnerable customers, with dedicated case managers as appropriate.

>> Instill in the corporate culture a sense of responsibility, and incentivize correct behavior and effectively manage poor conduct.

>> Introduce a customer-centric framework to enable digital transformation and improve metrics around real-time customer feedback.

>> Use artificial intelligence (AI) and Machine Learning (ML) solutions to enable analysis of data, rapidly and with greater distinction. While this technology offers significant potential benefits for customers, companies need to implement procedures around the potential ethical risks that are posed. (I discuss this in more detail in the next section.)

>> Introduce mandatory conduct objectives in annual performance assessments. Performance against these and other behavioral ratings is to be considered when determining rating levels and discretionary pay.

Data protection and privacy

In a nutshell, data protection is about securing data against unauthorized access, so it's more of a technical issue. Data privacy is about authorized access, but a firm needs to determine who has access and who defines that access, so it's more of a legal issue. In today's world, where collecting and processing personal data has become such a significant revenue driver, firms are investigating more ways of deriving revenue from their data but need to manage the downside risks of data security, management, and privacy requirements. Given that it can be difficult to determine whether certain information meets local or international regulators' definitions of personal data, these risks have naturally tended to increase.

However, the pace of change in technology, and the way that personal data is leveraged, has substantially outpaced that of data privacy regulation, entailing that people aren't sure who has their personal data, what it's used for, or whether it's protected. Given that there have been some highly publicized data breaches in the news, both regulators and end users are imposing greater restrictions on data usage.

The most important regulatory development on a global scale was the introduction of European legislation in the form of the General Data Protection Regulation (GDPR). This came into effect in May 2018, with the goal of giving EU citizens more control over their personal data. Moreover, GDPR explicitly has extraterritorial reach, and so any company conducting business with EU citizens has to be compliant. Many other countries, including Canada, Argentina, and Brazil, as well as the State of California, have now also introduced legislation or increased implementation requirements, taking their lead from elements of the GDPR model. This has resulted in most firms "cleaning house" and ensuring that their use of personal data is compliant. This invariably requires board oversight, the employment of a data protection officer (DPO), and further governance structures that require employees to prioritize data privacy and relationships with customers and suppliers.

In response, many companies have implemented a risk-based approach to reaching compliance by covering the more material elements of data that present the highest risk. The principal areas include making sure data is secure, reducing the amount of data stored, collecting only as much data as necessary to complete processing activities, and keeping data for only as long as required. The data should also be pseudonymized or encrypted, or both:

>> *Pseudonymization* masks data by replacing identifying information with artificial identifiers.

>> *Encryption* translates data into code, so that only people with access to a decryption key or password can read it.

Moreover, the increasing prominence of "Big Data," which is complex data sets that are too large to be processed by traditional data processing software, may intensify this issue. There are no clear rules to guide decision-making as Big Data and related AI technologies evolve, and so companies need to have ethical principles in place to ensure consistent and predictable decisions can be made.

REMEMBER

So, data privacy falls into the basic human rights bucket but is at odds with the business models of many successful companies. This increased reliance on data collection, processing, and distribution has also increased potential reputational, litigation, and regulatory risks where there is poor data stewardship. Therefore, ESG investors view such issues as a vital metric when evaluating which companies to invest in and are advocating that companies become more transparent in their processes and privacy safeguards. Effectively, they are pushing companies to self-police and self-regulate rather than act on regulatory decrees, as a reactive stance may be more damaging to long-term profitability. The costs associated with pro-active risk mitigation are small, compared to the potentially favorable increases in company valuation in the longer term.

Gender and diversity

Recognition of the existence of gender and ethnic inequalities, and the importance of addressing them in business, has been disappointingly slow, even though evidence of such discrimination has mounted in most occupational sectors globally. However, more recently, regulatory requirements have been imposed to document inequalities in the workplace, particularly equal pay for men and women, which have generated more debate and political consideration. By emphasizing and reporting on key indicators of inequality, such disparities become public and create reputational damage to the organizations involved, which encourages them to be proactive in their response. And multiple reports are showing that this should be beneficial to the performance of the company. In addition, companies that show strong diversity in their workforce, particularly in terms of race, ethnicity, gender, and sexual orientation, and at the board level are more likely to make better business decisions and therefore have financial returns above their national industry medians. Equally, companies with less diversity are less likely to achieve above-average returns.

REMEMBER

Such results can vary by individual country or sector, but increasingly, more diverse companies are finding that they are better able to win top talent and enhance their customer orientation, employee fulfillment, and decision-making, which help increase returns. Moreover, this promotes all kinds of diversity, including age, sexual orientation, disability (including neurodiversity), and social differences, which can bring a competitive advantage as it promotes an inclusive company culture that can strengthen organizational effectiveness.

Investors have increasingly emphasized the value of boardroom diversity, not purely from a social perspective, but also as a way to improve the mix of decision-makers at the board level. This reduces groupthink and legal risk while improving corporate governance. However, they need to actively push companies to disclose more information as there is a lack of basic data to evaluate diversity improvements. Those that have managed to integrate diversity also report that it helps decrease company-specific risk in the long term. This leads to a lower cost of capital, as they adjust their discount rate when valuing companies for factors that haven't been fully priced into the market.

Employee engagement

Research suggests that a strong corporate culture, a positive working environment, and engaged employees contribute toward the best-performing companies. Increasingly, questions are raised about corporate governance regimes that are only focused on the interests of capital, and not enough on the interests of labor:

» Does the typical "shareholder value" model, which emphasizes using corporate profits for share buybacks and returning dividends to investors, have an inherent bias toward value removal rather than value creation?

» Does this approach impede the promotion of internal, long-term re-investment in human and physical capital, productive capacity, and research and development?

» Do such entrenched incentives for asset holders and senior management create a natural tendency toward short-termism in both finance and industry?

Most European countries explicitly include employee representation on a company's supervisory board, which gives them formal rights to information and involvement in corporate decision-making. This isn't viewed as some form of social experiment but a recognition that employee voices at the board level increase trust and co-ownership, and improve insight by bringing different perspectives and information to the table. This encourages employees to feel more engaged and promotes longer-term horizons. After all, workers face the longer-term risks in a company more than other stakeholders and therefore should have more say in corporate governance. Reports conclude that satisfied employees work harder, stay longer, and produce better results for the organization. This will be even more relevant as the workforce becomes increasingly composed of millennials and Generation Zs who are more inclined to bring their values into the workplace.

REMEMBER

The ESG investor view is that exploiting employees, and local communities and environment, is no longer sustainable, and that some organizations aren't appropriately focused on employee engagement. After all, if a company's management treats other stakeholders that way, there is a good chance that they might treat their shareholders just as poorly! An organization's success should be built on motivated, engaged employees, so employers should reappraise their purpose if they want to attract and retain the best talent. Furthermore, in-work poverty is a reality in some business sectors, so creating a positive corporate culture must be difficult when its employees are struggling to get by. Therefore, some investment funds are heavily focused on explicitly targeting firms that promote human capital through areas such as personal development, autonomy, fairness, job purpose, and work environment.

The COVID-19 pandemic provides a real opportunity for firms to strengthen their commitment toward greater employee engagement. Given that flexible working, or "working from home," will prevail in the "new normal" environment, engaging with a more disparate workforce presents different challenges. This is intertwined with a corporation's approach to ESG issues, where companies that embrace their ESG strategy into the culture of their organization now seem to be rewarded. Many companies will reactively respond to regulation and investor community pressure, while those that have been proactive should gain a competitive advantage in the fight for talent when the recovery begins.

Community relations

Community relations represent the ways in which companies establish and maintain a mutually beneficial relationship with the communities in which they operate. By taking an active interest in the well-being of its community, a company gains long-term benefits in terms of community support, loyalty, and goodwill. Organizations are recognized as good citizens when they support programs that improve the quality of life in their community, including education, employment and environmental programs, urban renewal projects, recycling, and restoration. These can also include philanthropy, volunteering, salary sacrifice schemes, and in-kind donation programs. Even smaller businesses can achieve community visibility and create goodwill by sponsoring local sports teams or other events, through financial support or employee participation.

REMEMBER

Competition and social pressures require changes in the relationship between company and community. By making a commitment to the community part of their core business strategy, companies attract and retain top employees, position themselves positively among customers, and improve their position in the market. This strategic social investment helps establish a consistent brand image and market presence globally and can be the most significant communication activity undertaken by an organization. The company develops relationships to promote its brand, and the community receives assistance from the program — win/win.

Meanwhile, for some firms, particularly mining and excavation companies, a strong community relations program is required by law in some countries (including Australia, China, Nigeria, and South Africa). These Community Development Agreements (CDAs) are contracts between investors and communities under which the benefits of a mining project are shared with local communities and other stakeholders. A particular example is the Australian Native Title Act, which compels companies with mining licenses to agree and enter into CDAs with Aboriginal communities that have a legal right to the land as native title holders.

Human rights

International human rights law outlines the duties of governments to act in specific ways or to abstain from certain acts, and to endorse and protect human rights and fundamental freedoms of individuals or groups. These basic rights are based on shared values like dignity, equality, fairness, independence, and respect, and they are inherent to all human beings, regardless of ethnicity, gender, nationality, race, religion, or any other status, without discrimination. Some examples include the right to life and liberty, freedom from slavery and torture, freedom of opinion and expression, and the right to work and education. Therefore, human rights–focused frameworks cover a broader diversity and balance of social issues and tend to concentrate on a specific industry and their most material issues.

TIP

The standards most commonly used by investors are the Universal Declaration of Human Rights (UNDHR; www.un.org/en/universal-declaration-human-rights/) and the more recently issued UN Guiding Principles (UNGPs) on Business and Human Rights, which identify three pillars: Protect, Respect, and Remedy. Check out www.ungpreporting.org/resources/the-ungps/ for more information.

The United Nations has created a comprehensive body of human rights law, representing an internationally protected code that all nations can subscribe to based on internationally accepted rights, including civil, cultural, economic, political, and social rights. Investors should also ensure that companies act on these issues and support the fight against any human rights violations by international companies. As shareholders, investors have the power to change corporate behavior and end any practices that are contrary to human rights by proposing resolutions at a company's annual general meeting (AGM). Frequently, this is most apparent with companies' supply chain partners, and this prompted the United Kingdom to introduce legislation, in the 2006 Companies Act, that requires given companies to produce a statement each financial year. This highlights the steps they have taken to ensure that slavery and human trafficking aren't present in their business or supply chains. In addition, this holds companies accountable, and failure to comply may impact their reputation, their operational effectiveness, and ultimately their financial performance.

TIP

Investors have demanded more reliable, accessible information about the human rights track records of individual companies. In recent years, a growing number of labor and human rights experts have produced public ratings and rankings that focus explicitly on these issues. They aim to highlight leading and lagging companies in a particular industry, or on a certain social issue, by using indicators that include a range of human rights concerns. Given that they are created by human rights experts, in consultation with other stakeholders, these ratings more adequately reflect labor and other human rights issues (for example, www. corporatebenchmark.org/). They also have transparent methodologies and indicators that are used in creating their evaluations.

Labor standards

Labor standards are defined and protected through international conventions and instruments, including standards suggested by the International Labour Organization (ILO) and the United Nations (UN). It's assumed that a company's workforce is a valuable asset and that a positive worker-management relationship is important to the sustainability of a business. Any failure to create and support this relationship, and maintain good labor conditions, could result in a range of additional business costs and impacts. These can include low levels of worker productivity and low-quality output, strikes or other worker action, failure to secure contracts with major and international customers, fines or penalties levied by local regulatory authorities, and ultimately reputational damage.

On the contrary, positive labor conditions can enhance the efficiency and productivity of operations, leading to increased revenues and margins. Moreover, many companies require that their suppliers demonstrate policies that align with the ILO Fundamental Conventions and best practices and participate in third-party audits by accredited verifiers to assess compliance.

WARNING

Labor standard issues tend to be found in certain industry sectors and activities, such as "sweatshop" manufacturers in labor-intensive products, such as clothing and footwear, mining for physical commodities, construction activities, and hospitality. However, the legal frameworks in developing countries, where many of the issues are unearthed, don't comply with good internal practices, and many countries have poor records around the protection and enforcement of workers' rights (although, as frequently highlighted, such activities are also found in developed nations where the legal frameworks are supposed to protect workers).

International companies and investors should ensure that local companies have employment policies in place that at least comply with local laws and regulations and envision establishing the protections recognized by the ILO core conventions. Companies also should ensure that their own practices, and those of companies in their supply chain, ensure compliance with best practices. Investors should also check whether a company is audited regularly to confirm that it observes its own policies. Some companies have been known to create systems that "hide" their infringements! Therefore, a supplier's competitiveness could be directly related to harmful labor practices.

Meanwhile, technology has driven the emergence of the gig economy, which describes the creation of more flexible job opportunities, such as ride sharing or food delivery services, which operate under "zero hours" contracts (where an employer isn't obliged to provide any minimum number of working hours to the employee). These new business models don't fit traditional labor frameworks, as workers complete tasks similar to those of regular employees but they are classified as "self-employed" individuals or "freelancers." This entails that they don't have access to the same rights and benefits legally due to regular employees, including freedom of association and collective bargaining. Therefore, while the gig economy provides more flexible work conditions than regular employment, it presents worrying challenges to labor rights through insecure work, uncertain hours, poor pay, and involuntary overtime.

WARNING

Damaging media reports covering poor labor practices have become regular news headlines. The major difficulty here is that some supply chains have multiple tiers, extending beyond formal suppliers to a large number of less formally organized suppliers. Monitoring practices that ensure good labor standards can be extremely complex. Companies and investors should try to map their suppliers and determine the most material risks and any possible mitigation. However, the stark reality is that this could take months to produce and would involve considerable time, effort, and expense; therefore, there may be a natural exclusion policy that is pragmatic at times.

WARNING

In a worst-case scenario, all of the issues highlighted in this section can lead to a modern form of slavery, including debt bondage (where a person is forced to work for free to pay off a debt), child slavery, domestic servitude, and forced labor, where victims are threatened with violence. Again, some of these practices can be as prevalent in developed as well as developing countries.

Evaluating a Company's Social Performance

Corporate social responsibility (CSR) is effectively a voluntary self-regulating approach that encourages a company to be socially accountable to its stakeholders, the public, and itself. By adopting CSR as a part of their business strategy, companies are aware of their impact on different aspects of society. However, it's a wide-ranging concept that takes different forms, relevant to the company or industry, but incorporates the social indicators outlined earlier in this chapter. Furthermore, it also encompasses companies' responsibility to the environment, entailing ethical behavior and transparency that contributes to sustainable development.

Through CSR programs, businesses can benefit local communities and society more broadly while boosting their brands. Introducing CSR policies is now expected, with more companies placing CSR at the center of their corporate, digital communications, and broader strategy. On the other hand, companies that don't uphold societal standards and practices leave themselves heavily exposed to reputational and other risks. In turn, this can hit both their top and bottom lines through loss of sales, fines, and litigation.

The following sections list some tools and information for evaluating a company's CSR performance.

The results are in: Achievements

There are no independently objective criteria that define or evaluate how well a company is delivering on their social targets. In part, this is because each program can be as unique as the companies following it and the communities being helped. Many companies adhere to expected buzzwords and highlight "buy-in" from senior management, and "strategic alignment" between their services and their social impact. However, transparency on progress toward their goals, community assessment on their improvements, and peer evaluation, compared to firms that have a long track record of CSR, give a clearer picture of their achievements.

Generally, the CSR initiatives that achieve the greatest impacts incorporate feedback loops that enrich programs as they evolve. Constant refinement of what you measure, allied with clearly defined Key Performance Indicators (KPIs), will increase the efficiency of a program and lead to better results.

TIP

Some industry-standard tools that can assist further include the following:

- » **B Corp Certification,** which aligns company practices to social goals (https://bcorporation.uk/about-b-corps).

- » **CommunityMark,** which is a measurement tool for community involvement (www.laing.com/uploads/assets/CommunityMarks%20monitoring%20 boards%20-%20FINAL.pdf).

- » **Global Reporting Initiative (GRI),** which provides global standards for sustainability reporting, including but not limited to social considerations (www.globalreporting.org/standards/).

- » **International Labour Organization (ILO),** which ensures human rights within the supply chain (www.ilo.org/).

- » **Sustainability Accounting Standards Board (SASB),** which measures the financial impacts of sustainability, including but not limited to social considerations (www.sasb.org/).

When in Rome: Differentiating on a national or regional basis

Internationally developed standards and objectives, such as the UN Sustainable Development Goals (www.un.org/sustainabledevelopment/sustainable-development-goals/; see Chapter 1), guide countries and organizations toward greater sustainability and corporate responsibility. Some of these goals clearly highlight that the scope of social impact that companies can consider varies considerably in different jurisdictions. More broadly, this could be considered within a continent as much as within a given country, and developing countries will be evaluated differently than developed countries, as developing countries often don't have effective legal or regulation procedures, or don't systematically enforce them with respect to appropriate programs.

Moreover, the point of engagement may be different; for example, a large, multinational corporation may directly support social activities from its headquarters or certain regional offices, or provide that support indirectly through its suppliers in developing countries. Evaluation of how well those programs then perform may also require different metrics based on the organizations and indicators involved.

TIP

From an investor's point of view, reports suggest that there are differing focuses: Companies in different countries or continents tend to focus more or less on social activities within the ESG triumvirate. Evidence suggests that European companies engage in social responsibility programs more than those on other continents.

Determining Measurements for Social Performance

Given that research shows that socially responsible corporate programs are aligned with corporate success, the measurement of a program's performance — the topic of this section — has become essential. Such measurement allows organizations to make better choices about which programs to support, and how to improve the efficiency of their CSR initiatives and enroll stakeholders to support them.

WARNING

However, most social measurement assesses what is most convenient, not always what is most material. In the current environment, most measurement concentrates on data that companies have easy access to and are prepared to disclose. This ultimately rewards companies for developing programs that relate to social issues, but not for the results of those efforts. This system allows companies to produce a lot of information, much of which is not relevant; therefore, this doesn't deliver any meaningful benefit in assessing companies' social performance. Moreover, it's challenging to find objective measures for material impact, so there is a tendency to measure processes rather than specific outcomes.

REMEMBER

The lack of consistent standards for evaluating social measurement increases costs and doesn't highlight the true social leaders, as most people don't know what "good" looks like! Therefore, "social" evaluation trails behind its ESG "siblings" in terms of consistent indicators used to measure company performance in a way that is useful to investors. However, post COVID-19, companies will be more closely identified with the concept of "purpose." How committed were they to deliver value to customers, invest in their employees, deal fairly with their suppliers, support the communities in which they operate, and generate long-term value for investors? Both society and investors will hold companies accountable and include this analysis in their ESG research. Here are some important aspects to consider:

>> Was customer feedback moved to the center of decision-making so that companies could recognize issues and prioritize actions more efficiently?

>> Were actions taken proactively to assist employees' well-being, and what effect will company actions have on employee loyalty and approval in the future?

>> How was the handling of furloughs and layoffs dealt with, including the example set by executive management in sharing their load of the burden?

>> What did a company contribute toward broader societal impacts, and did they provide access to their capability or facilities to help society at large?

The alignment of social and economic responsibilities

Evidence suggests that more analysis is required to produce a useful system of reporting to validate the alignment of corporate programs with the needs of society. Commentators have suggested that it requires its own global accounting standard to improve comparability. Therefore, the need to integrate social issues is clear because, for example, a company's supply chain is unlikely to be secure if it has poor labor practices and human rights violations. Operational performance could be damaged by increased worker turnover and decreasing motivation and productivity. By successfully managing social issues, companies can obtain access to environmental resources, build human capital to safeguard a productive workforce, strengthen their supply chains, and benefit overall from a competitive advantage in the market.

Also, there is a growing awareness that good social performance can deliver better relationships with local communities. However, companies should remember that while they are genuinely delivering social programs, they should ensure that social and economic responsibilities are aligned and agree on such balance with key stakeholders. In this way companies can benefit economically, while being socially responsible, through increased sales and customer loyalty. Studies suggest that businesses that improve their social responsibility perception see consumer recommendations increase. Therefore, companies can establish themselves as socially responsible and good corporate citizens while adding greater value to their business.

REMEMBER

All of these aspects show that purpose can be aligned with corporate success. Asking companies to run their business with the main purpose of creating value for society seems a long way off, but it may increase the total value created in the future.

Long-term change for people and communities

The availability of skilled workers is one of the key aspects in becoming a successful company. To tackle the skills-gap challenge, companies must invest more in training and reskilling their workforce. According to the World Economic Forum (WEF), more than half of all employees will require significant reskilling by 2022, but the problem is likely to be even more acute in specific regions.

In addition, research shows that companies that prioritize their values, create social impact, and build a more diverse and inclusive culture are better placed to improve employee engagement and productivity, and they have an advantage in attracting and retaining skilled talent. Ultimately, companies will be measured on how well they have adapted to the new environment, and an indication of that will be whether they attract the right workforce and how they utilize those employees thereafter.

TIP

The WEF theme "Skills for Your Future" focuses on investing in training, education, and skills to optimize human resource management and help organizations attract and nurture the best talent. The nature of work, the workforce, and the workplace is being transformed by new tools and technologies, and companies need to use this opportunity. See `www.weforum.org/focus/skills-for-your-future` for more information.

The COVID-19 crisis has brought social factors to the foreground, and these have increased focus for many investors. There has been additional analysis of how companies deal with their customers, employees, suppliers, and stakeholders in general. Investors will appreciate more fully what stakeholder management means in their investment process, as going forward this will have an impact on company profitability and return on investment.

Deciding on Weight Factors

Investors haven't focused on how companies have performed socially in the past (as much as environmental performance; see Chapter 3) because companies haven't adopted uniform reporting on social issues in the same way that they have for other ESG factors. For example, greater attention to environmental factors has led investors to create systems and reporting methods for topics such as carbon emissions and clean energy usage. However, while social factors have been the trickiest part of ESG for companies and their investors to measure and monitor, as data related to social issues becomes more accessible and refined, it's anticipated that investors will systematically value social factors alongside other financial factors.

Furthermore, regulatory drivers related to social aspects — such as the UK's and Australia's Modern Slavery Acts or the increased attention created by the adoption of the UN Sustainable Development Goals (see Chapter 1) — support this alternative approach. But despite the positive progress being made, there is still a long road to travel before social issues are systematically integrated into investment decision-making processes. Nonetheless, more investors are considering how they integrate their relative weighting towards 'E,' 'S,' or 'G' issues for specific companies and sectors. Even within 'S' alone, there will be different weighting considerations based on specific social indicators, which may be driven by industry sector or region-specific considerations. The following sections dig deeper into weight factors (see Chapter 8 for more information).

Take your pick: Different social issues

Social issues cover a wide range of topics: consumer protection, product safety, labor law and safety at work, diversity, the fight against corruption, and respect for human rights throughout the supply chain. Therefore, they are inherently more qualitative and judgmental indicators, and so, investors find it challenging to integrate them into financial analysis and models because they are difficult to quantify.

To complicate matters further, social issues are evaluated differently in different countries. For example, some countries place greater emphasis on respecting human rights and avoiding child labor, while others may place issues around workplace diversity higher up their value chain, and such differences may also be amplified by the region of the world in which they are investing.

REMEMBER

As a result, it's more difficult for investors to highlight the financial impact that social issues have on risks and long-term investments. To change this perception, it's necessary to have clear definitions and measurements for what constitutes a "social" company. Furthermore, it's necessary to determine what weight to give to diverse social issues so that investors can better evaluate given companies and sectors in social terms. It has been more usual to analyze social factors through qualitative analysis, but investors are increasingly quantifying and integrating social factors into financial forecasting and company valuation models, in alignment with other financial factors. Some social issues lend themselves to quantification (for example, the gender pay gap), but there also needs to be an understanding of what the company's approach is to managing and addressing them, which can also be achieved through stakeholder engagement. By integrating social issues into fundamental analysis, investors can treat social factors in the same way as any other financial issue with existing quantitative methodologies. (See Chapter 15 and www.unpri.org/listed-equity/esg-integration-in-quantitative-strategies/13.article for more details.)

Think outside the box: Scenario analysis

Social factors can be integrated through a range of techniques, including revenue, operating margins, capital expenditure, discount rate, and scenario analysis. A common approach is for investors to forecast revenue, typically taking a view on how fast the industry is growing and whether a specific company will gain or lose market share. Social factors can be integrated into these forecasts by increasing or decreasing the company's revenue growth rate by an amount that reflects the level of investment opportunities or risks.

Social factors can also be used to estimate the influence on assets' future anticipated cash flow — such as by forcing long-term or permanent closures (as with the COVID-19 lockdown) — and thereby alter their net present value (NPV) by applying a discount rate to future cash flows. The impact is likely to be a reduction in NPV, resulting in an impairment charge, which brings down the book value accordingly. An asset revaluation can result in lower future earnings, a smaller balance sheet, additional operating and investment costs, and a lower fair value for the company.

Another example of an impact to asset book value is where a local community protest could lead to work stoppages at mines or even to mine closures, which reduces the future cash flow of the mining company. If an investor believes that future cash flow will be significantly less than the current estimate, the investor may charge an impairment charge to the book value of the mines and the income statement of the mining company.

Alternatively, a less common approach to help understand the impact of ESG factors on the fair value of a company is to conduct a scenario analysis, where an ESG-integrated company valuation is calculated and compared to an initial valuation. Quant strategies and smart beta providers tend to evaluate the differences between the two scenarios that can be used to calculate the materiality and magnitude of social factors affecting a company. This is particularly relevant for certain companies, given that social factors are more industry-specific and tend to appear in financial measures over a longer time frame.

These challenges help explain the facts suggested by surveys, that there are greater long-term returns to be made from environmental and governance factors than from social factors. Unfortunately, there seems to be greater anticipation of downside risk with social factors than upside benefits.

REMEMBER

On the other hand, research implies that companies with high social standards appear to react stronger to incidences such as inflation or periods of economic weakness, thereby reducing a company's systematic risk. Moreover, it suggests that the "social" factor pillar considerably reduces all three types of risk — namely idiosyncratic and total firm risk, as well as systematic risk — and that the social factor is the only one, within ESG, that reduces systematic risk. The conclusion is that social factors should be considered as effective, when managed well, in reducing corporate risk. Therefore, 'S' could help investors to build a portfolio that responds in a less volatile way to market changes.

TECHNICAL STUFF

In modern portfolio theory, systematic risk is defined as the risk to which all companies are exposed that cannot be reduced by diversification. Research suggests that factors that fall within the 'S' of ESG are as common as (and more so for some companies) those inside 'E' and 'G' in contributing to business risk and ultimately causing lasting damage to a company's reputation.

Some ways in which social factors could be integrated into an investor's portfolio to create a combined ESG score include the following:

>> Equal weighting applied to each of the three factors, regardless of the data transparency issues

>> Optimization of weighting based on historical data

>> Industry-specific weightings

Studies suggest that in the short term, both equal-weighted and optimized approaches performed better because they had higher exposures to governance issues. However, an industry-specific weighted approach that changed weightings over time showed the strongest financial performance.

The 'S' in ESG has never been more relevant for corporate productivity and, as a consequence, investment returns. And yet, from the plethora of ESG-related investment products, studies have revealed that a much smaller percentage of S-ratings-based products target investors as the primary audience, versus the vast majority of E- and G-ratings-based products. In addition, it's suggested that the UNGPs on Business and Human Rights should inform what analysts, raters, and investors measure when it comes to 'S.'

Chapter **5**

Give Me a 'G'! Decoding the Governance Component of ESG

orporate governance principally describes the systems a company uses to balance the competing demands of its diverse stakeholders, including shareholders, employees, customers, suppliers, financiers, and the community. Through this process, it provides the structure to deliver a company's objectives by covering all aspects of organizational behavior, including planning, risk management, performance measurement, and corporate disclosure. In total, it safeguards appropriate oversight aimed at ensuring long-term, sustainable value creation with due regard for all stakeholders.

As such, corporate governance has always been an important topic in its own right, before it took on additional significance within the broader ESG universe. Therefore, among the 'E,' 'G,' and 'S' factors, it can be considered the most relevant to performance as it controls the overall purpose and strategy of a company and how risks are mitigated. If you don't start with 'G,' the other issues aren't identified or managed, so it's more difficult to solve for them if a crisis situation occurs. Consequently, the 'G' in ESG is considered a mandatory element of any due diligence process, with some investors placing increasing emphasis on it as the core component of their investment approach. Moreover, governance data, unlike environmental or social data, has been amassed for a longer period of time, and the norms and standards for what encompasses good governance have been widely debated and accepted.

Therefore, the days when governance focused exclusively on maximizing shareholder value have gone; for example, the UK Corporate Governance Code was revised in 2018 to charge boards with establishing a company's purpose, values, and strategy. This ensures that companies consider creating long-term value for all stakeholders.

This chapter outlines how investors determine what "good" corporate governance looks like, how they evaluate governance values, how governance interacts with and influences the 'E' and 'S' factors within ESG, and how this differs from region to region. Of course, this is all reviewed against the backdrop of the COVID-19 pandemic of 2020, and how corporate governance contributes to management of the current crisis and any similar scenarios in the future. After all, governance can be viewed as the quality of leadership, and leadership is essential in times of crisis.

The Good Place: Defining What "Good" Corporate Governance Looks Like

In 2001 and 2002, the collapse of two big corporations, Enron and WorldCom, and the ensuing scandals (followed by further collapses at high-profile companies including Arthur Andersen, Global Crossing, and Tyco) were precipitated by corporate governance failures. A common starting point for defining corporate governance is to highlight the four pillars: the board of directors, management, internal auditors, and external auditors. Within this structure, there are a number of key tenets to achieve good governance, which include board quality, independence and attendance, executive remuneration and incentives, ownership, audit and accounting standards, bribery and corruption, and business ethics — all of which are discussed later in this chapter. These tenets need to be responsive to the current and future requirements of the company; they also need to apply caution in decision-making and ensure that the best interests of all stakeholders are considered. These elements have further stimulated the evolution of corporate governance globally.

REMEMBER

"Good" corporate governance, as you find out in this section, requires that companies respect the needs of all stakeholders, including shareholders, employees, customers, and suppliers, while recognizing any societal or environmental issues and being accountable for their actions. These governance factors allow companies to measure the quality and strength of their structure and practices. How good each company is at maintaining their position is open to conjecture, but there are also independent observers that attempt to score and rank each company's ability (see Chapter 14 for more on this). Governance factors indicate the rules and procedures for countries and corporations, and allow investors to screen for applicable practices, as they would for environmental and social factors (covered in Chapters 3 and 4).

The benefits of good governance

Research on governance factors has shown that companies ranking well below average on good governance characteristics are more disposed to mismanagement and risk their ability to capitalize on business opportunities over time. However, good governance is more an insurance policy than a guaranteed way to raise Return on Capital Employed (ROCE), although there is a clear correlation between financially strong firms and those that exhibit effective governance. Given the importance of good governance, investors are giving 'G' factors further consideration. In addition, to mitigate governance risks, investors also undertake "engagement," interacting with managers and directors of companies on business strategy and execution, including sustainability issues and policies. This also extends to agreeing to vote on certain key decisions at shareholder meetings. Consequently, investor engagement and stewardship, which focus on the effect of corporate activity on all stakeholders of the company, are increasingly seen as an integral part of good governance.

REMEMBER

So, while corporate governance is important to investors to confirm a company's direction and financial viability, it also needs to demonstrate good corporate citizenship through environmental awareness and ethical behavior. Good corporate governance produces a clear set of rules and controls in which shareholders, directors, and employees have aligned incentives. In turn, this helps companies build trust with investors and the community. Meanwhile, investors have confirmed their willingness to pay a premium for shares of well-governed companies.

For example, in the United States, leading institutional investors have continuously asked corporate boards to clarify their companies' purpose and contribution to society. This has culminated in the Business Roundtable's statement on corporate purpose, issued in August 2019, declaring their commitment to not only shareholders but all stakeholders. Their members are exclusively the CEOs of 181 of the major U.S. companies, and a key question is "Will they live up to the statement in times of stress?" (See the statement at `https://opportunity.businessroundtable.org/ourcommitment/`.)

On the other hand, bad corporate governance casts doubt on a company's reliability, honesty, and responsibility to stakeholders, which has consequences for a firm's financial health. For example, the scandal that hit Volkswagen in September

2015, where they deliberately manipulated engine-emission equipment in order to falsify pollution test results, saw their stock lose nearly half of its value in the days following the announcement. Moreover, the fraudulent practices that bankrupted Enron and WorldCom resulted in the introduction of the Sarbanes-Oxley Act in 2002. This imposed stricter recordkeeping requirements on companies, and introduced rigid criminal penalties for violating them, in order to restore confidence in public companies.

More "regular" types of bad governance practices include companies not cooperating sufficiently with auditors, resulting in the publication of noncompliant financial documents, poor executive compensation packages that fail to align with shareholder interests, and badly structured, poorly performing boards where it's difficult for shareholders to vote out unproductive members. In addition, it's important to highlight that where countries fail to establish acceptable standards of governance, the companies within those jurisdictions can be found "guilty by association" and find it difficult to attract foreign and institutional investment.

Practices and values

Corporate governance seems to have been in the news more often in the last 20 years due to the number of scandals that have been reported, leading to the collapse of companies due to mismanagement. This has provoked regulators all over the world to introduce numerous acts and rules to monitor and control negligent corporate behavior that causes harm to shareholders and stakeholders. This oversight essentially "helps companies to help themselves" when considering best practices and values in pursuit of profit maximization. This has acted as a wake-up call for the corporate world to "get its act together." However, it's clear that some of the lessons learned haven't prevented abuse of corporate power (Wirecard in Germany, which was brought down by accounting fraud, is the latest high-profile example) and have also shown that monitoring for ethical business behavior is a constant requirement.

Consequently, companies are required to provide increasing levels of non-financial information, especially concerning their ESG impacts. Such demands range from specific types of disclosure, such as board composition and executive pay, to calls for extensive periodic reports on companies' ESG performance. For example, corporate social responsibility (CSR) reporting, or sustainability reporting, has evolved from an ad hoc activity assumed by a few progressive companies to a routine practice at most of the world's large companies. While there isn't a legally mandated framework for this reporting, many companies have implemented the standards set out by the Global Reporting Initiative (GRI; see Chapters 1 and 15), which cover a broad range of issues from human rights to environmental compliance, anti-corruption efforts, and customer privacy. The abundance of sustainability issues has encouraged numerous attempts to narrow and categorize the field.

REMEMBER

This highlights the art of guiding and controlling an organization by balancing the needs of various stakeholders. This enables the resolution of conflicts of interest between stakeholders and ensures that the organization has the processes, procedures, and policies that they need to promote the principles of transparency and accountability. Such controls need to be balanced against companies' requirements to maximize profits while safeguarding against companies cutting corners in their pursuit of profits. So, companies need to be managed and directed in accordance with standard norms and procedures that promote ethical conduct.

Multiple stakeholder orientation

Stakeholder orientation is generally defined as an objective to benefit all parties that are affected by the future success or failure of an organization. Essentially, it's in companies' best interests to maintain positive long-term relationships with all stakeholders, understanding their needs and constantly aligning stakeholder requirements with companies' needs. The current environment has been created by essential changes in shareholder engagement, which has become a dominant topic for public companies and their investors in the 21st century. Public companies have embarked on unparalleled levels of proactive engagement with major shareholders and stakeholders. Institutional investors have also improved their engagement efforts, committing substantial resources to governance issues, company outreach, and the analysis of proposals on voting ballots and voting policies.

Furthermore, levels of shareholder activism remain at record highs, enforcing considerable pressures on targeted companies and their boards. Investors seek a greater voice in companies' strategic decision-making, capital allocation, and overall corporate social responsibility.

Many shareholder-driven campaigns are forcing changes to corporate strategies (through spin-offs) or capital allocation strategies (through share repurchase programs), suggesting that their voices are being heard in the boardroom. Given that shareholders are the ultimate owners of the company, this is appropriate; however, concerns are expressed by other stakeholders where activists' goals are too focused on short-term uses of corporate capital, such as share repurchases or special dividends. Longer-term stakeholders are demanding that the board consider both long-term and short-term uses of capital to determine the appropriate allocation of that capital to meet the company's business strategy. ESG considerations are naturally forcing companies to veer toward a longer-term approach with a broader set of stakeholders to be included.

Walk the Walk: Evaluating a Company's Governance Values

Governance has become a key focus for sustainable investing, particularly as firms navigate their recovery for after the COVID-19 pandemic. Their response to the pandemic has prompted a renewed focus on best practices and has highlighted the requirement for effective corporate governance and review of a company's purpose and values. While the greater focus on ethical and environmental issues will continue, there is a renewed emphasis on specific business issues around fairness and transparency, which has been the traditional focus for fund managers' stewardship recognition in the past. (One example of a basic question is "With COVID-19 destroying the economy and an impending uncertainty about the extent and duration of the crisis, should companies have been paying dividends?") As companies make decisions in circumstances that have never been faced before, stakeholders will be constantly scrutinizing and verifying any board decisions and resolutions. However, "no one size fits all" in relation to a company's response, so each company needs to determine the principles and values that are appropriate in light of its needs and circumstances. The following sections explain how to evaluate a number of these principles and values.

REMEMBER

All companies should adhere to some core principles:

>> In particular, decision-making at the board level should consider the interests of all stakeholders, including employees, customers, suppliers, and the community in which the company operates, in order to achieve long-term value creation.

>> The board and management should engage with long-term shareholders to understand concerns and issues that worry them and potentially affect the company's long-term value creation.

>> Shareholders who engage with the board and management in a way that affects decision-making are urged to disclose relevant identifying information and to accept some accountability for the long-term interests of the company and its shareholders.

>> As part of this responsibility, shareholders should accept that the board must constantly weigh both short-term and long-term uses of capital when deciding how to allocate it in a manner that is most beneficial to shareholders and to creating long-term value.

Board responsibilities

A corporation's board is ultimately responsible for the management of its business and directly responsible for given decisions, including relationships with the company auditor and setting executive compensation. Through its oversight function, the board selects and reviews the performance of the Chief Executive Officer (CEO) and ensures that they set a "tone at the top" that establishes an obligation to integrity and legal compliance. In turn, this should establish the basis for corporate culture that is communicated to employees throughout the organization. Furthermore, investors are increasingly expecting greater "buy-in" to ESG issues and for companies to have a strategic approach to corporate social responsibility (CSR).

The board needs to have significant participation in formulating the company's long-term strategy and needs to frequently assess implementation of the plans to ensure long-term value creation. Subsequently, the board and senior management should jointly agree on the company's risk appetite to achieve those goals and appreciate any major risks involved. This can be achieved by establishing a structure for risk oversight, assigning responsibility to committees, and supervising the designation of senior managers who are accountable for risk management.

Moreover, as the risks from ESG issues become more apparent, it's increasingly important for boards to understand how these risks affect the business. Resultant impacts can be financial, material, and spread across several areas of a business in every sector of the economy. A key part of directors' fiduciary responsibility is the "duty of care," where they sufficiently inform themselves on such issues prior to making business decisions. Therefore, the recruitment of directors with experience and exposure to the material ESG issues that the company faces helps satisfy this obligation. However, there is a need to educate the entire board on relevant ESG issues so that they appreciate and assess the risks and engage with relevant stakeholders and shareholders. A useful tool to evaluate the likely impacts of key environmental and social risks on corporate strategy is scenario analysis (introduced in Chapter 4).

The board should review all financial statements to ensure they accurately represent the company's financial situation and existing operations, and ensure full disclosure of other important information highlighting past results or future plans. To achieve this, the company's internal controls and procedures need to be designed to identify and discourage fraudulent activity. These procedures should also include oversight and approval of annual budgets and operating plans, and input on the capital allocation process, to ensure an adequate balance between short- and long-term funding. Meanwhile, the risk oversight function should focus on business resiliency, including topics such as business continuity, cyber-security, crisis management, and physical security. The company's compliance program also needs to be robust, and the board should be made aware of any meaningful compliance issues that arise.

TIP

Directors need to assess whether the company's Enterprise Risk Management (ERM) process is flexible enough to always identify ESG issues as both current and emerging risks. As a starting point, companies should review the guidance on integrating ESG issues within the company's ERM process, which has been developed by the Committee of Sponsoring Organizations of the Treadway Commission (COSO; www.coso.org/Pages/guidance.aspx) and the World Business Council for Sustainable Development (WBCSD; www.wbcsd.org/).

Board composition

Increasing attention has been focused on the relative diversity of a company's board, in terms of the mix of women, ethnic minorities, and others with diverse cultural backgrounds, which has been proven to avoid "groupthink." Diversity should also promote representation from a broader range of society, which has been shown to improve board performance and encourage the creation of long-term shareholder value. BlackRock, one of the largest global asset managers, has made it clear that boards looking for their support will have to focus on board diversity, with generational diversity seen as an indicator for greater integration of ESG factors.

REMEMBER

These traits should be combined with the general characteristics of integrity, strength of character, sound judgment, objectivity, and an ability to represent the welfare of all stakeholders. This also assumes that the directors are independent and don't have relationships that might impair their ability to apply independent judgment. As such, a significant majority of the board's directors should be independent, according to appropriate rules and regulations or as determined by the board. In addition, the tenure of long-standing, independent board members should be reviewed and limited, as there may be a perception that they are not, over time, as independent.

Audit committee structure

The audit committee's role has traditionally been to provide oversight and monitoring of the financial reporting process, the audit process, the company's system of internal controls, and compliance with laws and regulations. However, as investors persist in requiring more insight into organizations' strategies, impacts, and dependencies related to ESG issues, they may expect an independent group, such as the audit committee, to take ESG oversight as part of their regular risk and regulatory compliance activities. While the board should participate in recognizing the ESG risks that influence corporate strategy, oversight should be formalized in a specific committee, and the audit committee could be best placed to cover that function given their responsibilities for overseeing the organization's assurance and disclosure processes.

REMEMBER

But the audit committee should ensure that executive management identify and assess any significant ESG threats, policies, and judgments required to systematically identify ESG risks and determine how they should be improved, including particular risk (for example, climate change and diversity) and macro trend analyses. The board should then establish systems for committees to work together on ESG risk oversight and provide disclosures that meet investor expectations on material issues.

ESG risks are established across industry sectors and can present systemic risks that need to be addressed by companies. The audit committee must understand how to oversee ESG risks through their regular approach of risk identification, prioritization, and mitigation processes. In turn, they need to adequately structure and disclose their ESG oversight to investors and other stakeholders. Yet, in many jurisdictions, no regulatory body or mandate explicitly requires organizations to provide ESG disclosure. As a result, no single standard or structure guides organizations on how to present such information to stakeholders.

A number of sustainability standard-setting and reporting initiatives are developing standardization and consistency in ESG disclosure, such as the Global Reporting Initiative (GRI), Sustainability Accounting Standards Board (SASB), and Task Force on Climate-related Financial Disclosures (TCFD). In addition, several jurisdictions mandate some form of corporate ESG disclosure through their capital markets regulators, or through stock exchange listing requirements. Such standards are gaining traction, and the vast majority of firms are providing some form of sustainability disclosure to the market. Find out more about these initiatives in Chapter 1.

Given their oversight of the financial reporting process, audit committees are best positioned to proactively engage and challenge management in appropriate discussion and advise how information is presented to investors. For example:

>> They are familiar with requesting information from finance, treasury, investor relations, operations, supply chain, and even third parties through their oversight of internal controls and compliance.

>> Their risk assessment and management responsibilities should contribute to an understanding of whether ESG issues are being considered in isolation or proactively through an ERM lens, covering the full range of risks relevant to the organization and investors.

>> They should establish an internal governance structure around ESG factors in the company, developing roles, responsibilities, data management, reporting, and disclosure.

>> They also have responsibility for selecting and retaining external auditors; therefore, they could analyze the current plethora of external market ESG evaluators (providing scores, ranking, and analysis) and determine which firms to engage with to "showcase" the company's ESG profile. However, this should also entail establishing procedures for any compliance concerns related to the company's code of conduct that ESG risks create.

REMEMBER

Ultimately, the audit committee should mirror its regular responsibilities for the financial reporting and audit process into the ESG reporting and oversight process. They should be satisfied that the ESG reporting and related disclosures prepared by management present the company's ESG "credentials" accurately and ensure that internal ESG reporting staff have adequate resources and support to carry out their role. This process should consider ESG regulations and potential litigation, with anticipation of any fines or penalties that might arise from ESG violations. Depending on the type of company, this might include extreme weather events disrupting operations, workplace injuries or deaths, or data privacy or security breaches. The key factor is to guard against risks such as market devaluations, loss of assets, reduced profits, or reputational damage from an ESG liability. However, it should also be viewed as an opportunity to determine how the organization can leverage any ESG opportunities by fully integrating and embracing any emerging ESG trends.

Bribery and corruption

Even though the 'G' of ESG is largely identified with aspects of board oversight, from board structure and responsibility to specific sustainability targets, it's bribery and corruption that remains one of the biggest business risks, with the United Nations (UN) stating that it is "one of the biggest impediments to achieving the Sustainable Development Goals (SDGs)." Many institutional investors are concerned about corporate corruption and its impact on both investment returns and economic growth. Corruption takes various forms, including bribery, embezzlement, money laundering, and tax evasion, and it costs the global economy over US$3 trillion each year, according to the UN.

REMEMBER

Bribery and corruption risks tend to be more prevalent within developing economies, where the rule of law can be weaker and enforcement may be lacking, but it's in reality a global issue. For example, in many developed countries, it continues to be an issue in the real estate and construction sectors. However, while corruption isn't unique to lower-income countries, it has a disproportionate impact on the poor and most vulnerable economies and people, reducing access to education, health, and justice services. And both the World Bank and the World Economic Forum (WEF) have reminded people that much of the world's corruption couldn't happen without the actions of organizations in wealthy nations!

Investors know that bribery and corruption are ESG factors to be considered in their investment portfolios and recognize that there are regional difficulties in terms of governance structures. Investors are mindful of certain affiliations and recognize that many developed countries accept the export and enablement of bribery and corruption by their corporate and individual citizens, whether that be financial institutions accepting corrupt proceeds or intermediaries facilitating fraudulent transactions. Corruption can add up to 10 percent of the cost of doing business globally and up to a quarter of the cost of procurement contracts in developing countries!

REMEMBER

ESG due diligence should not only look at the effectiveness of controls for risk prevention and uncovering bribery and corruption, but also at how they interact with the business model of the company and the "incentives" that are available for misdemeanors. In addition, standards introduced should also consider the advantages for the business of receiving more revenue for products sold, given that money "escaped" through corruption can be reduced or slashed from the purchase process. Therefore, many companies view a budget allocated to such measures as an investment rather than an expense. Moreover, companies that establish these policies and procedures are building a sustainable business for the future by meeting the UN Global Compact's 10th Principle against corruption and are in a better position to fulfill SDG 16. (Read about these principles at www.unglobalcompact.org/what-is-gc/mission/principles/principle-10 and www.un.org/ruleoflaw/sdg-16/.)

Ultimately, this helps companies reduce damage to their brand, reputation, and share price, potential exclusion from new business opportunities, liability to pay substantial fines, and use of management time dealing with investigations or prosecutions. Furthermore, investors risk reputational damage and reduced return on assets if they are implicated in corruption, especially if the resulting scandal is badly managed by the portfolio company.

TIP

Given that corruption represents substantial legal and economic risk for companies doing business around the world, the U.S. Department of Justice (DOJ) and the Securities and Exchange Commission (SEC) are waging an international fight against corruption by increasing the number of investigations, settlements, and prosecutions for violations of the Foreign Corrupt Practices Act (FCPA). The FCPA contains both anti-bribery prohibitions and accounting requirements, the latter being designed to block accounting practices intended to hide fraudulent payments and ensure shareholders and the SEC have an accurate overview of a company's finances. To prevent violation, the SEC and DOJ can administer hefty fines and imprisonment. Find out more about the FCPA at www.justice.gov/criminal-fraud/foreign-corrupt-practices-act and www.sec.gov/spotlight/foreign-corrupt-practices-act.shtml.

Executive compensation

In general, executive compensation should align the interests of senior management, the company, and its shareholders to promote long-term value creation and success for the company. Therefore, it should include performance-based components that reward the realization of targets tied to the company's strategic plan, but that are discarded if the targets aren't met. Executive compensation represents one of the major components of corporate governance discussions and tensions between institutional shareholders and companies, and it's accepted that executive pay should incentivize long-term performance. However, such packages need to optimize financial results and promote sustainable behavior without creating systemic risks that damage investors' long-term interests.

Companies have started studying alternative ways to integrate ESG factors into incentive programs, but there is no standard method to link ESG metrics to executive pay. In addition, companies from different sectors and industries are influenced by different market forces or constraints; subsequently, distinct materiality can be applied to different ESG factors. For example, while environmental issues are specifically relevant to companies with a large environmental impact, other sectors will focus on community relations or ensuring health and safety in the workforce. However, this may not always be practical due to difficulties in measuring ESG factors or the lack of evidence highlighting the precise impact on overall company performance. Therefore, there is no "one size fits all" approach to integrating ESG factors into executive compensation schemes.

Sustainable value creation will have different definitions for each company, so it's necessary to determine appropriate ESG metrics that impact the long-term viability of operations and introduce assessments that include unique definitions for sustainability. These may include industry-specific regulations, regional economic conditions, access to resources and capital, environmental or political conditions, workforce composition, and growth opportunities. ESG metrics related to external sustainability indexes are discouraged because they aren't necessarily relevant to companies' circumstances. For example, Royal Dutch Shell introduced a scheme to tie executive pay to three- to five-year targets for their net carbon footprint from 2020. This sets an important precedent and should encourage their peers and other industry players to consider similar programs.

REMEMBER

More generally, the inclusion of ESG and CSR targets within executive compensation highlights that, rather than aligning incentives only with shareholders, there should be a broader focus on key stakeholder groups; it also signals a commitment to the company's value objectives as much as the value of the company. Therefore, companies should introduce clear guidance on how material ESG metrics are identified and related to sustainable shareholder returns, company strategy, and executive compensation. ESG targets should also be integrated into an appropriate time horizon that is in line with business, and form a meaningful component of the overall remuneration compensation. It goes without saying that this should sit within a proper governance structure (if not alongside the existing compensation approach) and be conducted in an ethical way such that ESG targets are rigorous and challenging to ensure outperformance is incentivized.

Lobbying

In general, *lobbying* can be described as the act of lawfully attempting to influence the actions, policies, or decisions of government officials or members of regulatory agencies through persuasion or interest representation. In a worst-case scenario, political donations and lobbying expenditures are used to unduly exert influence over public policy and regulatory systems. Despite this, most companies don't have a formal lobbying oversight system and don't fully disclose how those monies are spent. In some cases, companies may engage in activities that are effectively corrupt, but permissible by law!

In the United States, in particular, companies have substantial sway over public policy resolutions at federal and state levels via direct lobbying, as well as through think tanks and third-party trade associations. Studies suggest that business interests spent over US$30 billion on federal lobbying over the last 20 years, without there being an effective system for citizens to check the full scope of corporate influence. Disclosure databases only provide an aggregated quarterly total of money spent, and lobbying through trade associations provides companies with "political cover" when supporting policies that are unpopular or untransparent with respect to SDG sub-target 16.6. This target aims to "develop effective, accountable and transparent institutions at all levels." (Visit `www.un.org/sustainabledevelopment/peace-justice/` and click the tab "Goal 16 targets.")

REMEMBER

The level of spending on lobbying can lead to an unfair representation of company interests over public interest, and the lack of accountability can also enable companies to support public policy positions that prevent action on other SDGs, such as SDG 13 (climate action; visit `https://sdgs.un.org/goals/goal13`). However, a company may face reputational and/or operational risks if its lobbying activity is exposed and conflicts with stated company goals or implicates the company in public controversy. Therefore, far-reaching lobbying disclosure can offer broader public accountability and guarding against corruption. This ultimately helps increase trust in people and institutions, while allowing the signposting of critical ESG issues with company leaders.

Political contributions

Contributions are the most common source of election campaign support, whereby a contribution is considered as anything of value given, loaned, or advanced to influence a federal election. However, a board should reflect on its position with respect to political contributions by considering their purpose, benefits, risks, and boundaries. After all, by definition, a donation is a gift made without expectation of return, and any political contributions must assist the political process and not be linked in any way to a direct business advantage!

Therefore, due to stakeholder misgivings of corporate political engagement, the potential for erroneous perceptions of companies' objectives, and the risk of bribery, it's reasonable that many companies prohibit all political contributions. This trend is further reinforced by the conclusion that they benefit more from lobbying (see the previous section) and other forms of political activity. They have greater legitimacy, permit a higher degree of management and control, and allow for simpler measurement of returns.

In principle, companies shouldn't make political donations; however, if they are made, they should be as a representation of corporate responsibility, offering general support to the political parties to support a genuine democratic process. As such, they could be made in emerging or fragile democracies where, for example, the company has a leading market share and the international community agrees that funding could strengthen the democratic process. It should ensure that there is no suggestion of any immediate business advantage for the company and in all cases that donations are being appropriately disclosed.

Moreover, many companies are being challenged by shareholders and corporate governance advocates to disclose information on their political contributions. Therefore, many firms are increasingly voluntarily disclosing their political contributions, even though no mandates are forcing them to do so, as an indication of best governance practice.

Boards should also consider benchmarking their political contributions disclosure versus their peers and their industry to monitor if their disclosure practices vary from those of their competitors. If this is the case, they should analyze the motives behind that strategy and decide whether an alternative approach could be in the best interest of the board, the company, and its shareholders and other stakeholders.

For example, the large asset manager BlackRock states that companies can engage in certain political activities where they want to influence public policy in line with the companies' values and strategies; however, it believes that it's also the duty of boards and management to determine the appropriate level of disclosure of such types of corporate activity. Consequently, some firms believe that engagement in the political process is critical to their success, as their growth is dependent on forward-thinking legislation and regulation that improves public infrastructure. Without the benefit of information from the commercial sector, policymakers may risk missing opportunities to fully exploit technology or cause unintended consequences; therefore, they suggest that their contributions are designed to educate policymakers.

Whistleblower schemes

Whistleblowing is a term used when a person passes on information concerning wrongdoing. This is referred to as "making a disclosure" or "blowing the whistle." The worker informs on a person or organization they regard as being involved in illegal and unethical practices. Corporate or employee misconduct presents challenges to corporate governance, largely because it undermines positive corporate culture and ethical business conduct and impedes economic growth; therefore, whistleblower policies are seen as an indication of good-quality corporate governance.

Workers are often the first people to witness wrongdoing within an organization, and their information can prevent escalation of the problem, which may damage an organization's reputation. However, where an organization hasn't created an open and supportive culture for whistleblowing, workers may not feel comfortable making a disclosure, for fear of any consequences. The two main issues they fear are concerns of reprisal and that no action will be taken if they make the disclosure.

TECHNICAL STUFF

One high-profile example of this was the case of whistleblowing at Barclays Bank in 2016. Barclays was found to have violated local banking laws and its own procedures during the handling of a whistleblower disclosure by the New York State Department of Financial Services (DFS) and subsequently fined US$15 million. The information was not dealt with by the bank's investigations and whistleblower team, but distributed among senior management, at which point the CEO allegedly asked for the whistleblower(s) to be uncovered. The DFS investigation uncovered actions that exposed the bank to risk and created an atmosphere in which employees might hesitate to raise issues of concern. The CEO himself was also fined £642,430 by UK regulators for breaking rules by trying to find the people who forwarded the information, and his bonus was cut by £500,000.

REMEMBER

So, the landscape is changing, and companies with poor whistleblowing policies potentially increase risk for their investors by losing the chance to recognize misbehavior taking place internally and subjecting themselves to litigation. As an employer, it's good practice to generate an open, clear, and safe working environment where workers feel able to speak up. Even though the law doesn't require employers to have a whistleblowing policy in place, the existence of such a policy demonstrates an employer's responsibility to listen to the concerns of workers. By having transparent policies and procedures in place, an organization shows that it welcomes information being shared with management, and it's a vital component of an effective corporate compliance program. Progressive corporate leadership is also directing similar procedures to critical workforce-culture concerns such as bullying, gender inequality, sexual harassment, and any other issues of personal conduct and ethics.

Lead the Way: Emphasizing How 'G' Can Dictate the 'E' and 'S' Factors

Governance can never be isolated from environmental and social issues, as you find out in this section. Excelling in governance requires an understanding of the spirit of an issue or regulation rather than mastering the letter of the law. Therefore, identifying potential violations before they occur or ensuring transparency and discussions with regulators, rather than "ticking the box" and submitting a report, highlights that understanding the 'G' in ESG is critical. Ultimately a company's governance approach will determine how they respond to environmental and social issues relating to the company, as well as covering cultural, economic, and political concerns. Governance can expand authority, policies, and procedures to address sustainability issues and create a culture that supports its acceptance.

Likewise, when sustainability permeates governance, executives become more accountable for environmental and social performance, such as energy, water, and emissions issues; equal opportunity, health, and safety; and well-being topics. The ways in which sustainability governance can affect environmental and social performance include developing a comprehensive set of policies, directives, and standards that direct fulfillment, creating a sustainability office that coordinates corporate-wide environmental and social strategy and activities, and appointing a board committee with primary responsibility for reviewing such matters.

Governance as an overarching principle for ESG

Good governance was deeply rooted in the culture of many firms well before environmental and social issues began to take center stage. Similarly, fund managers and investors have included corporate governance quality within their investment decision-making long before the exponential interest in ESG investment that has been seen in recent years. The stewardship investor influence in high-quality governance is still critical, including understanding the management, their long-term planning, and executive compensation structures.

This is demonstrated by the recommendation of the Principles for Responsible Investment (PRI) to changes in the UK Corporate Governance and UK Stewardship Codes, suggesting more attention should be paid to ESG issues. Furthermore, in particular, the UK Stewardship Code explicitly states that environmental and social issues are important drivers of long-term investment value and are part of the fiduciary duty that investors owe to their clients and beneficiaries.

Research suggests that external ESG ratings are able to measure up to 80 percent of environmental and social impacts within a company but fail to capture 20 percent of governance issues, even though governance may be considered to be the most important of the 'E–S–G' triumvirate. For example, in the climate change–related bankruptcy of the Pacific Gas and Electric Company (PG&E), external ESG ratings failed to fully gauge the governance component of ESG. While it highlighted the climate change component expected in a utility company, it failed to fully assess the internal management of those risks. Meanwhile, industry peers suggested that the company's internal ESG risk management processes weren't particularly strong.

Furthermore, such different assessments of ESG governance between outside ESG-ranking entities and industry peers can be even more relevant, given that reports suggest that the vast majority of investment firms view governance as the highest influence on investment decisions among ESG factors. The reality appears to be that companies don't always act on red flags, even when they are staring them in the face. Moreover, investment research company MSCI undertook research on ESG factors on the performance of companies in different sectors to establish whether the governance factor is the most important driver of performance for companies, and whether the weighting of 'E,' 'S,' and 'G' factors makes any difference to long-term performance. Their findings showed that governance does have more impact on companies' performance in the short term (one year). However, over longer time periods, all three ESG factors are vital to outperformance. The research also showed that the weighting of 'E,' 'S,' and 'G' factors within each industry can have a great bearing on the performance of an ESG index over long time periods.

For example, governance is considered to be the main ESG risk for banks. Governance quality is primarily essential for banks because they operate with greater leverage and are usually more confidence-sensitive than businesses in other sectors, especially regarding their funding arrangements. The results of a governance violation usually go beyond the direct impact, such as a financial penalty, but can lead to reputational damage, causing franchise erosion, a loss of business, or clients withdrawing funds. Yet, in public disclosure documents, many banks treat the governance factor of ESG almost as an afterthought, focusing more on environmental issues that may not be material. Despite this, governance failings continue in the banking sector, leading to clients being disillusioned by reputational damage caused by those failings, which affects their profitability and liquidity and therefore banks' earnings capacity.

The role of governments

In parallel to actions by companies, investors, and ratings agencies, governments, policymakers, and regulators are also driving change to take ESG into account. Here are some examples:

>> The UK government has launched a Green Finance Strategy, requiring that it will be mandatory for all listed companies and large asset owners to disclose the environmental impact of their activities by 2022. This approach is in line with the Task Force on Climate-related Financial Disclosures (TCFD), a body that exists to promote disclosure of climate-related risks (and opportunities) in order to enable assessment of investment risks and ultimately risks to the financial sector, thereby enabling more informed decision-making by investors about how investee companies are managing climate change–related risks and opportunities. The UK government is an early adopter of the aims of the TCFD, and their policy is to associate private sector financial flows with clean, environmentally sustainable, and resilient growth. All listed firms will have to be fully transparent about the climate effect of their actions. See www.gov.uk/government/publications/green-finance-strategy and www.fsb-tcfd.org/ for more information.

>> The European Union (EU) Taxonomy is a classification tool that includes a list of economic activities and performance levels specifying what threshold of environmental performance a service should have to influence Europe's environmental objectives. The adoption of the Taxonomy Regulation follows the entry into force of the Sustainable Finance Disclosure Regulation (SFDR) in December 2019, which effectively assumes that good governance is a prerequisite of good corporate sustainability. The first phase of integration reviews activities that can noticeably contribute to climate change mitigation or adaptation. An action will only be coherent with the taxonomy if it does no substantial harm to the other environmental targets, and meets minimum safeguards, specified in line with the OECD Guidelines for Multinational Enterprises and the UN Guiding Principles on Business and Human Rights.

The taxonomy is a significant effort by financial regulators to mandate disclosure against a sustainability objective, rather than a financial one, and will transform EU-wide sustainability goals into a tool that investors and corporations can work with. Taxonomy disclosures will help corporations and issuers access green financing to decarbonize high-emitting sectors and grow low-carbon sectors (see Chapter 15 for more information).

Initially, the climate change mitigation objective is Europe's pledge to net-zero carbon emissions by 2050. The taxonomy will be supported by regulation, with the list of economic actions and performance levels being issued as part of the precise legal requirements from the European Commission by the end of 2020. Financial market players and businesses will be required to finalize their first set of taxonomy disclosures, including activities that significantly contribute to climate change mitigation and adaptation, by December 31, 2021. Investors with funds in Europe will be obliged to reveal against the taxonomy where the fund is marketed as contributing to an environmental objective. See `https://ec.europa.eu/info/business-economy-euro/banking-and-finance/sustainable-finance/eu-taxonomy-sustainable-activities_en` for details.

Around the World: Underlining Regional Differences in Governance Activities

Both academic and industry research tends to view corporate governance at country and company levels. It's felt that the quality of corporate governance varies more by country than by company. Therefore, it's critical to appreciate the legal and regulatory requirements linked to corporate governance that are enforced by each country. This section looks at corporate governance in countries in three regions: emerging markets, North America, and Europe.

REMEMBER

In addition, country-level governance laws and regulations play an important role in producing a favorable environment for executing policies relating to the 'E' and 'S' of ESG. Economic studies have shown that countries with an open, honest, and transparent economy outperform those that do not. As such, evaluating countries for their ability to generate an environment beneficial to high-quality corporate governance is critical, and applying country governance is the next generation of responsible investing; thus, portfolio construction should begin with the 'G' as a leading indicator of future environment and social improvements.

Unfortunately, the current information on country-level governance hasn't been standardized and is fundamentally qualitative. Most governance information is offered on a company level, and it typically includes stakeholder, corporate social responsibility, and similar analysis. While many non-governmental organizations (NGOs) perform significant research on countries, including economic statistics

(GDP, trade balances) and social welfare (child labor, environmental quality), they don't provide insight into the legal, regulatory, and economic infrastructure most suited to good corporate governance.

Investors review the quality of a market's public institutions, which is indicated by the strength of its property rights, disclosure standards, and other features, to establish how much they can trust the market with their capital. Laws, regulations, and policies that form the investment environment predictably take center stage and form the institutional framework in which businesses operate. Better frameworks provide greater access to financing, lower cost of capital, and more favorable treatment of all stakeholders. Many studies highlight that these channels operate at the level of firms, sectors, and countries, although voluntary and market corporate governance mechanisms have less effect when an overall country's governance system is weak.

Investors should also be aware of the International Corporate Governance Network's (ICGN) mission to promote effective standards of corporate governance and investor stewardship in order to advance efficient markets and sustainable economies worldwide. ICGN is an investor-led organization whose policy positions are implemented by influencing policy, providing a reliable source of investor opinion on governance and stewardship, connecting peers to enhance dialogue, and informing dialogue through education (visit www.icgn.org/about).

Emerging markets

Emerging markets play an increasingly significant role in the global economy, given their high economic growth projections and their developing physical and legal infrastructures. Reports suggest that, combined, these countries account for nearly 40 percent of global gross domestic product (GDP). For some investors, emerging markets offer an attractive prospect, but they also involve multidimensional risks at the country and company levels. These risks compel investors to have a clearer appreciation of the company-level governance factors in different markets.

In emerging markets, the dominance of family- and state-controlled companies, and the probability for minority shareholders' interests to be compromised, creates a unique challenge due to the concentration of company ownership (although where incumbents, particularly family-owned businesses, have a long-term interest in the success of the business, this shouldn't always be seen as a negative, despite Western-biased models suggesting this). In the 21st century, some emerging markets have moved faster than others to plug their governance gaps, caused by economic storms and corporate scandals driven by governance failures. Without required safeguards, controlling shareholders will control corporate resources to meet their own objectives at the minorities' expense.

In the context of these macro factors, corporate governance rules and regulations present some valuable measures that increase the level of confidence in capital markets. Codes, listing rules, and legislation offer mandates connecting to board practices, shareholder rights, disclosures, voting mechanics, and environmental and social risks. While corporate governance codes commonly operate on a comply-or-explain basis, they have proven successful in shifting markets forward toward improved governance practices. On the regulatory front, most emerging market economies have maintained progress, having not only implemented corporate governance codes and regulations to create their standards, but also supervising periodic reviews to further progress these standards. Indeed, most major emerging market economies have revised their codes in the past three years. This recent activity shows that corporate governance has become a policy precedence for these countries and has led to better disclosure standards, higher levels of board independence, and more shareholder protections.

However, bureaucracy, corruption, lack of transparency, and the level of observance to the rule of law at the home jurisdiction may affect a company's own governance practices while also subjecting it to substantial risks. The 1997 Asian financial crisis was a major turning point for economies and corporations that had borrowed excessively, fueled in part by lax governance. The 2008–2009 global financial crisis emphasized the dangers of debt excesses and unproductive oversight. More recently, the aspiration to gain entry to major market indexes and attract more capital have been key; however, governance measures figure among the range of criteria they have to meet. The accessibility, competence, and transparency of their financial markets, combined with the strength of their regulatory systems, are just some aspects that index providers also consider.

TIP

An assessment of public governance at the country level may help set expectations of the types of risks related to investing in individual corporations. Resources include the following:

>> Indexes established by international organizations, such as the World Bank's Worldwide Governance Indicators (https://databank.worldbank.org/source/worldwide-governance-indicators) or Transparency International's Corruption Perceptions Index (www.transparency.org/en/cpi), may serve as helpful indicators.

>> The World Bank, as part of its Doing Business report (http://documents1.worldbank.org/curated/en/688761571934946384/pdf/Doing-Business-2020-Comparing-Business-Regulation-in-190-Economies.pdf), has established a Protecting Minority Investors score, which, among other factors, evaluates the ability of shareholders to bring suit, director's liability, and transparency toward minority investors.

Political risk may also be an issue, as political decisions could in some cases endanger relatively weak institutions. The challenge for institutional investors is how to weigh country factors, even if the investors assume that optimal governance is firm specific. Ultimately, investors can and should play a role in influencing governance practices in emerging markets through educated voting and, perhaps more importantly, continuing engagement with companies and regulators.

North America

Commentators suggest that the United States has struggled with its corporate governance framework due to its multiple facets of legal, securities, and accounting rules designed to protect the interests of shareholders in a transparent way. However, the perception is that the overall system lacks rigorous implementation to the point of favoring executive management over shareholders, in some cases allowing *poison-pill tactics* (generally a defensive maneuver used by a corporation's board against a takeover), which force the bidder to negotiate with the board rather than negotiate with the shareholders. This has culminated in a number of regulatory changes being applied in the United States and Canada:

>> The U.S. Securities and Exchange Commission (SEC) has introduced amendments to its rules governing proxy solicitations, designed to ensure that clients of proxy-voting-advice businesses — firms such as Institutional Shareholder Services (ISS) and Glass Lewis, which provide investors with research, data, and recommendations on proxy proposals that are voted on at a company's annual meeting — have reasonable and timely access to more transparent, accurate, and complete information on which to make voting decisions. They also approved new Human Capital Management (HCM) disclosure requirements on how public companies manage their workforce, particularly talent management; however, they allowed companies to decide whether they feel the information is important enough to warrant disclosure, and this will be based on a concept of materiality.

>> In Canada, the Business Corporations Act is set to come into force, codifying mandatory input on board and management diversity disclosure, pay, legal majority voting, and the method that corporations use to send information to their shareholders. See https://laws-lois.justice.gc.ca/eng/acts/C-44/ for information.

A change in corporate purpose from shareholder primacy to stakeholder capitalism is potentially underway, reinforced by the U.S. Business Roundtable's Statement on the Purpose of a Corporation (see https://opportunity.businessroundtable.org/ourcommitment/). Essentially, stakeholder capitalism is a corporate governance theory related to the benefits of a wider group of stakeholders than just a company's shareholders. There is no broadly established definition of stakeholders, but it's usually taken to encompass customers, employees, suppliers, creditors, the community, and the environment. In an election year that has experienced a global pandemic and a resurgence of the Black Lives Matter movement, the broader stakeholder inclusion seems to be firmly in favor.

Europe

Corporate governance has been high on the agenda in Continental Europe, as well as in the United Kingdom. The European Commission is concerned about the gender imbalance on corporate boards and has proposed a directive that aims for a 40 percent presence of women on listed company boards. It also wants to improve the transparency of the non-financial information reported by publicly listed companies with more than 500 employees through the EU Non-Financial Reporting Directive (NFRD). A key component of the NFRD is that asset managers need such data as a key source of mandatory reporting by portfolio companies in Europe of non-financial information, which European-based asset managers will need to use to meet their own responsibilities under the new regulation on sustainability disclosures in the financial services sector.

Moreover, the EU has been supporting studies for many years that compare and contrast the laws and policies between member states in areas such as the duties of corporate boards, acquisitions, accounting, and institutional investor oversight. Some have successfully resulted in the adoption of legislative initiatives that further some form of harmonization in the respective areas. The future governance agenda on the relationship between corporate governance and sustainability is also front and center, with a final report published on July 29, 2020.

Recently, the concept of defining corporate purpose has been a key trend in Europe as well. In France, more companies are expected to adopt a *raison d'être* (corporate purpose), with an anticipation that this may become a legal requirement. The *raison d'être* gives a sense of meaning to stakeholders and puts ESG at the center of corporate strategy. Climate change and transitioning to a lower-carbon economy are also main concerns for European stakeholders.

Furthermore, boards will have to understand and discuss ESG data (and its impact on key issues) with investors, with the number of CAC 40 board committees focused on ESG doubling in recent years. (CAC 40 is a benchmark French stock market index.) This is a significant improvement, as ESG is the focus of a quarter of the questions raised at general assemblies and half of the resolutions submitted by shareholders. Meanwhile, in Spain, investors will begin to exercise their vote on non-financial reporting, and regulators are also extending corporate governance principles that promote key components of ESG to private companies in 2020.

Chapter **6**

Highlighting Corporate Greenwashing

There are many different definitions for *greenwashing*, but essentially, they all come back to the impression that a company is making unsupported or misleading claims about how environmentally friendly or socially responsible the company or their product is. In a number of cases, some of the environmental claims are partially true; however, companies engaged in greenwashing usually exaggerate their claims or the benefits of their products or services in an attempt to mislead consumers and other stakeholders.

This chapter covers corporate greenwashing and some issues to consider there, and then discusses how this also translates into greenwashing within financial products and investments. The chapter ends with an overview of a new practice, dubbed "coronawashing," which has similar traits to greenwashing and was brought on by responses to the global COVID-19 pandemic of 2020.

The Grass Isn't Always Greener: The Basics of Greenwashing

REMEMBER

Greenwashing, from a product perspective, generally comes in two forms:

» Where companies spend more time, effort, and money promoting their products as being eco-friendly, rather than creating them as eco-friendly

» Where companies claim that their products are made from alternative materials that are apparently more eco-friendly, when actually they have a larger carbon footprint than conventional materials

Moreover, confirmation of corporate greenwashing is seen when companies unveil eco-friendly marketing campaigns, where they have spent more on the campaign than on any environmentally positive practices.

The following sections delve into the basics of greenwashing, including its prevalence and how to combat it.

Tracking the growth of greenwashing

On August 19, 2019, in the United States, the Business Roundtable announced a new Statement on the Purpose of a Corporation, which was signed by 181 CEOs committing to lead their companies for the benefit of all stakeholders, including customers, employees, suppliers, communities, and shareholders. You can read the statement at `https://opportunity.businessroundtable.org/ourcommitment/`. This was quite a groundbreaking statement for so many big companies to make, and they all, no doubt, increased their ESG credentials as a result.

However, at least one of the companies has recently decided to cut insurance for their part-time workers, which potentially has a negative financial impact on their employees (although those employees are now less likely to be absent, which doesn't drain productivity for the company but is contrary to the spirit of the statement to look after all stakeholders!). Therefore, on the back of a major corporate responsibility initiative, there are still doubts about some firms' intentions to become more responsible and sustainable. So, do investors view this as a positive, new commitment to their communities, employees, and the environment, or as an example of greenwashing?

Previously, adhering to ESG principles was a nice-to-have, but for most firms it's becoming a must-have, so there is persistent pressure on companies to "do good." Therefore, in exaggerating their green credentials, firms are seeking to avoid any public criticism, whether or not it leads to more business or investment. This has led to a greater emphasis on accountability, and the demonstration of standards is growing. One example of greenwashing could be companies claiming their products are from recycled materials or have energy-saving benefits, while the flip side is regulators calling out asset managers on their use of marketing that represents their products or activities as positively "green" when they are not.

REMEMBER

Today greenwashing appears to have become more prevalent, but it's difficult to prove, given the lack of a common definition for what constitutes good corporate behavior, whether at the company level or from an investor perspective. Consequently, there is great ambiguity as to what ESG-friendly practices are, and therefore what eligible investments are. Companies and fund managers are aware of the premiums they can extract if their products or services are considered to be green or sustainable. However, deciding whether they really "walk the walk" entails in-depth knowledge of corporate culture, environmental impacts, labor relations, management quality, supply chain practices, and risk profile. The expectations of investors and other stakeholders regarding corporate conduct is changing and becoming more demanding. Companies are responding but perhaps not always in a manner that is genuinely aligned with improved corporate performance on social or environmental issues. Therefore, analysts should be scrutinizing a company's ESG claims in the same way they have traditionally viewed a company's financial statement fundamentals.

Specifying the details

It's important for fund managers to be frank and transparent about inclusions and exclusions within their ESG investing methodologies and the leeway that they have to veer from the original course. In return, investors should prudently review any investment prospectus, particularly for ESG funds, prior to investing in order to fully understand exactly how the fund invests. The "devil is in the details," and both parties have a duty to ensure it meets their objectives.

A review of many fund prospectuses highlights that several fund managers take a fairly broad approach to ESG investing strategies. While nothing is fundamentally wrong with such an approach, investors may find, for example, additional risk in their returns if they haven't checked a fund's exclusionary investment practices. Moreover, if a fund states that impact investing is a goal, the investor needs to hold them to impact metrics and performance standards, such as job creation and increased diversity.

There isn't general industry agreement on which non-financial factors are material to a company's performance. Some funds rely on strictly quantitative ESG scoring provided by external providers, while others rely on proprietary ESG measures determined by internal quantitative measurements, which are combined with information gathered from company management. Therefore, it isn't surprising that the weighting of various ESG factors may vary from fund to fund. Furthermore, investors should be aware that different fund managers employ diverse screens and exclusions for different companies. Should they only exclude weapons companies on the basis of producers and distributors, or also exclude the retail outlets that sell ammunition and firearms?

Some of the things that investors could request in order to unearth any green-washed products include the following:

>> Determining the firm's formal pledge or mission statement concerning ESG investing

>> Understanding the firm's availability of ESG investment professionals, comprising portfolio managers and analysts

>> Meeting with the asset manager's ESG team to evaluate their procedures

>> Asking about the firm's capacity to weight ESG data and analytics in security analysis from a risk perspective

>> Analyzing the firm's policy and track record on shareholder proxy voting and engaging directly with company management and directors

Until the industry agrees on standard definitions and practices around ESG invest-ing, the responsibility normally rests with the financial advisers to review and understand the variables of any strategy marketed as including ESG factors. Meanwhile, the CFA Institute (www.cfainstitute.org/en/ethics-standards/codes/esg-standards) has received widespread support from the investment community to develop a standard to reduce misunderstanding and enable better alignment of investor objectives with products offered. This should allow inves-tors and clients to carefully assess whether an investment product meets their needs. It isn't meant to determine disclosure obligations for corporate issuers, recommend prerequisites for the labeling of securities or investment products, or specify best practice for a particular strategy or approach.

Using plain language

One of the biggest challenges with ESG investing has been the lack of uniformity in definitions. Terms such as "responsible," "sustainable," and "green" are used interchangeably and mean different things to different people. This is part of the reason why it has been difficult for investors to know exactly what a fund was offering, aligned with a plethora of funds being launched that incorporated one of the terms stated. Of course, with hindsight, it was clear that some funds' proce-dures had little to do with ESG.

Given that the industry has been aware of this problem for some time, the UK's Investment Association (IA) produced a report in November 2019, outlining a responsible investment framework aimed at standardizing some of these terms. The IA included definitions for some of the key phrases used in ESG investing, such as "ESG integration," "exclusions," "sustainability focus," "impact investing," and "stewardship." This has provided a first step to a homogeneous approach to ESG investing, although it's likely that there will be more progress in the future. See `www.theia.org/sites/default/files/2019-11/20191118-iaresponsibleinvestmentframework.pdf` for details.

Using the IA responsible-investment framework, there are three different levels to fund ESG investing:

>> **Exclusions:** This level involves the exclusion of investments in certain companies and sectors from the fund or portfolio based on pre-defined criteria.

>> **Sustainability:** This level is a philosophical framework where investment is made in companies that fulfill sustainability criteria and/or deliver on specific sustainability outcomes. This can involve positive screening, where investments are made in businesses that are "best-in-class" based on ESG ratings, or sustainability-themed investing, where investments are made in companies that target specific sustainability themes such as climate change mitigation, pollution prevention sustainability solutions, and approaches that relate to one or more of the UN Sustainable Development Goals (SDGs; see Chapter 1).

>> **Impact investing:** This level concerns investments that are made with the intention of generating a positive and measurable social or environmental impact.

The European Commission has linked its sustainable finance plan to protecting "EU consumers and investors from greenwashed financial products." Find out more at `www.e3g.org/wp-content/uploads/E3G-A-Vision-for-Sustainable-Finance-in-Europe_Chapter-4-Inclusion.pdf`.

They have also developed a classification system, or "taxonomy," for identifying environmentally sustainable economic activities, and labels and standards that should help with this identification. This is related to the idea that greenwashing is primarily a consideration for retail investors, although, as discussed earlier in this chapter, the potential for greenwashing is much broader than that. Find out more at `https://ec.europa.eu/info/business-economy-euro/banking-and-finance/sustainable-finance/eu-taxonomy-sustainable-activities_en`.

Setting up a system

Another major challenge for ESG investing has been the lack of consistency among ESG rating providers, both in terms of fund and company ESG ratings. The plethora of ESG data points and the lack of homogeneity among rating providers, which have their own criteria, weightings, and other differences in methodology, has resulted in a situation where the correlation between the scores of the many ratings agencies is generally low. Low correlations also cause problems for investment managers who rely on company ESG ratings, given that the results of their screening can change radically, depending on which data provider is used.

Due to this inconsistency, many funds now disaggregate the ESG data and apply their own weightings. However, this entails that it's even more important for investors to be aware of which methodology the fund uses and what the criteria are with respect to their own weightings. Ultimately this creates greater uncertainty around which portfolio constituents are likely to be in a given fund and how they may be rebalanced.

A TALE OF THE PRINCIPLES FOR RESPONSIBLE INVESTMENT

The UN-backed Principles for Responsible Investment (UNPRI; see www.unpri.org/) investor initiative, set up to raise ESG standards, increased their requirements in recent years to retain the highest PRI rating. Asset owners have seen a significant increase in requirements around the selection, appointment, and monitoring of fund managers, including ensuring that a minimum of 50 percent of assets held has integrated ESG, as well as integrating changes to the fund manager selection process. Ironically, the PRI had to place 10 percent of its approximately 2,000 signatories on a watchlist for failing to meet their targets last year. While two-thirds of these signatories have improved their standards, or will meet their standards by the end of the year, one-quarter of them, with more than US$1 trillion of assets under management, have failed to improve or even refused to meet the PRI!

Now, most managers experienced a large fund's inflow after they declared their commitment, regardless of the fund's prior ESG performance, and yet studies suggest that the managers' ESG scores remained the same after they had signed; therefore, they must not have changed their portfolio ESG holdings to incorporate ESG factors. Moreover, it was found that compared to their peers, PRI members were a third more likely to *not* speak up on environmental issues, and their portfolio holdings subsequently underwent an increase in environment-related controversies!

The nearby sidebar "A tale of the Principles for Responsible Investment" highlights some of the issues that may even apply to members of the UN-backed Principles for Responsible Investment (PRI) investor initiative, which was set up to raise ESG standards.

REMEMBER

Documentation should outline a systematic approach to specified ESG issues throughout the entire investment process, which should facilitate increased returns and reduced risk. Moreover, ESG investing should involve searching for and including companies based on desired ESG features, rather than just excluding firms with undesirable business activities. (Some investors argue that investment strategies that only apply exclusions should not be labeled as sustainable, but other investors will argue that some exclusions are acceptable based on ethical determinations.) If investors are asked to limit their universe, they potentially risk underperformance or worse because they aren't selecting what might be seen as the most efficient set of investments.

Just When You Thought It Was Safe: Coronawashing

The term *coronavirus,* along with associated words and phrases, invaded our language in 2020, and now it's quickly become a route to brand self-awareness and questionable attempts at corporate caring, with many companies jumping on the new bandwagon. The very companies that have been called out as polluters, tax dodgers, and persistent outsourcers are now urging us to #StaySafe. All companies, sincerely or not, have their corporate communications teams working on their new image as a public-spirited entity that has stepped up to help others during the pandemic, while trying to ensure that their profits aren't further impacted than they have been already.

Those with short memories perhaps forget that these are some of the same companies that have contributed to and benefited from unsustainable use of natural resources, weaker public services, and the reduced standards of living that the pandemic has unfortunately highlighted. The following sections discuss both sides of coronawashing: the corporate aspect and the investor aspect.

Coronawashing on the corporate side

And so, "coronawashing" has started! As Winston Churchill was famously quoted as saying, "Never let a good crisis go to waste!" The PR machine is in overdrive, with companies highlighting how they are helping to fight the crisis while ensuring that they can't be blamed for worsening it! Social media streams are catching every soundbite and any camera footage that can possibly be used to position their company in the soft lighting of good corporate citizenship.

Meanwhile, behind the scenes, the same companies are requesting government bailouts and leveraging the crisis to push for favorable legislation and reductions in regulations that are sometimes more necessary now than they were before. There has been an influx of consumer goods that are feeding off the fear of coronavirus, which highlights the stark reality that there's no safer time for capitalism to excel than during a global pandemic!

However, while COVID-19 has propelled these issues, and the ESG pillars on which they stand, to the front of our collective thinking, sustainability is still establishing itself as a core business strategy, and many of the Key Performance Indicators (such as emissions, ocean plastics, water scarcity, and social engagement) are still pointing in the wrong direction. Prior to COVID-19, the potential consequences of these issues still seemed too obscure for many companies to grasp. Some saw endorsing sustainability best practices as a "nice-to-have" rather than a vital element in their competitiveness and future success. Many organizations were still looking to maximize shareholder value in the short term, without thinking of their long-term corporate health and ongoing shift to "stakeholder capitalism." And they are likely to be the firms that get caught out by coronawashing as they pay "lip service" to a short-term opportunity that should highlight their failings.

Coronawashing on the investor side

Company ESG objectives are one side of this story, but ESG investing will witness some of the outcomes. Skeptics had predicted that the booming investor appetite for ESG would wane when times got tough, while staunch supporters maintained that ethical and sustainable companies would prove more resilient. Thus far, evidence suggests that the supporters have been proven correct as green bonds and ESG share indexes have outperformed benchmarks.

However, some of these facts may implicitly be victims of "coronawashing," as most ESG-focused exchange-traded funds (ETFs), which have seen the lion's share of investor flows, are by their nature passive instruments that are heavily weighted toward companies that have proved resilient in the pandemic, such as pharmaceutical and technology companies. Indeed, given that a number of ETFs are based on indexes that use exclusion rules, to deliberately exclude companies failing ESG principles that have generally exhibited poor performance of late, they have indirectly dodged underperformance!

But investors need to observe closely what they are buying, as ESG scores within different indices are subjective, and not all indexes are created with the same objective. Sometimes, ESG ETFs include shares that explicitly contradict how they are sold to investors. This is typically because the fund has been primarily designed to closely track the broad market, rather than be "fossil-free," and is designed for investors looking to integrate ESG factors into their core investments without drifting too far from the overall profile of their benchmark index.

WARNING

While ESG investing has become even more popular, and rightly so where funds are invested in firms that are expected to be more resilient to change in the long term, there is a *caveat emptor* ("buyer beware"). Ultimately, it's difficult to know how the current COVID-19 crisis will play out or what effect it will have on sustainable issues. The current warm glow of bonding against the common enemies to ESG pillars suggests positive change for the future, but others propose that governments and organizations are focused on fighting the economic slowdown and will be diverted away from sustainable projects in the near future. Consequently, some of the support offered by asset managers and "talking heads" for ESG as a "safe haven" investment now verges on coronawashing, and appropriate risk management should be observed!

Furthermore, the "build back better" mantra post-pandemic needs to be considered carefully for all stakeholders. There is a view that this is a once-in-a-lifetime opportunity to reshape economies globally to be more environmentally sustainable and socially inclusive. However, the economic strain post-pandemic may cause a narrower focus on just getting the economy back on track, regardless of the environmental consequences that this may entail in the short term. It's certainly a difficult balancing act, but the once-in-a-lifetime approach requires a global unity that may not be forthcoming.

2

Investing in ESG through Different Instruments

Evaluate the tangible investment results behind the use of ESG ratings and metrics.

Identify the use of equity and fixed income–based investments behind portfolio construction and management.

Get the highlights of the listed derivative and alternative investments used to build a sustainable portfolio.

See the growth in investment dollars in ESG in Europe, North America, and Asia.

Chapter **7**

Approaches to ESG Investing

I n Part 1 of this book, you get a good understanding of why investing in ESG is an important consideration for your portfolio. This part of the book focuses on the approaches to ESG investing that different investors may employ, and the types of instruments that they use to implement their strategy.

This chapter, in particular, emphasizes that many terms have been used interchangeably to describe the incorporation of ethical, environmental, and social factors into investment fund management, such as ethical investment, green investment, and socially responsible investment. The definitions of these various terms all overlap, and many have particular significance for different industry participants. With the growth in investing in recent years, these industry terms have proliferated. However, distinct differences exist that influence how client portfolios should be structured as well as which investments meet social or environmental impact goals.

Understanding Socially Responsible Investing

As outlined in Chapter 1, the integration of ESG factors is used to augment traditional financial analysis by recognizing potential risks and opportunities beyond technical valuations. While there is an overlay of social awareness, the main purpose of ESG valuation remains financial performance.

Socially responsible investing (SRI) — the subject of this section — moves a step further than ESG by actively removing or choosing investments that correspond to particular ethical guidelines. The underlying motivation could be personal values, political ideology, or religious beliefs. Unlike ESG analysis, which influences valuations, SRI uses ESG factors to direct negative or positive screens on the investment universe. The definitions for SRI given by industry representatives include the following:

>> The UK Social Investment Forum (SIF) defines SRI as an "investment which combines investors' financial objectives with their commitment to social justice, economic development, peace or a healthy environment."

>> Eurosif defines SRI as an investment that "combines investors' financial objectives with their concerns about social, environmental and ethical (SEE) issues."

Looking at reasons for SRI

Regardless of the various definitions, there appear to be three common motives for SRI:

>> To avoid investor participation in activities that they object to

>> To inspire companies to improve their impact on society, the environment, or the economy

>> To generate investment outperformance

The first of these motives has historically provided the inspiration for SRI, but more recently, the other two factors have become increasingly important and are now the primary motivation for many SRI investors. Nevertheless, different SRI strategies are selected to respond to different investor motives, and each strategy could deliver a different result depending on the focus outcome, but traces of each motive are generally found in every strategy.

Therefore, the key consideration is to view SRI as a long-term investment approach that integrates good ESG practices into the research, analysis, and selection process of securities within your investment portfolio. It combines fundamental analysis and engagement with an evaluation of ESG factors to identify companies with sustainable business goals (positive screening), while avoiding those with questionable practices (negative screening), in order to better capture long-term returns while benefiting society. Consequently, SRI promotes corporate practices other than profit maximization through capital investment.

REMEMBER

SRI strategies tend to follow the political and social dynamics of the time. This is an important factor for investors to recognize, because if a strategy is focused on a particular environmental, ethical, or social value, the investment may suffer if that particular value isn't considered as relevant among investors in the future.

TIP

Moreover, given that interest has grown in socially conscious investing, numerous funds and pooled investment vehicles are available to investors, including mutual funds and exchange-traded funds (ETFs), allowing exposure to multiple companies across many sectors with a single investment. However, investors need to read carefully through fund prospectuses to establish the precise philosophies that are employed by the fund managers, in order to ensure that they meet their own intended goals.

It's important to emphasize that there is a difference between SRI — which involves actively excluding or choosing investments based on explicit ethical guidelines — and impact investing, which looks to help an organization to complete a project or develop a program or do something positive to benefit society. (I cover impact investing later in the section "Evaluating Impact Investing.") The main factors motivating SRI are primarily linked to investors' desire to, for example, address climate change, the use of renewable energy, and water management, along with other environmental and social issues. Meanwhile, where exclusion screening persists — it's still the most prominent strategy in terms of assets under management in Europe — tobacco is seen as the most popular exclusion criteria.

Comparing a best-in-class strategy to an exclusion strategy

TIP

One way to determine which companies may have the greatest positive impact is to adopt a best-in-class (BIC) strategy, which allows investors to choose those companies that have the best ESG scores in a particular industry sector. This also allows investors to choose a given criterion or target, and the final rating realized can be connected to the weighting of the criterion, which can depend on the sector. A BIC portfolio usually incorporates companies that meet both SRI/ESG and conventional financial evaluations. However, some BIC portfolios don't differ meaningfully from non-SRI portfolios, and so investors are increasingly searching for benchmarks or indexes that can be applied to implement a BIC approach. In short, getting best relative performance in terms of ESG scores doesn't guarantee positive impact.

The oldest SRI strategy is the exclusion strategy, which traditionally focused on the avoidance of "sin stocks," such as companies concerned with the production or sale of alcohol, pornography, tobacco, and weapons. This approach systematically excludes companies, sectors, or countries from the acceptable investment universe when they are involved in activities that are considered questionable or unethical. This strategy can be applied at an individual fund or mandate level, but progressively even more so at an asset manager or owner level, across the entire product range of assets.

However, some investors believe that for an exclusion strategy to be meaningful, it could be applied together with some attempt at engagement and stewardship policies, which implies that investors should hold symbolic amounts of stock in exclusion companies to be able to exercise voting rights. This allows active investors to show their commitment to creating a positive impact and better sustainability in portfolio companies. If they just sell the stock, the company may simply continue to operate in an unsustainable way that goes unchecked, which isn't positive; however, they have to weigh any reputational risks that may be associated with continuing as an investor. Therefore, divestment may still be the best route with certain companies.

Weighing the potential return on SRI decisions

REMEMBER

Some investors presume that integrating ESG factors into an SRI process will lead to lower returns, but there are growing indications that SRI could lead to greater returns. The principle is clear: The corporations that are most likely to operate effectively in the future are those with convincing social responsibility profiles, that trade in an objective and progressive way, with an executive team that tackles short-term risks while ensuring that the business is positioned to adjust to long-term transformational changes.

Conversely, you shouldn't expect that the returns from SRI indexes will be constant in the short term. There are likely to be short-term divergences in performance relative to the point in the economic cycle or market conditions. For example, SRI emerging market indexes have a fundamentally lower allocation to China than their non-SRI equivalents. This could cause return on investment (ROI) to diverge between these two indexes or portfolios if the Chinese equity market experiences strong gains or losses.

In addition, there are concerns about the potential lack of diversity offered by ESG shares, given that many companies that meet the SRI criteria are predominantly large-cap stocks, which can limit the potential for diversification within investor portfolios. This could entail that investors find fewer opportunities within small-cap, mid-cap, and emerging market domiciled companies, while potentially excluding entire sectors, which enhances the risk of concentration within given sectors. The counterargument to this is that ESG incorporation into the SRI process allows investors to screen out companies engaged in unsustainable practices; this will exclude companies expected to underperform their competitors and result in a smaller but higher-quality investment universe. This suggests that any loss of portfolio efficiency will be more than offset by the more appealing investment characteristics of the remaining companies.

Moreover, there are concerns over the ROI repercussions of limiting the universe of asset managers by excluding those that don't observe a predetermined threshold of ESG integration. Many smaller asset managers have the ability to generate persistent *alpha* (in other words, consistently finding excess return in their portfolio) but haven't fully incorporated sustainable investing strategies or integrated ESG factors into their processes. Meanwhile, larger traditional asset managers will increasingly integrate SRI principles into their investment process in order to boost returns.

Nevertheless, there is a growing need to boost the supply of SRI investment proposals to meet the expected demand with more familiarization among finance professionals to engage successfully with clients when distributing information about SRI opportunities. Conversely, although fund fees have dropped in recent years, the fees for SRI strategies are naturally higher than passively managed funds as managers charge higher fees to counterbalance their need to monitor corporations' activities to ensure that the criteria of the fund are being maintained. Higher fees can have a material effect on performance.

Still, in general, the SRI momentum has influenced the adoption of responsible or impact investing strategies by several institutional investors, and numerous quasi-sovereign institutions have well-defined SRI policies:

>> The Canadian Pension Plan completely integrates ESG into its investment decision-making approach.

>> The Norwegian Sovereign Wealth Fund (Norges) deploys exclusionary screening and active corporate engagement to enhance the practices of its investee companies.

>> Adoption in the United States has generally been slower than Europe; nonetheless, a notable exception is the Ford Foundation, which has pledged to invest US$1 billion of its endowment into mission-driven impact investments.

>> In his 2020 annual letter to company CEOs, BlackRock founder Larry Fink, as head of the largest asset management company in the world, publicly demanded that every company show how it makes a positive contribution to society.

>> Morgan Stanley has created the Institute of Responsible Investing, which is tasked with integrating SRI strategies across all departments of their business.

>> Many conventional asset management firms have launched impact investment funds, including Apollo, Bain Capital, KKR, TPG, and Wellington.

REMEMBER

However, investors need to differentiate between those strategies that they feel have been created as asset gathering tools versus those with a discernible track record of creating genuine impact. At the extreme, Chapter 6 covers issues around greenwashing and what needs to be monitored for that issue. Otherwise, undertaking some due diligence on the SRI or impact credentials of a fund can highlight what track record or experience it has in the field or whether it's jumping on the bandwagon.

Evaluating Impact Investing

The demand for impact investing — covered in this section — has resulted from the continuation of substantial societal challenges (for example, demographic changes, inequality, social exclusion, and unsustainable development) and the failure of current institutions, such as governments, charities, non-governmental organizations (NGOs), and philanthropic organizations, to meet those challenges.

REMEMBER

Unlike SRI or ESG investing, impact investing isn't just about sidestepping sin stocks or "doing no harm," but also actively employing capital to tackle social and environmental objectives while creating financial returns for investors. It requires purpose, where portfolio companies must proactively track, measure, and report on their social and environmental impact. Where successful, impact investing is releasing significant capital from mainstream investors.

Defining and tracking "impact"

Despite the growing interest in such goals, more recently driven by the identification of the UN Sustainable Development Goals (SDGs; see Chapter 1), there is still no agreement on what impact investing specifically covers, which is reflected in the wildly different estimations in the size of assets under management from industry representatives such as the Global Impact Investing Network (GIIN) and the Global Sustainable Investment Alliance (GSIA). The SDGs are commonly highlighted as part of the impact frameworks that investors are creating, using them as a road map to help recognize where investment opportunities lie or how their current investment methodology aligns. They help investors communicate the contribution that they are making to provide solutions for the bigger-picture questions that society faces and to facilitate a unified stance for the industry.

Impact investing is an approach to investing in initiatives, organizations, and funds that pursue the development of both financial returns and quantifiable social and environmental impact. Investors pursuing financial returns and impact refer to this as the "double bottom line," borrowing an accounting term to convey how both facets need to be measured and reported. Impact investments are frequently made through closed-end private equity and venture capital funds, whereby debt funds have seen increasing popularity, more recently among impact investors. A number of traditional private equity firms have opened dedicated funds, introducing billions in new capital and pulling in institutional investors. Furthermore, this interest isn't only coming from the "usual suspects," such as foundations and health- or faith-based organizations, which have a natural disposition to consider impact. Mainstream institutional investors, including corporations and pension funds, are also showing real enthusiasm to be involved.

TECHNICAL STUFF

In the UK, the private Social Impact Investment (SII) market peaked in 2019; however, the pandemic has hit activity in the SII market harder than the broader investment market, with a 25 percent drop in the number of announced deals completed in the UK in the first half of 2020, compared to the same period in the previous year. Nevertheless, greater activity is expected to rebound as impact investors look to support the economic recovery post-pandemic.

REMEMBER

The difficulty in tracking "impact" is an issue that still hampers the development of this market, as uncertainty remains with respect to precise definitions of positive impact. Such definitions vary as investors tend to track outcomes with their own distinctive metrics based on specific objectives, which may also vary at different parts of the investment cycle. Following are some of the measurement methods used to determine impact:

>> **Expected return method** evaluates the estimated benefits against the projected costs to determine which investment yields the highest impact.

>> **Theory of change method** outlines the projected process to realize social impact, using a tool that maps the connections between input, activities, output, outcomes, and ultimately impact (logic model).

>> **Mission alignment method** measures the implementation of the project against its mission and end objectives over time, using scorecards to scrutinize and govern key performance metrics on finances, operational performance, organizational efficiency, and social value.

>> **Experimental and quasi-experimental methods** represent after-the-fact assessments that use randomized control trials to conclude the impact of an intermediation compared to the situation if the intermediation hadn't taken place.

Measuring social and environmental outcome targets

Investing for return and impact is complicated, as many projects targeted at social and environmental challenges are relatively expensive without having immediate or explicit financial returns for investors; as a result, compromise is typically expected between returns and impacts. Consequently, international best practices and models for impact investing should be categorized and analyzed. Based on insights from past projects, sound methodologies can be created to facilitate identification of prospects that can produce measurable market rate financial returns and social and environmental impact. Practical lessons should also be drawn from past projects to determine how to fruitfully engage with optimal opportunities.

WARNING

For an impact evaluation, it's difficult to categorize projects that are both realistic and measurable. Focusing on overly elaborate projects may be counterproductive as it may take many years and require a controlling stake in the entity in order to achieve meaningful impact. Therefore, rather than chasing multifaceted targets, it may be better to emphasize projects with a higher probability of success that can be achieved in a relatively short time frame. In addition, targeting impact goals that can be certified and audited by third-party entities and adhere to ISO (International Organization for Standardization) standards is important in the long run. (Examples can be found in this article: www.responsible-investor.com/articles/the-world-s-official-standards-body-has-begun-writing-sustainable-finance-rules.)

For impact investing to scale, products must be able to address the breadth of institutional requirements, comprising the capacity to absorb large pools of capital, and provide sufficient liquidity and stringent risk management practices, while producing measurable return and impact. These have usually been provided by investment strategies targeting blue-chip securities, primarily bonds. However, this results in directing funds to investments where it's harder to proactively produce impact, as bondholders and minority shareholders have fewer opportunities to directly influence senior executives of large corporations. Moreover, blue-chip securities are concentrated in mature markets, whereas the maximum need for impact capital is in emerging markets or less established areas.

Conversely, research shows that specializing in fixed income does allow opportunities to scale up impact investments. In particular, a focus on emerging markets, servicing principally undercapitalized small and medium-sized enterprises (SMEs) in developing countries, highlights the opportunities in less efficient markets where better arbitrage opportunities may be found.

Calculating impact metrics

Although the commercial world has several universally acknowledged tools, such as the internal rate of return, for evaluating a potential investment's financial yields, no equivalent exists for calculating social and environmental rewards in dollar terms. Projecting returns is often a matter of conjecture. For example, the reporting of ESG issues is now standard practice at the majority of large and mid-cap corporations, but this is usually restricted to information about commitments and process, and seldom scores actual impact. Impact investing has been described as the "third stage of responsible investment," succeeding the stages of ESG integration and risk management.

Nonetheless, the measurement of positive impact of products and services is still comparatively new, with methodologies and protocols still being established. There are a series of methodological challenges in the data, including concerns over the borderlines of corporate reporting and the capacity for "double-counting" of impact data, reporting over consistent time frames, and correctly evaluating or guesstimating product- and service-level impacts. Consequently, a number of obstacles need to be overcome first. Methodologies need to be standardized, and data quality and equivalence need to be substantiated, as more than 130 impact measurement initiatives need to be considered.

While widespread research has been conducted in this area, the evaluation of impact normally incorporates a number of identifiable metrics that the investors consider to be applicable to the social or environmental issue being tackled. Both impact funds and traditional asset managers are initiating annual reports that monitor the development of such metrics during the life of the investment. One example of the research undertaken in this field is that conducted by the Impact Management Project, a collaborative, multi-stakeholder endeavor facilitated by Bridges Fund Management, an impact investment firm founded in 2002, and funded by such large institutional investors as BlackRock, Hermes Investment Management, and PGGM. They have considered five dimensions of impact: what, how much, who, contribution, and risk. Another example is the Harvard Business School Impact-Weighted Accounts Project, which aims to drive the creation of financial accounts that reflect a company's financial, social, and environmental performance (visit www.hbs.edu/impact-weighted-accounts/).

In addition, NEF (the New Economics Foundation) has developed a framework based on cost-benefit analysis, social accounting, and social auditing, with the goal of capturing social value by transforming social objectives into financial and non-financial measures. Social return on investment (SROI) analysis is a process of understanding, measuring, and reporting on the social, environmental, and economic value that is being created by an organization. SROI measures the value of the benefits relative to the costs of achieving those benefits by creating a ratio between the net present value of benefits and the net present value of the investment. This provides a further framework for exploring an organization's social impact, in which tangible monetization plays an important, but not exclusive, role.

TIP

You can find information on how SROI could help organizations better understand and quantify their social, environmental, and economic value here: www. nefconsulting.com/our-services/evaluation-impact-assessment/prove-and-improve-toolkits/sroi/.

Focusing on Faith-Based Investing

In many ways, faith-based investing — discussed in this section — was the original forerunner of socially responsible investing and subsequently impact investing. Therefore, the exponential increase in assets under management and a general interest in ESG principles and framework have naturally led to increasing awareness of faith-based strategies.

Reviewing religious principles of finance

Investors looking to invest in a manner coherent with Christian values frequently consider avoiding investing in companies that support non-Christian approaches — for example, from supporting abortion to building controversial weapons. Alternatively, they often favor firms that support human rights, environmental responsibility, and fair employment practices via the support of labor unions.

The top three SDGs that faith-based investors seem to favor include decent work and economic growth (Goal 8), affordable and clean energy (Goal 7), and reduced inequalities (Goal 10). These SDGs also appear as top themes for impact investors in the GIIN's flagship research report summarizing the largest industry survey of impact investors. The harmony between faith-based investors and impact investors' concentrations in the same SDGs implies that there are opportunities for these entities to collaborate on common social and environmental goals.

This is particularly true where impact investors can support faith-based investors in mobilizing more of their capital to realize positive, measurable, social, and environmental impact results. Multiple entities now provide assistance in investing in a manner that supports Christian values, and mutual fund firms and other funds are committed to such parameters for investors who don't want to take the do-it-yourself approach.

Indeed, faith-based investors are often ahead of the game when spotting potential alpha in certain trades because they are engaged earlier than other investors in issues such as climate change, where they consider the issue to be morally unacceptable. Before such investments appear on the radar of ESG investors as materially relevant, faith-based investors may have already excluded such entities from their portfolios or begun an engagement exercise.

Meanwhile, investors specifically looking to pursue Islamic religious principles normally avoid so-called sin stocks, such as those issued by firms that profit from alcohol, pornography, or gambling, and investments in pork-related businesses are also prohibited. They are also forbidden from owning investments that pay rates of interest on their funds, or companies that receive a significant part of their revenue from interest payments. As an extension of this, many Islamic investors also try to avoid companies that carry heavy debt loans (and therefore pay considerable amounts of interest).

Examining exclusion screening and divesting

Faith-based investors from many faiths were at the vanguard of negative screening and divestment strategies, given that they were intentionally and publicly eradicating from their portfolios corporations whose practices were against their convictions. For example, in the 1970s and 1980s, such investors divested from Dow Chemical to protest against its production of Agent Orange, and from South African companies in response to their support of apartheid.

Even more so today, considering the "no harm" principles of faith-based and ESG investors, portfolios are constructed to specifically exclude certain companies that produce goods or services considered to do social or environmental harm. These generally include sectors such as alcohol or tobacco, as mentioned in the previous section. Some large and well-known funds, such as the Norwegian Sovereign Wealth Fund, have their own exclusion list, which excludes firms engaged in "unacceptable greenhouse gas emissions," due to their involvement in oil sands production, for example.

Moreover, when considering whether to include negative screening in an investment strategy (and which sectors or stocks need to be excluded), investors also need to determine the quantity of the portfolio that they are considering. Within a fund structure, this might only apply to the fund's passive investments, or where they don't have direct control. Alternatively, it might be related to all assets in the fund structure that require compliance of all the underlying active managers.

REMEMBER

Positive screening is a comparatively new, but progressively popular, investment approach that involves actively seeking values-aligned investments for your portfolio by using ESG ratings to identify best-in-class stocks. Negative screening is purely an exclusion process to remove unsuitable stocks, whereas positive screening allows investors to add stocks to their portfolio that are considered to be positively engaging with ESG factors.

Advocating for values through proxy voting

Shareholder advocacy calls for investors to use their voices as "part-owners" to influence demands for socially or environmentally responsible company policies and practices. Through discussion and meetings with company management, shareholders should directly support the adoption of good corporate governance and socially responsible approaches. Investors should also consider filing shareholder proposals that would be voted on at the company's annual general meeting. Many faith-based investors are active participants in order to ensure promotion of corporate social responsibility.

However, for those investors interested in bringing a company to task, there are minimum threshold levels that apply to ensure that a filing is submitted, which varies according to jurisdiction. The types of thresholds include a minimum monetary holding and/or percentage holding in the company or a minimum number of shareholders who support the proposal. The requirements to be met should be available on your local regulator's website — for example, www.sec.gov/news/press-release/2020-220.

Investors should also actively vote on proposals submitted by management or other investors in advance of company annual meetings, or ensure that their proxy vote will be submitted by a delegate. Similar to exercising your democratic right to vote, investors should carefully review their annual proxy materials to consider how they should vote on given proposals. Historically, this has been something of a "rubber stamp" exercise to reinstate specific board members whose terms had elapsed, or to confirm the auditor company assuring the accounts. However, with increasing activism, those issues and others are being questioned. If you have concerns over the performance of a company, this is usually your main opportunity to make your voice heard, particularly with respect to topics such as executive pay.

Central to ESG integration is engagement with the underlying asset managers to confirm that the managers are determined to improve their ESG integration practices over time, and also to ensure that the asset managers are engaging with underlying company management teams to influence their behavior in a way that is supportive of good corporate governance, environmental policies, and social practices. For further information, visit `https://partners-cap.com/ publications/a-framework-for-responsible-investing`.

Alternatively, many large shareholders engage an external investment advisory service that, in addition to providing investment advice, will liaise with the third-party asset managers to scrutinize and foster adoption of policies in support of the investors' desires for impact and ESG-related investing standards and engagement with company management. The primary advisory firms are Glass Lewis and ISS, but given that some firms play such an important role in shareholder voting, particularly in the United States, regulators have started to impose restrictions on some of their activities.

Chapter **8**

Analyzing Equity-Based Instruments

Typical equity-based investment funds are either *actively managed* (the portfolio manager decides where and what to invest in) or *passively managed* (a fund tends to follow market indexes, with no active decisions made by the portfolio manager). This approach applies equally to ESG funds:

» Some managers determine their ESG universe based on a given number of stocks, which naturally increases the *active risk* (the measure of risk in a portfolio that is due to active management decisions) within a portfolio.

» Other managers take a more passive approach by following a specified index and its composition of securities, some of which may exclude given stocks (for example, fossil fuels, tobacco, and arms-related stocks). In other words, the index company selects the portfolio of companies that the fund manager then follows.

This chapter investigates how different equity-based strategies have been applied to the growing demand for ESG exposure. This ranges from how ESG factors are integrated into existing funds and strategies, including adjusting index-based or sector- and theme-based approaches, to how such factors are incorporated within smart beta or quantitative strategies.

Integrating ESG Strategies into Investment Decisions

Awareness of the benefits of ESG integration is increasing, and the types of applications are growing. What do I mean by "ESG integration"? Glad you asked. *ESG integration* is the systematic and explicit inclusion of material ESG factors into investment research, analysis, and decision-making. This is one of three broad approaches to adding ESG analysis into investment decisions, along with screening and thematic investing (covered later in this chapter). All three ESG procedures can and often are applied simultaneously.

The following sections run through the basics of getting started, discuss both active and passive investment approaches, and note where the respective ESG scores and risks can be recognized within given strategies.

Just the basics: Getting an overview of the process

REMEMBER

Most investors will begin the process of ESG integration by following four common steps:

1. **Qualitative analysis:** Collecting relevant intelligence from different sources, including company reports and research, and determining material factors that are influencing the company. When I say *material factors,* I mean financially material issues that are most likely to impact the financial condition of a company and are consequently most important to investors.

2. **Quantitative analysis:** Measuring the effect of material financial factors on equities in existing portfolios or the wider universe, and modifying valuation models accordingly.

3. **Investment decisions:** Using this analysis to decide whether to buy (or increase weighting), hold (or maintain weighting), or sell (or decrease weighting).

4. **Active ownership/stewardship:** Using the prior analysis to inform company engagement and proxy voting decisions. This information can be used to support any future monitoring and investment analysis and to advise subsequent investment decisions.

After this process, the evaluation of material issues from ESG factors can determine the following:

- » Financial and financially material ESG factors

- » The potential effect of material financial and ESG factors on company, sector, economic, and country performance

- » Investment decisions to buy, hold, trim, or exit positions

Adopting such an approach may involve changes to an investor's processes, which requires a development of the skills needed to decide how ESG issues (covered in Chapters 3, 4, and 5) may impact individual company performance. Particularly, investors need to develop the skills to identify and integrate material ESG concerns, which are believed to affect company and investment performance. This can reduce the analysis required for those companies where ESG issues aren't considered to be material at that time. Investors who are collecting ESG information from multiple sources — including company reports, filings, and ESG research providers — to identify the most material ESG issues per company or sector build this skill and experience over time.

To achieve stock-level integration, investors will then commonly adjust financial statement forecasts and valuation discount rates in their financial models to reflect material ESG factors as well as any industry-related ESG issues. Given that companies can be scored using material ESG characteristics, portfolios can be constructed to overweight or underweight individual securities that match such characteristics in an optimized tilt. This balances the potentially opposing features of increasing a portfolio's ESG score and decreasing the portfolio's tracking error relative to its benchmark, thus permitting investors to integrate the ESG influence. Therefore, ESG indicators have been added to traditional financial measures, taxes, and other fundamental information to assess the value of public companies.

However, many early-stage investors in ESG have primarily used simpler approaches, employing negative screening techniques, which effectively exclude certain types of stocks such as alcohol, tobacco, and fossil fuels. Alternatively, investors have expanded on this approach by focusing on given themes or sectors, either from an exclusion perspective, as per individual stocks, or from positive screening where they add stocks, sectors, or themes that exhibit positive ESG scores. (These approaches are covered in the later section "Constructing equity portfolios that integrate ESG factors.") This has been particularly true in Europe, where the largest quantity of ESG-related assets under management reside. This is largely because companies haven't traditionally reported or explicitly identified material ESG data that could affect their financial performance, so the only way to accomplish that is through investors proactively engaging with companies.

REMEMBER

On a positive note, there are more industry-wide efforts to increase the standardization of ESG data and reporting requirements, which should greatly improve access to data. As standardization continues to improve, more institutional investors should follow the material ESG factor integration approach. This is already true for the United States, where ESG integration into analysis of listed equity investments is the most common ESG approach. However, greater integration in the United States isn't due to U.S. companies reporting material ESG factors any better than elsewhere, so greater standardization of ESG data providers' input is still required.

Using active strategies

The development of ESG investing is being driven by bottom-up pressure from asset owners and top-down policy initiatives. More investors are now concentrating on maximizing ESG performance through risk-return constraints, rather than the more traditional approach of prioritizing risk-adjusted returns. In other words, more investors are now focused on maximizing ESG performance, subject to their own risk-return limits, rather than purely focusing on an investment's return subject to the degree of risk taken to achieve it (hedge funds and investors commonly refer to this as the Sharpe ratio).

Market participants suggest that active managers have traditionally focused on issues that are most relevant to underlying investment performance through fundamental bottom-up approaches, and so they have the aptitude to explore and evaluate ESG issues that are financially material. Moreover, active management approaches have focused on shareholder engagement with management in a consistent manner. Active managers, due to their deep knowledge of companies, should play an important role in engaging with management on material ESG data points, providing a value-added proposition that could positively sway company behavior and push sustainable long-term value for investors.

REMEMBER

Because ESG issues are embedded with business issues, a single source of data isn't always sufficient to decide on investment pros and cons. Many active ESG strategies will have a team of fundamental equity and credit research analysts, supported by expertise from an in-house ESG team, who assess material ESG themselves rather than relying solely on external ESG data providers. These multiple sources of data should provide greater flexibility and the capacity to concentrate on the most material issues relevant to the investment theme. Active ownership should also entail communicating with firms to enhance their ESG policies and practices. Engagement beyond formal data can be more meaningful than the data on its own, as the data providers each have a slightly different approach to evaluating ESG practices in companies.

Moreover, ESG analysis is equally essential to active fundamental analysis. Issues that are material to performance are constantly evolving, and so investors' approach to corporate engagement and analysis should also continue to evolve. Where analysts are directly engaged in the business context, procedures, and industrial requirements of a company and its sector, they should also be on top of ESG issues that are evolving, which provides confidence in measuring and establishing the credibility of the fundamental investment process. Furthermore, they should be able to attune allocations to reflect changes to ESG assessments as they arise. This ability to respond immediately to changing dynamics can allow active managers to unearth opportunities or risks that could be missed by passive ESG strategies, which may be more important in the current environment as corporations struggle to comply with changing disclosure regulations and investor expectations.

Analyzing the impact of different ESG scores

REMEMBER

There's an increasing body of evidence that corporations prioritizing ESG issues generate superior long-term performance across a variety of metrics, including sales growth, return on equity (ROE), and even alpha (a measure of market outperformance). Companies pursuing a stakeholder approach to value creation by integrating ESG into their long-term strategies are able to attract the best talent, develop loyal customer bases, benefit from sound corporate governance oversight, moderate risk, and push profitable growth by investing in sustainable innovations. So, shareholders should still benefit, but not at the expense of employees, customers, suppliers, or the community. Consequently, modeling a business around ESG factors can be an underappreciated source of sustainable competitive advantage, given the strong business fundamentals and ability to create market outperformance that such companies possess. Furthermore, this has been confirmed by testing the effect of material ESG scores on stock returns.

REMEMBER

Material ESG scores, which identify and evaluate only those issues that are financially important to a company, enhance forecasts of financial performance in comparison to total ESG scores. This finding has been particularly true for total ESG scores (an aggregate of the individual scores given to the ESG issues) as opposed to ESG score changes (the relative change in a total ESG score), which is in line with the long-term value-generation attribute of ESG performance:

- >> **Total ESG scores** are claimed to be a more accurate forecaster of longer-term business performance.

- >> **ESG score changes** are guided by short-term events and accordingly have a greater influence on short-term performance.

This analysis can be used to validate the view that long-term material ESG factors are currently mispriced by the market. So, by having a more qualitative incorporation of material ESG data in the valuation approach, investors could benefit from this mispricing. As long as such information isn't transparently available, there is a competitive advantage for those analysts who can deliver such information, and given that the market has been slow to adapt, this mispricing may be available for some time. Moreover, if this information is combined with data provided in a business sustainability assessment questionnaire, they are even more significant as a forecaster of financial returns than broadly available public information, particularly for companies in industry sectors that exhibit more environmental risks.

Watch out: Thinking about risks and disclosures

Investment managers need to be able to measure and understand risk in order to manage it. Risk management is the essence of investment management, so analyzing ESG risk factors, alongside more traditional statistical and quantitative risk factors, helps deepen understanding of potential downside risks. Correspondingly, time invested now in evolving investment research to integrate an ESG framework will help differentiate the funds that will be successful in the future. In addition, analyzing more conventional quantitative-risk measures, such as tracking error or *beta* (the volatility of a security or portfolio in comparison to the market as a whole), alongside more qualitative ESG risk metrics ensures a multidimensional perspective.

As the quality and availability of ESG data and analysis continue to evolve, asset managers who understand the data can use it to further inform their investment evaluation. ESG data should provide new perspectives to unearth any risks that are hidden in the balance sheets and financial ratios and identify new investment opportunities. In addition, the information offered by proprietary ESG scoring and ranking techniques has helped investors build a granular picture of corporations' ESG performance. This has been driven by the increasing scope of mandatory ESG disclosure obligations.

For example, under the EU's Non-Financial Reporting Directive (introduced in January 2017 but currently being revised), listed EU companies with more than 500 employees need to disclose a range of information in their annual reports concerning employee, environmental, and social issues; respect for human rights; and corruption. Moreover, voluntary standards and frameworks, such as the Carbon Disclosure Project (CDP), the Financial Stability Board's Task Force on Climate-related Financial Disclosures (TCFD), and the Science-Based Targets (SBT) initiative, are encouraging more standardized reporting that should lead to more informed ESG scores.

Meanwhile, the Global Reporting Initiative (GRI; www.globalreporting.org/), the most widely used reporting standard, allows companies to determine which issues are material for reporting purposes, ultimately allowing investors to compare companies' ESG performance and companies to incorporate guidelines into financial reporting. In addition, the Sustainability Accounting Standards Board (SASB; www.sasb.org/) takes an investor's viewpoint to recognize which sustainability metrics are anticipated to have a material effect on the financial state or operating performance of companies. The definitions that SASB has determined as material per industry and sector have become reference points for many market participants. (Flip to Chapter 1 for more about the GRI and SASB.)

Investigating how companies with higher ESG scores outperform

Investors have traditionally been concerned that sustainable investing requires a risk/return trade-off when investing in corporations with strong ESG practices, an approach that provides lower risk but also lower return. This may have become more of an issue in recent years as more ESG-focused investment vehicles have been offered to investors and a record number of assets have been invested in ESG funds. Nevertheless, analysis suggests that in recent years, and during the COVID-19 pandemic, ESG-based funds have performed well.

One explanation for this could be that companies with high ESG scores have already succeeded in achieving better governance, lowering operational risk, and building in greater flexibility due to better employee relations and more reliable supply chains, and have thus minimized the risk to their business reputation. Consequently, they tend to be of higher quality, to exhibit lower volatility, and to be larger in market capitalization and more mature, with higher earnings and dividend yields. These factors have allowed them to protect their earnings better, and therefore to have gained wider acceptance than companies with lower ESG metrics.

Conversely, a counter-explanation is that ESG funds' outperformance can be better explained by what they *don't* hold than what they do. Actively managed ESG funds have strict selection criteria, actively engage with companies in their portfolios, and avoid poorly rated ESG companies and sectors. Such funds are often underweight in, or exclude entirely, sectors such as airlines, tobacco manufacturers, and energy sourced from coal, oil, and gas, thus avoiding underperformance of those stocks in their overall return.

Put more succinctly, generally speaking, buying "best-in-class" stocks and selling the "worst-in-class" should have generated an annualized excess return in recent years. Historically, this could have been explained away by cyclical rotation in and out of given sectors in line with the cyclical performance of macro indicators. However, a paradigm shift seems to have been observed in recent years, initially driven by climate change concerns but exacerbated more recently by the impact of the pandemic.

REMEMBER

Further examination of the return drivers for different components within ESG shows that 'E' components (environmental; see Chapter 3) exhibit positive excess return by the outperformance of "best-in-class" stocks and underperformance of "worst-in-class" stocks. Alternatively, 'S' (social) and 'G' (governance) components appear to generate their positive excess return from the poor performance of "worst-in-class" stocks (see Chapters 4 and 5 for more about social and governance factors). Moreover, the 'S' component seems to have come to the fore in more recent years and is likely to receive even more attention after the pandemic. To compute ESG ratings requires a mixture of qualitative, quantitative, and engagement-based approaches by identifying material ESG risks and opportunities for each sector, allocating weights to the key indicators based on their materiality, and then combining quantitative ESG ratings with analysts' financial recommendations.

Take it easy: Applying passive strategies

REMEMBER

Two prominent investment developments in recent years have been the increase in assets that are passively managed and the growth in sustainable investing. Replicating both these developments, index-based funds that feature ESG factors have grown in both number and assets. While the majority of sustainably invested assets remain in actively managed ESG funds, net flows into passively managed ESG funds have outstripped net flows into active funds for four of the past five years. Investors have been drawn to passive strategies, such as passive index funds and exchange-traded funds (ETFs), in general due to their performance since the financial crisis in 2009 and the demand for lower-cost exposure to market beta. Meanwhile the shift to ESG indexes has seen responsible investing command an increasing share of the global ETF market, and this trend is likely to increase further. Index benchmarks are now being used by fund managers as tools to position investor selections and to redirect investment flows.

The following sections go over the pros and cons of passive methods for integrating ESG into investment decisions.

The pros

Although many ESG investors use an active stock selection approach, passive (index-based) methods can also be well suited for ESG-driven portfolios. An index's selection criteria for ESG issues can range across many different approaches, including ESG quality, sustainability, and thematic and sector exclusions. Passive strategies have democratized access to the financial markets at a low cost, characteristics that are consistent with an emphasis on passive ESG goals, and both approaches are data driven.

Assuming that an appropriate index, either ESG or non-ESG, has been selected, asset managers can create one of the following routes to offering, for example, a passively managed ESG fund:

>> **Purchase an ESG index license,** which provides the initial investment universe of constituent companies, and design a fund to replicate the index.

>> **Purchase an ESG index license and apply ESG methodology approaches,** such as exclusionary screens, ESG integration and/or thematic filters (all covered in this chapter), to refine company selection and narrow the investment universe to a smaller set of companies based on defined rules.

>> **Weight the index constituents once they are selected.** They can do this following index rules, such as by market capitalization, equal weighting, or "tilting" to underweight or overweight given companies based on specific rules.

Given that passive investment funds are based on indexes, they share certain features that are appealing to investors who want to use their investments to contribute toward positive ESG impacts:

>> They provide simplicity, as the indexes they are based on are transparent and rules-based, and are therefore easy to understand.

>> As the underlying portfolio seeks to replicate the index, the companies in the portfolio will change as the constituents of the index are revised.

>> They create performance benchmarks and help evaluate the broad performance of ESG and non-ESG universes. This generally requires less maintenance than for actively managed funds, so they tend to have lower fees and operating expenses.

>> However, investors should note that the "low-cost" character of passive investing via ETFs and index funds is significantly different in the ESG framework.

Net total expense ratios for passive funds and ETFs are generally higher than in the non-ESG universe, with passive ESG products levying a wide range of fees, the median expense ratio of equity ETFs being in the range of 40 to 50 basis points. Investment firms justify this additional expense through the need to perform additional due diligence or screening for ESG funds, but in practice they generally depend on ESG vendor ratings and third-party data. Nonetheless, market acceptance of higher expense ratios reveals an acknowledgment of the due diligence requirements for ESG analysis. Passive managers tracking broad-based indexes can use ESG integration to overweight companies with better ESG scores and underweight peer companies. Furthermore, some passive managers deliberately differ from conventional benchmarks' industry weights by excluding controversial companies, such as fossil fuel companies.

The cons

WARNING

Critics of passively managed funds feel that ESG variations of those funds are just compounding the fact that conventional indexes, such as the S&P 500, don't reflect the true economy, reward size, and liquidity, and take no account of, for example, corporate governance. Therefore, any funds with traits inherited from such indexes are inconsistent with the aim of moving toward genuine sustainability. Moreover, passive strategies are normally applied by utilizing a single third-party source for ESG research and data that rely heavily on voluntary company disclosure. This can create limitations in the quality, disclosure, and other biases inherent with ESG data, as this data is backward-looking, meaning that investors are missing a complete risk-reward analysis, which may result in skewed allocations to portfolio optimization and sector weighting. In addition, different third-party ESG rating providers often have contradictory views on the same company, which is difficult for the passive manager to understand as they are unaware of the source of the analysis, criteria, or assumptions made in giving a company a certain score in the first place.

This is further exacerbated by the number of holdings in the chosen passive index, leading to a lack of in-depth understanding of the companies' fundamentals and how the fund will be able to pursue active ownership strategies such as ensuring company engagement, filing shareholder resolutions, and developing proxy voting guidelines to ensure improvements in a company's ESG policies and practices. Many observers are calling for greater commitment to improving corporate ESG practices from passive managers entering the sustainable investing space. Particularly with respect to proxy voting records, the largest index fund managers — BlackRock, Vanguard, and State Street, which together hold around 80 percent of indexed assets — have been criticized in the past for regularly voting in support of management and in opposition to ESG shareholder resolutions. Given the size of their holdings, their support is often vital in securing such shareholder resolutions.

On the contrary, concerns aimed at index-like characteristics are less relevant to passive funds based on narrower thematic or industry-focused indexes, such as clean energy, where filters ensure that all companies in a fund contribute to the specific theme. Further examples of ESG issues addressed by sustainable investors include environmental issues, such as clean technology, water use and conservation, sustainable natural resources, and agriculture, while social issues include human rights, gender and racial equity, and workplace concerns. Also, rather than focusing on a way to determine ESG risks, a new generation of ESG benchmarks are being established to have a measurable impact, such as helping to meet climate transition goals under the Paris Agreement.

Finally, while active managers are more concentrated on stock-picking portfolios, many institutional investors prefer to employ ESG investing through optimized benchmarking portfolios that fit their strategic asset allocation (SAA) policy. For example, they typically define an SAA portfolio based on market-capitalization indexes and observe their investments by computing any tracking error between the invested portfolio and the strategic portfolio. Therefore, they accept a maximum level of tracking error, prompting some managers to build ESG-based, optimized portfolios by minimizing the tracking error with respect to the cap-weighted index for a given ESG excess score.

TIP

Effectively, this indexation with an ESG overlay approach offers investors a competitive solution to compete on price with traditional market-cap passive strategies. Consequently, ESG index tracker funds can offer a feasible, cost-effective solution for passive investors who, while mandatory holders of the index, are seeking a pragmatic solution to escape the unsustainable practices of many listed companies.

Reviewing relative returns and performance of ESG stocks

The general mantra from researchers and the market, based on more recent performance metrics, suggests that ESG investors don't have to compromise on performance in order to pursue competitive market returns. Positive screening strategies based on ESG scores (whether created externally by ESG scoring providers or in-house by dedicated analysts) can raise the ESG quality of both passive and active traditional and smart beta portfolios, without reducing risk-adjusted returns. However, instead of focusing on maximizing financial performance from ESG criteria, many investors are now concentrating on maximizing ESG performance subject to risk-return constraints.

TECHNICAL STUFF

Most market participants have reviewed the performance of ESG portfolios before and after the stock market sell-off caused by fears over the COVID-19 pandemic in 2020. During this period, the S&P 500 ESG Index, which tracks large U.S. companies with high ESG ratings, outperformed the established S&P index by 0.6 percent. Similarly, MSCI's emerging markets ESG leaders index, and the more Asia-focused

AC Asia ESG leaders index, outperformed their parent indexes by 0.5 percent and 3.83 percent, respectively. Indeed, BlackRock calculated that 88 percent of a globally representative selection of sustainable indexes outperformed their non-sustainable peers over the same period. And this isn't a new phenomenon as BlackRock has also suggested that similar outperformance was seen during market downturns from 2015 to 2016 and also in 2018.

Of course, some investors may see the demand for ESG stocks with high ratings as a potential bubble, given the weight of funds that are deployed in those stocks. Could the current outperformance lead to overstretched valuations, which in turn may lead to long-term underperformance? This is causing some investors to analyze stocks where their current ESG ratings aren't so high, but they are making credible efforts to improve their ratings through strong, sustainable business practices.

The other regular explanation for ESG outperformance is that, through their exclusion or reduced weighting policies due to fossil fuel screens, most ESG funds have low exposure to fossil fuel assets, which has protected their portfolios when oil prices and energy stocks have fallen. Some analysts suggest that such factors account for only a small amount of any outperformance and propose that, apart from the momentum of investors' buying supporting prices, better supply chain management and corporate governance have contributed to their effectiveness. To maintain high ESG ratings, corporations need to also maintain high levels of corporate disclosure for issues such as auditing of their supply chains, employee practices, and environmental stewardship. Often companies will use reporting frameworks such as the Global Reporting Initiative (GRI) or the Sustainability Accounting Standards Board (SASB; see Chapter 1 for details). This practice also helps businesses improve their own processes and benchmark their performance versus their peers.

However, investors should be aware that ESG screening techniques can lead to increased exposure to large, profitable, and conservative companies, which may also result in increased exposure to certain industry, sector, or geographical biases. The bottom line is that there isn't as much historical performance data for ESG funds as there is for the broader market; therefore, researchers are still building on conclusions drawn from sustainable investing data. This has been further complicated by changing classifications or definitions for what constitutes a sustainable investment strategy over time (the previous "sin stocks" exclusion focus may be more of a "fossil fuel" exclusion focus today), making evaluation and comparisons more difficult. This leaves plenty of room for researchers to develop algorithms that optimize the portfolio's ESG profile while managing exposures to different risk factors within given limits.

Verifying Quantitative Strategies

The vast increase in the amount of material stock market data and the parallel increase in the amount of computing power available to analysts and researchers have enabled the development and growth of quantitative trading strategies. Similarly, as the availability of material ESG data has increased, there has been an increasing focus on quantitative strategies for ESG portfolios and stocks. As mentioned earlier in this chapter, quantitative approaches are one of the four common steps to consider when incorporating an ESG strategy and can be used in conjunction with integration, screening, or thematic strategies.

One approach to quantitative investing is to help investors avoid the unintended risks of industry, sector, or geographical biases, mentioned earlier in this chapter, by targeting exposure to given risk factors. Such strategies target the intersection between companies that are efficiently managed, are profitable, and have strong cash flows while simultaneously exhibiting given ESG factors.

To determine the ESG properties of targeted companies, quantitative strategies increasingly incorporate non-financial performance indicators that can be gathered from corporate sustainability reports or external ESG data providers using artificial intelligence (AI) techniques, such as Natural Language Processing (NLP). Moreover, quantitative managers who implement ESG integration construct models that incorporate ESG factors alongside other factors, such as growth, momentum, size, value, and volatility. ESG data and ratings are integrated into the investment procedure, which can result in the weights of individual stocks being adjusted upward or downward.

REMEMBER

Often investors have a limited understanding of the impact of incorporating ESG criteria into their portfolios, or to what extent the risk and return characteristics of the portfolios are modified, and style or factor tilts can develop as a result. Quantitative techniques are used to assess and control these results to allow investors to maintain their financial and sustainability targets.

In addition, corporate ESG transparency is growing as the number of non-financial disclosure and reporting initiatives increase, such as the GRI and SASB (see Chapter 1), providing better data for quant techniques. A potential benefit of quantitative strategies is that there is no human judgment or discretionary buy-sell decision-making, as decisions are made by the model, which removes any predetermined biases, conscious or subconscious, from the investing process (although some would argue that there is an inherent bias in the way decisions are made when constructing the models). When dealing with emotive topics such as climate change or diversity and inclusion, natural biases can creep into the investment process. The growing body of research around ESG-based quantitative strategies suggests that ESG compliance and alpha generation aren't mutually exclusive outcomes.

The following sections build on the principles of using quantitative approaches to identify the ways in which ESG factors are utilized. The quant approaches include constructing an equity portfolio, adjusting the weighting of particular indexes, and determining which ESG factors are considered more important.

Constructing equity portfolios that integrate ESG factors

ESG information identifies many risk factors that aren't recognized through traditional financial metrics. Quantitative ESG analysts can scrape and scrutinize social media content to help update and allocate value to company intangibles. ESG intelligence should be reflected as a risk factor that doubles as an investment theme that has established correlations to returns, providing value to stocks with exposure to those factors. They can be included with conventional thematic factors, such as momentum, value, quality, growth, and volatility, and also offer diversification benefits because of their low correlation to traditional factors. Consequently, as ESG data becomes more established, statistically accurate, and comparable, more investors will use statistical techniques to pinpoint correlations between ESG factors and price movements that can create alpha or reduce material risk in their portfolio construction.

Four key approaches are taken towards ESG portfolio construction:

>> **ESG integration:** Investors increase or decrease the exposure to particular ESG factors by adjusting the weights of constituent companies based on the strength of material ESG issues or on their total ESG rating (also referred to as a "positive tilt" in favor of companies that fulfill certain sustainability criteria). This approach also incorporates investing in "best-in-class" companies with high ESG ratings or excluding "worst-in-class" companies with low ESG ratings. (ESG integration is covered earlier in this chapter.)

>> **Exclusionary screening:** Investors simply exclude specific companies or sectors participating in activities considered unacceptable, unethical, or controversial.

>> **Exclusionary/inclusionary screening for thematic filters:** Investors specifically exclude companies based on their exposure to particular industries (such as fossil fuels, arms manufacturers, gambling, and alcohol) or include companies (such as those focused on pollution prevention or that address one or more of the United Nations Sustainable Development Goals, covered in Chapter 1).

>> **Norms-based exclusions:** This differs from regular exclusion policies in that it focuses on investors excluding companies on the basis of violation or non-compliance with international norms or standards of conduct as defined by the Organisation for Economic Co-operation and Development (OECD) or the United Nations, such as the UN Human Rights Declaration.

From this starting point, managers can run different strategies — for example, performance based against relative returns (against a benchmark index) or total returns. Both strategies assume that certain elements of the stock markets realize stronger risk-adjusted returns than other segments over longer holding periods. Moreover, research indicates that financial markets are inefficient in determining material ESG scores and don't necessarily price different levels of ESG performance well in the short term, and particularly not in the long term. Naturally, companies with higher ESG scores have a greater chance of being included in such portfolios, as many managers ensure that their portfolio's ESG score is comparable to that of the benchmark index. Therefore, managers will positively screen stocks, as well as negatively screen them, for inclusion and exclusion strategies.

Where managers don't have their own internal ESG ratings, they will need to use data from a larger sample of ESG rating agencies to build a model that extracts the required information, or aggregate individual scores from specific rating agencies into one total score; this will help them to account for the differences in methodologies used by different providers. Research shows that a combination of *alpha* (a measure of the active return on an investment compared with a market index return) and ESG investment targets entails a higher active–risk acceptance from investors. Given the percentage of assets under management that are predicted to be linked to ESG factors in the future, investors and managers may need to review whether current market benchmarks (standard market capitalization–weighted indexes) are appropriate benchmarks given their sustainability and risk/return objectives.

TIP

Investors should also be aware of the appropriate time horizon for ESG integration in their portfolio construction:

>> Highly active portfolio managers that build focused stock portfolios with comparatively high turnover (generating higher costs) may concentrate on isolating and mitigating short-term event risks. As a result, they will be more concerned with potential ESG issues that occur more frequently.

>> Portfolio managers constructing broad, diversified portfolios with long-term investment horizons, such as indexed or buy-and-hold investors, need to focus on these long-term risks in their choice of ESG criteria and integration, mitigating event risks through diversification.

Moreover, it has been found that companies with high ESG ratings outperform companies with low ESG ratings, and they also show a lower incidence of stock-specific events, leading to lower levels of systematic risk.

Adjusting stock index constituent weights

The objective of any of the many ESG indexes available from index providers is to help investors measure the performance of ESG-aligned portfolios. They are often designed to provide risk/return characteristics that are similar to the underlying universe, while offering the additional benefits of enhanced index-level ESG performance. For example:

>> Some of these indexes will use different methodologies to modify company weights based on the index providers' ESG ratings, thereby allowing industry-neutral re-weighting to ensure that the industry weights in each index match the underlying benchmark universe.

>> Other indexes may focus on the stocks with the highest ESG scores, combined with the equally weighted performance of the largest stocks, by market capitalization, within specific regions.

REMEMBER

However, ultimately investors need to consider the ESG issues that are material for investment performance, and whether broader ESG indicators provide value relative to specific data on given ESG factors.

Incorporating ESG "momentum," by buying companies showing improved ESG ratings, has improved performance relative to concentrating on the ESG rating itself. In addition, combining ESG scores with traditional financial metrics has produced more positive results than using ESG data on a stand-alone basis. Nonetheless, ESG-based stock selection can introduce size, sector, or geographic biases relative to standard index-based exposure. This problem can be further exacerbated by the methodology used for ESG ratings by the index provider. Different approaches can lead to markedly different ESG scores for individual companies, which can naturally result in different index constituents or weighting per ESG index for given sectors or geographies.

Determining which ESG factors matter most in quantitative strategies

Research studies from financial institutions such as Amundi and MSCI highlight that not all ESG data is "fit for purpose" when looking for ESG trends and performance:

>> The most relevant data for interpreting risks and returns comes from ESG ratings based on industry-specific financially material scores. It's also clear that different ESG issues can be material for different industries, which is supported by the SASB's approach to corporate disclosure, where industry-specific indicators are required.

>> ESG issues don't necessarily impact all stocks, with a disproportionate effect on "best-in-class" and "worst-in-class" companies in the market. In addition, increasing investor demand for ESG exposure has created more investment in "best-in-class" stocks, which naturally lifts stock prices and performance in those names, while exclusion policies for "worst-in-class" stocks lead to falling prices and underperformance in those entities.

>> The research highlights that time (the holding period), size (the investment universe), and scope (of the investment strategy) are three additional factors that investors must consider when gauging what impact ESG screening has on returns, volatility, and drawdown for their portfolios.

REMEMBER

Given that different ESG issues are material for different industries, these issues can be selected and weighted for each of the Global Industry Classification Standard (GICS) sub-industries based on potential exposure to the corresponding issue. The most commonly utilized issues that are considered when calculating a company's ESG rating are as follows:

>> **Environmental ('E' segment):** Carbon emissions, water scarcity, toxic emissions, and waste (see Chapter 3)

>> **Social ('S' segment):** Labor management, health and safety, human-capital management, and privacy and data security (see Chapter 4)

>> **Governance ('G' segment):** Corporate governance, business ethics, corruption and instability, and anticompetitive practices (see Chapter 5)

When considering which of these ESG segments has the greatest impact, it's important to remember that some key issues are interrelated and can be focused on capturing risks related to events, such as fraud or an oil spill, which tend to affect companies' stock price in the short term. Meanwhile, other key issues focus on long-term risks that can erode a company's stock price over longer periods, such as carbon emissions. Of course, some key issues can also show features of both short- and long-term risk.

REMEMBER

Environmental issues tend to suffer more from long-term risks that play out over time. Social issues show a mix of short- and long-term risk characteristics, and governance issues have the highest short-term risk profile due to the greater propensity for event risk. In deciding how to apply this information, active portfolio managers may want to focus on mitigating short-term event risks, depending on how actively they trade and what their time horizon is. Conversely, portfolio managers who are building diversified portfolios with long investment horizons may be more focused on long-term erosion risks.

The distinct differences across the 'E,' 'S,' and 'G' pillars are summarized in the following sections.

Environmental issues

The three key environmental issues — carbon emissions, water scarcity, and toxic emissions — are driven by long-term risks, with individual company performance showing positive long-term differences between the "best-in-class" and "worst-in-class" scoring companies. There are generally insignificant differences in the tendency for event risks between such companies.

Social issues

The key social issues show differing results, with labor management (including labor conflicts) showing both strong event risk and long-term risk features; however, this was far less prevalent for best-in-class scoring companies.

Health and safety showed similar traits for the benefits of best-in-class, but there is negligible distinction between high- and low-scoring companies on event risk.

Despite some high-profile cases, differences in companies' management of privacy and data security haven't historically contributed to positive performance, and high-scoring companies haven't avoided more negative events than low-scoring companies.

Governance issues

Governance-related issues generally show the strongest results from both risk perspectives. However, business ethics and anti-competitive practices show much stronger event-risk characteristics with negligible long-term risk. Low-scoring companies on business ethics are far more likely to experience a severe stock-price loss than top-scoring companies, while the differences are much less noticeable for corruption issues. However, corporate governance, particularly with respect to corruption issues, shows greater long-term risk characteristics and less event-driven risk differentiation.

In general, companies with strong corporate governance exhibit much better profitability and lower stock-specific and systemic risk than low-scoring companies for key governance issues.

Putting it all together

Within individual key issues, carbon emissions ('E' segment) show the most meaningful outperformance of all key issues, with health and safety as well as labor management (both 'S' segment) and corruption ('G' segment) representing the next-most important issues. These "top-performing" key issues indicate that long-term risks are more evenly distributed across the ESG segments than event risks, which tend to be more concentrated in the 'G' segment. This explains why governance issues have consistently shown the strongest significance for stock-price risks over shorter periods of time.

REMEMBER

Having identified the key ESG issues within each component, it's important to consider how individual factors are aggregated within a portfolio. Assuming an investor has selected stocks with different ESG issues and weighted them for given sectors or industry classifications, thereby making up an overall ESG composite score or rating, this approach can make a significant difference to financial performance over time. Combining the 'E,' 'S,' and 'G' components together in a random way will be less effective than taking a dynamic approach to adjusting by industry-relevant issues, materiality, and appropriate weightings on a predetermined basis. This should allow investors to integrate relevant ESG factors in a way that captures emerging risks and opportunities.

Identifying Smart Beta Strategies

Two of the most significant trends in the global asset management industry have been the growth in ESG investment and smart beta strategies. *Smart beta* can be defined as a rules-based investment strategy that sits between active management and conventional passive management (market cap–weighted). Therefore, smart beta can be seen as an overlay strategy to the approaches mentioned earlier in this chapter to build ESG portfolios, in that smart beta strategies typically capture specific factor exposures.

The growth of smart beta strategies has been driven by a mixture of low costs and returns potential, with the promise that they typically cost less than actively managed funds but offer outperformance compared to traditional passive products. The relative significance of both smart beta and ESG has increased considerably in recent years, and further growth is anticipated as investors combine these strategies. Some market commentators suggest that passive strategies, including both smart beta and market cap–weighted approaches, will reach an estimated 25 percent of global assets under management by 2025.

Currently, smart beta ESG isn't a mainstream offering, but research suggests that adoption rates are increasing, even more so in Europe than the United States and Asia, with larger investors currently more active than smaller investors. Three broad approaches for combining smart beta and ESG have been identified:

>> **Extending negative screening,** such as excluding companies involved in tobacco or controversial weapons, to smart beta strategies. This straightforward approach is also the most popular and can be achieved through mandates, dedicated funds, or internally managed portfolios.

>> **Using ESG metrics,** which are calculated through internal quantitative testing (covered earlier in this chapter). Many investors use this approach to add financial value to traditional factor strategies to improve the risk/return performance of their internal smart beta indexes.

>> **Blending ESG information and smart beta strategies.** A smaller number of investors follow this approach, using portfolio tilts based on specific ESG metrics, such as climate change.

Some barriers to these approaches continue to be an insufficiently long track record of ESG data and disclosure, while others feel that continuing developments in Machine Learning (ML) could identify relevant correlations between ESG performance and stock returns, which could increase the inclusion of smart beta ESG strategies in the future.

Combining ESG data with recognized risk premia factors (the amount by which return on a risky asset is expected to outperform the return on a risk-free asset) is a valuable development in the smart beta industry, with some investors viewing ESG as an established factor on its own. Moreover, a significant amount of research, testing, and planning has been made into smart beta ESG, which is likely to materialize in the near future. Investors appreciate the clarity that rules-based smart beta brings to ESG integration, giving a clearer view of which ESG inputs are being used and facilitating targeted ESG exposures. Others feel that ESG metrics are more insightful than overall scores in an ESG integration context and that the quantitative focus of smart beta is expected to help create higher-quality ESG data over time.

Conversely, incorporating ESG information into smart beta strategies could potentially lead to factor bias, as some investors have found ESG to be negatively correlated to value stocks and positively correlated with quality. In addition, some investors feel that active management (discussed earlier in this chapter) offers a better platform for engagement, due to the greater concentration of portfolios and the fact that active managers have more flexibility than smart beta managers to make tactical portfolio changes in response to new ESG information, such as event risk.

The following sections outline how ESG factors can be incorporated into smart beta and portfolio construction approaches to more explicitly avoid unwanted exposures or achieve specific weightings in their portfolio.

Extending negative stock screening to smart beta strategies

ESG scores can be used to exclude "bad" stocks from a portfolio, which leads to improved scores for standard passive portfolios, without worsening their risk-adjusted performance; however, they can also improve smart beta strategies even further. One approach is to extend negative screens, by excluding companies involved in tobacco or controversial weapons, to smart beta strategies. This is normally realized through mandates, dedicated funds, or internally managed portfolios. Some investors may focus their screening on specific ESG issues, such as carbon-related measures, to highlight a company's carbon intensity relative to its industry peers. This approach is taken by the majority of smart beta strategies.

Alternatively, other investors use ESG metrics that they have discovered through quantitative testing to add financial value to traditional factor strategies. For example, by developing ESG factors around issues such as corporate environmental, carbon, or governance data, it's possible to improve the risk/return performance of existing, internal smart beta indexes.

Using ESG equity factors and scores to weight portfolio construction

Institutional investors who want to integrate ESG factors into their investment strategies require the right tools to evaluate portfolio risk features and performance. In addition, the composition of an ESG portfolio hangs on the investor's objectives. The reason for an ESG investment may be driven by ethical factors, such as social activism, and financial considerations, such as alpha generation or index tracking. This varied set of objectives leads to a detailed set of technical conditions that enable portfolio construction. The subsequent technical specification relies on the quality of the material ESG data, as well as the investor's level of risk aversion and comfort level with stocks that are correlated with agreed exclusions and underweights.

In any portfolio, unwanted exposures or underperformance relative to a benchmark are feasible; however, the developing library of ESG data and the expansion of portfolio construction techniques continue to allow investors to hold the components that align with their ethical and financial views.

Most investors want to build optimized portfolios with enhanced ESG scoring, while keeping risk, performance, country, industry, and style attributes similar to their established benchmarks. In addition, expected improvements in ESG scoring allow investors to go beyond traditional exclusion-focused strategies. Supporters believe that markets don't price ESG factors efficiently because they address long-term risks that haven't been understood by the economy, and so alpha generation is possible as markets begin to recognize these undervalued effects. Therefore, overweighting companies whose ESG scores are improving — benefiting from ESG momentum — or underweighting companies with lower ESG scores are two ways of improving portfolio performance. However, it's important to identify systematic sources of return from common market factor contributions, relative to asset-specific returns that benefit from material ESG factors, while maintaining acceptable levels of tracking error from the established benchmark.

WARNING

Research suggests that the market penalizes companies with lower ESG scores more than it rewards companies with higher ESG scores. This may be due to investors' views that poor ESG practices are sources of risk, forcing them to price in ESG risks more quickly based on events (pollution, fraud, and so on) than to incorporate long-term upside of ESG opportunities into stock prices. The lower ESG ratings anticipate event-driven news that threatens stock returns more than they recognize higher ESG ratings reflecting material and long-term upside, offering discounted values in such stocks.

Focusing on a Given Theme

Investors can get exposure to many ESG investment themes in their portfolios. These largely focus on environmental or social themes such as renewable energy or health and well-being, and they tend to address a given investor's values, where they want explicit exposure to a theme. Sector exposure can be considered an implicit approach to a similar goal by investing in given sectors that address those themes rather than specific companies.

Sector exposure

ESG investment funds are often skewed toward industries, such as pharmaceutical and technology stocks, but are underweight on sectors, such as airlines or energy. These sector biases, largely driven by ESG rankings or exclusions, have insulated ESG funds against any downturn in recent years and driven a performance boost for most.

REMEMBER

The Global Industry Classification Standard (GICS) has 11 sectors and 158 sub-industries. Of these 158 sub-industries, only about 100 find their way into portfolios composed of the top 30 percent of ESG-scored companies. Therefore, industries' weights in a portfolio roughly align with associated industry ESG scores. Moreover, the five industries with the largest weights have higher ESG scores, and the five industries with either minimal or no exposure have lower ESG scores. As a result, sector and industry selection has helped ESG funds outperform the main benchmark indexes in recent years.

It's currently unclear how much year-to-year proactive sector rotation takes place within ESG portfolios; therefore, industry "tilts" may cause a long-term bias that ESG portfolio managers should be aware of, and they should adjust sector or industry selection, or associated weightings, as necessary.

TIP

Sector or sub-industry performance can also vary from year to year, but the principal way for sector weights in ESG portfolios to change is for businesses from different sectors to increase their ESG ratings and become integrated or to move down and drop out. In addition, some industries don't have companies rated by ESG scoring vendors, so those industries are ineligible for inclusion in an ESG portfolio. Where a manager feels that a portfolio's sector weights need to be adjusted, they may consider executing an active sector overlay strategy to enhance the existing portfolio.

Thematic exposure

Investment themes linked to the Sustainable Development Goals (SDGs; see Chapter 1) have become more prominent on investors' sustainability road maps as they attempt to create positive impact while capturing opportunities in the global equity market. The SDGs have provided central pillars in forming the sustainability approach of many investors, governments, and civil society groups. The new decade has begun, leaving just ten years to achieve the SDGs by 2030. However, recent progress reports issued by the European Union (EU) and the United Nations suggest that most of the 17 SDGs are unlikely to be met on time.

Nonetheless, the SDGs capture many of the more exciting upside opportunities in today's equity markets and are closely linked with global economic growth and overall macroeconomic health. Of these, five key ESG themes stand out: clean, efficient energy; environmental protection; sustainable infrastructure and development; health and well-being; and social equity. In addition, improved data and analytics for ESG investing creates an opportunity for investors to better manage risk and performance around SDGs.

The focus on SDGs has prompted the emergence of thematic fund launches in areas such as clean water, renewable energy, and social housing. However, the transition from fossil fuels to renewable energy, for example, will impact countries, industries, and sectors beyond fossil fuel exporters and the energy sector. Entire industries and sectors that aren't making the transition to a low-carbon future face possible downgrades, while research estimates that a quarter of the value of global equity and fixed markets is tied to the fossil fuel value chain.

TECHNICAL STUFF

About 20 percent of global carbon emissions were covered by some sort of carbon tax in 2019, which is likely to grow to more than 50 percent as close to 100 countries are enacting new regulations. In addition, the Principles for Responsible Investment (PRI) warns that up to US$2.3 trillion of company valuation could be lost by 2025 because of government policies to tackle climate change, including support for renewable energy and bans on coal and carbon prices. Increasingly, investors want fossil-fuel-free portfolios, and the call to fund climate-change solutions through their investments is growing. Meanwhile, companies will face higher fuel costs, updated building codes, and clean-energy requirements, so new strategies to support companies with products and services that support a lower carbon transition are prevalent.

Resource shortages are becoming more of a focus with, for example, a variety of sectors being heavily dependent on access to water resources, such as utilities, apparel, and agriculture. Companies with operations in dry locations are particularly exposed to these risks, and developed countries aren't immune from these issues. Estimates suggest that nearly half of the rivers and lakes in the United States may not meet the needs of people in the next 50 years because of aging infrastructure, population growth, and lower annual rainfall. Investors are monitoring how well companies are managing water shortages and embracing efficient solutions, while funds dedicated to supporting water regeneration are cropping up.

Chapter **9**

ESG and Fixed Income Instruments

B ond investors have typically trailed their equity colleagues when integrating ESG factors into their portfolios. Contrary to stocks (see Chapter 8), bond investors' primary focus is on alleviating the risk of default rather than gaining upside potential (which is naturally capped) and returning the principle invested ("Will we get our money back?") at a future date. However, because of ESG's increasing influence over credit ratings and investors' increasing engagement with debt issuers, the fixed income sector is starting to play catch-up. Particularly given the distinct range of debt instruments, issuers, and maturities, fixed income investors are integrating ESG considerations into their analysis, as ESG investing expands to all areas of the market and ESG metrics help spot new risk factors.

Another consideration is that for many years, ESG investing wasn't considered relevant for fixed income, as bond holders don't have voting rights and therefore have less influence on a company than equity investors. Nonetheless, with fixed income investment, due diligence has always been strongly influenced by governance ('G') factors, especially for corporate bonds. And with the increasing issuance of social ('S') and green ('E') bonds, and developing awareness of the impact of climate ('E') and COVID-19 ('S') risks, 'S' and 'E' factors are equally applicable to fixed income investment. (See Chapters 3, 4, and 5 for more about environmental, social, and governance factors, respectively.)

This chapter analyzes how ESG is integrated into mainstream fixed income investing and emphasizes some of the differences that arise among different bond issuer types. It also highlights the increasing use of fixed income indexes to represent a fixed income portfolio and identifies some of the specific ESG exposures that investors should be aware of.

Analyzing Fixed Income (Bond) Factors

REMEMBER

The key factors that affect the prices of fixed income securities include interest rate changes, default or credit risk, and secondary market liquidity risk. Bond rating systems are mainly driven by three factors: duration, credit spread, and liquidity. Of course, one of the biggest risks emanating from ESG is some form of event risk, driven by news that may affect a company's reputation and that leads to concerns around its credit risk, so the process of analyzing ESG factors as part of the investment decision is as natural an extension to fixed income as it is to equity investments (see Chapter 8).

The following sections discuss various ESG considerations with respect to risk, bond portfolio strategies, issuers, and integration factors, ending with the differences and similarities between credit ratings and ESG ratings.

The importance of risk

Using ESG factors to inform fixed income investment decision-making is primarily about identifying risks and opportunities that might otherwise be overlooked. While there are a variety of approaches to ESG integration, there is one consistent theme, that of capturing financially material risks. (And by *financially material*, I mean having a meaningful impact, either positive or negative, on a company's business model and value drivers, such as margins, required capital, and risk. Also note that material factors can differ from one sector to another.)

As clients look for evidence of ESG integration, they are expecting verifiable examples that ESG is integrated into fundamental analysis, particularly for long-term mandates. Therefore, some firms have adopted a more systematic approach to including ESG risks by recognizing material risks that are applicable to different company sectors, which is a similar approach to that used by equity investors. By identifying a given number of industry sectors, it's easier to highlight indicators specific to those sectors' issues and decide whether companies are managing them adequately. Given that the investable bond universe is so large, this allows investors to develop "red flags" in their portfolio and to benchmark companies against their peers in terms of ESG performance.

These indicators can be generated by using a cross section of data provided by external ESG providers. The generated scores can be broken down into specific 'E,' 'S,' and 'G' scores or kept as an overall ESG score, with weightings assigned to each of these categories as part of the peer group analysis (see Chapter 14 for more information). Meanwhile, macro indicators can also be applied to identify other country, region, or geopolitical-type risks that are relevant to a sector or given company. Given that fixed income bonds can have greater duration, it can also be appropriate to combine ESG scores that represent potentially long-term risks.

This analysis can be supported by the view that investing in the wrong bond generally has greater consequences than investing in the wrong equity, given that equity returns are largely driven by sentiment relating to earnings or profit projections rather than predominantly by fundamental risk analysis. This suggests that equities show a more immediate and direct response to ESG factors, while fixed income has a lagged effect as the creditworthiness of the issuer can act as a cushion to the ESG risk, possibly mitigating or delaying the impact. Therefore, an ESG risk can be deemed as meaningful from a business risk perspective but may not be sufficient to cause a change in credit rating or affect the price of a company's bonds materially.

WARNING

There has traditionally been a greater focus on 'G' risks within fixed income, acting as the driver in credit analysis and safeguarding returns from investment-grade bonds. It's rare to have a default due to 'E' or 'S' failures — such as the Exxon Valdez or BP catastrophes — but given a 'G' failure, the company can collapse and default on its debt, and there have been many examples of this over time.

Strategies for adding ESG to fixed income portfolios

REMEMBER

Approaches to the combination of ESG factors into fixed income portfolio strategies include the following:

>> **Negative screening:** This excludes entire sectors from the portfolio, but it depends on the size of the sector relative to the investment universe.

>> **Positive screening:** This picks the best ESG performers in a sector or universe, but if, for example, a portfolio only has the good ESG–quality corporates, then the return on those bonds won't be as high, so investors will tend to blend the portfolio with corporates that have lower ESG scores but are improving their ESG ranking.

>> **Best-in-class:** This separates investment grade (IG) and high yield (HY) issuers within a given sector but depends on the requirement to choose bonds from part of the universe, rather than all available bonds.

>> **Engagement:** This is an emerging practice for corporate bond strategies, particularly around issuance or re-issuance points (where the company is originally issuing a new bond or subsequently replacing a maturing bond issuance), when general discussion around the terms of the bonds will be ongoing, although bond investors should realize that this can be more difficult without the formal voting rights available to equity investors.

>> **Thematic:** The scale of investments needed to tackle thematic issues, such as climate change, has seen the demand for green, sustainable, or even pandemic bonds increase greatly over the last five to ten years.

REMEMBER

So, ESG factors are increasingly being blended into common fixed income portfolio factors, but they are still behind the curve when compared to the sophistication of ESG approaches employed by equity portfolios. However, rating agencies have always considered governance, or management strength, as an important part of their standard credit risk assessment framework. Therefore, this helps explain why there is higher correlation between ESG credit ratings among the big three providers (Fitch, Moody's, and S&P) than there is for equity ESG rating providers.

Bond issuer goals

For many companies, there is a preference to raise funds through bond issuance, as this can be more efficient and less expensive than giving up equity, particularly when benchmark interest rates are low. Therefore, the bond market is considerably bigger than the equity market, and many companies are realizing the increasing relevance of good ESG processes to attract bond investors.

In addition, issuers (which can be companies, municipal entities, or governments) often revisit the bond market to refinance old debt or look for new funding, giving bond investors a unique oversight for identifying risks, engaging issuers, and building relationships to effect change. Hence, fixed income investors can exert the most influence through the primary issuance cycle, when issuers are more open to investor requirements and are more likely to include demands in the terms of the new bond. As such, ESG-focused investors can not only influence issuers that already advocate an integrated approach to ESG; they should also engage with issuers looking to enhance their own proposals and who are keen to work with lenders to realize their ESG targets.

As mentioned earlier in this chapter, investing in bond issuers showing the best ESG scores can reduce the available yields, which is good for the issuer; as a result, risk-adjusted returns can be better. Therefore, issuers should be aware that investors are looking to increase returns and influence proactive developments by financing issuers with improving ESG scores as well. This also allows investors to take advantage of yield compression (where a stronger investment grade leads to a lower risk profile and therefore is purchased at a lower yield/return) as an issuer improves its ESG score and therefore its creditworthiness.

Meanwhile, the market appears to be welcoming further issuance in social bond securities related to ESG issues. Examples include gender, health, and other social-related infrastructure areas (such as food distribution and transport), sanitation, and water access, particularly given the requirements after the coronavirus pandemic. Development banks and agencies are working more closely with private finance and institutional investors to locate deals and co-invest. In addition, the UN Sustainable Development Goals (SDGs; see Chapter 1) are forming a central ESG framework to guide issuers on delivering returns to investors while simultaneously ensuring a positive impact on society. Hence, the UN's estimates — that to achieve the SDGs by 2030, investment between US$3 trillion and US$5 trillion annually is required — should trigger further new issuance, with most of this investment coming from the private sector.

The long-term nature of the SDGs, and the requirement that most of the funding needs to be used for long-term social and environmental projects, suggests that new issuance of fixed income bonds is best suited to meet the obligations. Moreover, the UN Global Compact has developed a "Blueprint for SDG Bonds," which offers guidance to companies and investors on the definitions, development, and impact measurement for issuance (check out www.unglobalcompact.org/library/5713). Therefore, there is a strong prospect of a growing market in SDG bonds by sovereigns, development banks, and companies, with some following specific themes to target given goals, such as the Asian Development Bank's launch of a gender bond in 2017. In addition, the evolution of green bonds highlights that many investors are mainly concerned with environmental, particularly climate-related, issues; the specifics of green, social, and sustainable bonds are covered in greater detail later in this chapter. Investors should recognize that there is a distinction between bonds that apply ESG ratings as a credit evaluation tool and those labeled bonds that are explicitly issued as sustainable instruments.

Defraying interest rate costs

ESG factors can impact borrowers' cash flows and the probability that they will default on their debt obligations. ESG factors are therefore important components in evaluating the creditworthiness of borrowers. For corporates, concerns such as the stranding of assets (where assets have suffered from unanticipated or premature write-downs or devaluation) linked to causes of climate change, labor relation challenges, or lack of transparency around accounting practices can cause unexpected losses, litigation, regulatory pressure, and reputational impacts.

Studies show that ESG and credit ratings are positively correlated. To identify the marginal effects of ESG, investors need to recognize the need for an integrated ESG credit-pricing model. Some evidence suggests that ESG affects the cost of capital in a positive way: Bond issuers with higher ESG scores have a lower cost of capital than issuers with lower ESG scores for the same credit rating. There is a clear yield spread difference between best-in-class and worst-in-class corporations, which is generally wider for Euro-denominated bonds than U.S. dollar–denominated investment-grade bonds (those that are believed to have a lower risk of default and receive higher ratings by the credit rating agencies). This has become more pronounced in recent years, whereas this ESG impact due to better data availability wasn't identifiable, say, ten years ago. As ESG ratings continue to be integrated into the fixed income arena, bond issuers must consider these benefits for their financing costs.

All together now: ESG integration issues

Given the restrictions on some of the strategies described earlier in this chapter, many investors prefer a full ESG integration approach to allow for the inclusion of the diverse characteristics of bonds and an investor's ESG risk profile. However, there are also reasons why investors question integrating ESG:

>> Credit rating agencies (CRAs) such as Moody's and S&P maintain that they integrate ESG risks already as one of their metrics, but there is a perception that it's still difficult to integrate ESG factors into credit analysis.

>> Liquidity issues are more widespread in the fixed income space, which may make it harder to rebalance actively managed portfolios using ESG signals.

>> Given that a bond holder knows the return on their debt instrument, their primary goal is to minimize the risk of default within the maturity of the instrument. As such, an equity investor should be more sensitive to ESG risks than a bond investor.

In addition, improvement is needed in the quality and availability of issuer-level ESG data, ESG credit rating analysis (incorporating the time horizon of credit analysis relative to the long-term nature of some ESG risks), and experience of ESG investment strategies customized to fixed income. Moreover, ESG data vendors have generally focused on publicly listed companies, overlooking smaller companies and those that only issue bonds. Therefore, while U.S. dollar and Euro investment-grade companies normally have good coverage, the high-yield universe and emerging-market companies have a much lower coverage.

CRAs are already integrating sustainability into their ratings frameworks, and the way this analysis evolves will generate greater interest as many sectors, with an aggregate of more than US$2 trillion of rated debt, are at risk of credit downgrades. This is primarily because of their exposure to environmental risks, such as carbon transition. The electric utilities and coal sectors face more of the pressing risks, while automakers, makers of commodity chemicals, and oil and gas companies are tackling threats on a three- to-five-year horizon.

TIP

Investors following an active strategy have more freedom to consider other mitigating approaches to these challenges. For example, they can invest in countries with poor ESG ratings, assuming they are attractive enough as stand-alone investment decisions, provided that the overall ESG score of the portfolio is relatively high. They can assign weightings to each country — for example, for their ESG emerging market portfolio. Based on both their current ESG practices and on any indicators of improvement, they can increase the country weighting; where there are signs of decline, they can reduce the country weighting. This dynamic approach can either increase or reduce exposure to improving or worsening credit quality, respectively.

Bond pricing

Unlike equities, the ultimate value of a bond is capped by its par value (the face value that a bond is issued at). As such, there is a greater focus on downside risk than upside potential, with most analysis focused on repayment and default risk. This increases the significance of dispute scores and other "red flag" ESG measures. Therefore, the key challenge is separating the influence of ESG risk in bond prices, given that coupon, term structure, and rates all influence credit spreads. Bond investors operate in a broader investment pool, where there are considerable differences in the quality and number of instruments, and they can experience lower levels of liquidity than in established equity markets.

REMEMBER

Bond prices are measured against their credit rating and the risk of default, so there is generally less volatility. Fixed income investors also need to consider the following:

>> Fixed maturity of fixed income bonds relative to equities potentially being held permanently

>> Position of fixed income instruments in corporate balance sheet structure

>> Different rights relative to shareholders, particularly in terms of voting and engagement

>> Sovereign, multinational agency issuers and asset-backed securities that don't exist in equity markets

Fixed income research has centered on adjusting key equity ESG factor considerations to corporate bonds. However, they don't always reflect some of the issues that are material for fixed income investors. While corporate bonds have traditionally been broken up into maturity, rating, and industry buckets, some investors have created models that also include liquidity, quality, value, and momentum. So, while there has been significant growth within equity market factor investing, largely driven by the movement toward lower cost and potential outperformance of passive investments, new studies show that factor investing can be extended to fixed income. These strategies include reducing risk through low volatility or risk bias, security screening strategies, looking for value within a particular universe, and tilting the portfolio toward higher-quality bonds.

Mix it up: Credit and ESG ratings

Credit ratings should signal all factors that materially affect an issuer's credit-worthiness. Therefore, long-term factors concerning an issuer's ESG performance should be incorporated, but the inclusion of ESG factors in credit analysis has been comparatively limited to date. However, material ESG factors are now being considered as part of the standard credit risk assessment model, with credit risk materiality depending on industry sector, company, and time horizon.

In addition, the European Securities and Markets Authority (ESMA) has distributed technical advice on how credit rating agencies (CRAs) are integrating ESG factors (visit www.esma.europa.eu/sites/default/files/library/esma33-9-321_technical_advice_on_sustainability_considerations_in_the_credit_rating_market.pdf). The publication determined that, although CRAs were bearing in mind ESG factors, they had a different approach depending on the asset class or sector. As such, ESMA ruled that credit ratings couldn't be depended on to offer an opinion on the sustainability features of an issuer and should thus focus on transparency. In response, CRAs (Fitch, Moody's, and S&P) have been developing further ESG data–generation capabilities and have made changes to their rating methodology to accommodate all industry sectors.

Consequently, Fitch (ESG relevance scores) and S&P (ESG evaluation tool) are now generating separate ESG scores to supplement their credit ratings, while Moody's is incorporating ESG analysis within its ratings. All of the CRAs have indicated that their current credit ratings haven't changed, despite initiating the new ESG approaches; however, investors will now be able to evaluate whether there are correlations between their ESG and credit ratings.

Meanwhile, the ESG in Credit Risk and Ratings Initiative created by the Principle for Responsible Investments (PRI) group has tried to improve the clear and systematic integration of ESG factors into credit risk analysis. They have facilitated dialogue between CRAs and investors to promote a standardized language and to debate ESG risks to creditworthiness, which started with the *Statement on ESG in credit risk and ratings,* which has been signed by more than 160 investors, with over US$30 trillion of assets under management (AUM) and 23 CRAs. By signing this statement, CRAs and fixed income investors pledge to incorporate ESG into credit ratings and analysis (check out `www.unpri.org/credit-risk-and-ratings/statement-on-esg-in-credit-risk-and-ratings-available-in-different-languages/77.article`).

The 'G' element of ESG (covered in Chapter 5) has always been a big part of the credit equation, as good corporate governance is a clear gauge of creditworthiness; therefore, CRAs are familiar with evaluating governance characteristics. It's currently unclear how the performance of ratings will be affected now that 'E' and 'S' factors will be considered more explicitly, but a greater emphasis on ESG factors may cause an increase in the cost of capital for those firms that are behind on ESG integration, or at least help investors recognize potentially dangerous events on the horizon. Initial research suggests that employing an ESG filter moderates risk in fixed income without decreasing returns, while highlighting that companies with low ESG ratings tend to show high market betas; therefore, reducing the share of such companies in portfolios reduces risk. However, just as the financial crisis of 2008–2009 highlighted some misgivings on credit rating methodologies, the effect of the coronavirus pandemic in 2020 has called into question the validity of the quality of some ESG credit ratings.

REMEMBER

Therefore, stakeholders should acknowledge that credit ratings indicate an assessment of an issuer's creditworthiness only. CRAs have to maintain full independence in deciding which criteria are material to their ratings. While ESG analysis of an issuer can be considered a significant part of a credit rating, the two measurements shouldn't be seen as interchangeable. Although ESG factors can be material to the credit rating, other criteria such as financial strength are generally perceived to be more significant. Financial strength can allow an issuer to adjust to ESG risks over time, but it's also a good proxy for the corporate management of ESG risks, as CRAs tend to focus on the 'G' of ESG. However, good governance won't, in isolation, positively affect a credit rating.

Emphasizing Bond Issuer Differences

The financial materiality of different ESG segments varies greatly across sectors. Research suggests that the 'E' segment (see Chapter 3) has a bigger influence on financial institutions than generally thought, as loans to fossil fuel producers expose banks to financial risks in any conversion to a low-carbon economy. Therefore, overweighting exposures to the more material ESG factors by industry can enhance portfolio performance.

Research further suggests that ESG factors explain a significant share of the deviation in credit spreads across emerging-market government issuers. As suggested earlier in this chapter, poor ESG performers generally pay a higher market premium to issue debt, with the opposite being true for good ESG performers. Therefore, fixed income markets seem to already be pricing in ESG-related risks, even though the correlation between credit spreads and ESG scores can be overwhelmed by macro forces such as "risk-off" periods, as regulatory pressures are causing issuers to pay more attention to sustainability issues.

There is also ESG potential in sectors that have been overlooked by sustainable investors, including U.S. agency mortgages, which make up around one-third of the Bloomberg Barclays U.S. Aggregate Bond Index. There is capacity to focus on the 'S' segment via exposure to programs that sponsor access to credit, assist underserved populations, and promote community development. Likewise, the U.S. municipal bond market is progressively grabbing the attention of ESG investors. Again, around one-third of issuance in the U.S. municipal market is related to the UN Sustainable Development Goals (SDGs; see Chapter 1), so a focus on issuers who do well in terms of environmental stewardship and social impact is attracting capital. Meanwhile, as discussed in more detail later in this chapter, sustainable investing is more regularly including specific mandates such as green and SDG bonds.

The following sections analyze further the different types of issuers, from government debt to emerging markets, with an evaluation of how ESG ratings are incorporated.

For king and country: Sovereign issuance

Government bonds make up a large amount of fixed income issuance, but ESG factors for countries are far less developed than for companies. Credit analysis of government debt has conventionally concentrated on macroeconomic indicators, such as debt-to-GDP (gross domestic product) ratios or other relationships that emphasize debt sustainability. Related to this are the issuer's current account position and its commitment, or ability, to meet its debt obligations. This can be driven by factors such as political stability or government effectiveness, which tend to be covered by the 'G' in ESG. However, the correlation between sustainability factors and government bond spreads is often obscured by macroeconomic factors that are considered more financially material. Changes in interest rates and inflation, or risk sentiment from "risk on" to "risk off," trigger changes in appetite for government debt.

Sovereign bond issuers require an alternative approach to regular credit analysis. There aren't as many openings to engage with governments on ESG issues as would be the case at the corporate level. Also, corporate bonds can be ranked relative to the ESG rating system used for the underlying equities. When evaluating government debt, it's important to make an objective ESG assessment of the country's issues rather than a subjective view of the government's policies, so that there is little risk of being accused of political interference. For example, some might argue that the United States fails to meet required ESG standards, given its support for the manufacturing of arms, social equality concerns, use of the death penalty, record on pollution emissions, and withdrawal from the Paris Climate Agreement (at the time of writing). Nonetheless, it's the world's largest issuer of debt; therefore, could a pension fund exclude U.S. Treasury bonds from a large, diversified bond portfolio?

Even in developing markets, ESG-based sovereign bond investment can be difficult. ESG assessments tend to be based on social and macroeconomic indicators, such as data on educational standards, labor markets, and social mobility, although research suggests that there is a correlation between ESG scores and per capita GDP. However, analysis of the SDGs could help investors recognize key factors aligned to the sustainability of a public debt issuer in less developed economies, although it may mean that a middle-income developing country such as Chile could be rated more highly than, for example, Bangladesh. Thus, specific ESG factors may risk denying countries that most need funding and instead support those that have better access to the financial markets already. Nevertheless, this requires reconciling viewpoints on general ESG principles with investments in emerging or frontier markets, which can suffer from higher levels of corruption, inferior governance with weaker application of laws, and progressively more polluted than developed markets.

REMEMBER

Some important drivers can be considered to influence an economy's performance from an ESG viewpoint, including how sovereign issuance is impacting the environment and how exposed the country is to climate risk. Moreover, a focus on how funds that a government receives are being invested in the country's citizens, and how effectively they are governing their people, is taking center stage. At a sovereign level, risks associated with public health standards, natural resource management, and corruption can affect trade balance, tax revenues, and foreign investment. These factors can result in bond price volatility and increase the risk of defaults.

TIP

Principles like these, or similar ones, can guide the selection of underlying indicators that are available from the World Bank's ESG data portal in producing a more complete view of each country's sustainability. The ESG portal allows investors to identify metrics such as renewable energy output and CO_2 emissions ('E'), unemployment and literacy rates ('S'), and measures covering the rule of law and corruption ('G'), which can highlight sustainability issues that aren't captured by established economic indicators. The underlying indicators can be used to formulate scores for each of the three key pillars: 'E,' 'S,' and 'G.' An equal-weighted combination of the three pillar scores provides an overall ESG score for each country. See `https://databank.worldbank.org/source/environment-social-and-governance-(esg)-data` for more information.

Corporate issuance

Many investors and managers have focused on adjusting material equity-factor ESG classifications to corporate bonds. So, how does ESG affect the credit rating of corporate bonds, given that corporate bond performance is normally established by a variety of factors? On a portfolio level, issuer selection and diversification are important factors, but traditionally, credit risk has been quantified relative to bond price volatility, credit default swap prices, and credit spreads. More recently, the PRI initiative (mentioned in the earlier section "Mix it up: Credit and ESG ratings") was launched to expand on workable solutions for more systemic and transparent integration of ESG into credit ratings and analysis.

ESG risks are already seen as a vital element in the analysis of the corporate credit criteria framework, but the goal is to provide a holistic view of an issuer's profile by considering ESG factors as part of the process. The primary focus for any CRA analysis is to use ESG factors to enhance the identification of any downside credit risk before any favorable factors are considered to improve the credit rating outlook. Governance, specifically, is only scored on a neutral or negative scale. Other factors that are evaluated include adherence to legal and regulatory requirements; employee, customer, and community relations; climate change policies; environmental pollution; and resource depletion. However, CRAs generally argue that 'E' and 'S' factors are implicitly included in their evaluation due to their appraisal of a company's approach to other credit factors. Consequently, ESG concerns are captured when a CRA believes they will materially affect the main focus of their ratings systems to evaluate the probability of default of a debt issuer and expected credit loss in the event of default.

Room for more: Emerging markets

The integration of ESG factors into investment practices in Asia has trailed in comparison to the United States and Europe for many reasons, including reduced understanding of the benefits and a comparative absence of commercial incentive. Asia inhabits a unique place at the crossroads of sustainability and finance. The region generates nearly 40 percent of global GDP, houses around 60 percent of the global population, is home to two of the top three energy-consuming nations, is the source of the majority of the world's modern slavery, and has an expanding trillion-dollar credit market.

Therefore, ESG factors are delivering a noticeable impact on Asian fixed income outcomes, in fields such as credit quality, defaults, and spreads. Investing with an ESG lens can help strengthen portfolios through enhanced risk management. For many participants, active investing using local knowledge and presence introduces the added benefit of a more refined method to recognize risks and opportunities. This can also assist with corporate engagement, and governance issues continue to be the most frequent and material factors for rating changes.

Regulations and institutional investor demand are the main drivers of environmental factor screening in Asia. In certain sectors (including energy, metals and mining, and utilities), environmental factors play an increasingly critical role due to growing awareness of climate change and sustainable financing. For example, the Asian palm oil industry, which produces most of the global supply, has been subject to scrutiny for alleged deforestation and destruction of wildlife, and in recent years, large institutional investors have divested their holdings in the sector.

Highlighting Fixed Income Indexes

Studies suggest that based on historical data, active equity portfolio managers have on average underperformed their benchmark indexes after transaction costs. However, in contrast, fixed income active managers have outperformed their respective benchmarks after transaction costs. As such, the need for passive management hasn't been as in demand as has been seen for equities. However, with more data and transparency, further research is emerging that could lead to changes in how investors will allocate funds going forward. Fixed income ESG indexes are likely to become strategic benchmarks for numerous investors in the near future.

REMEMBER

The various approaches to fixed income ESG investing aren't dissimilar to those for equities (see Chapter 8):

>> They use exclusion screens that eliminate companies (or issuers) on the basis of a poor human rights record (norms-based exclusion), sustainability approach, or "worst-in-class" assessment relative to peers based on their ESG rating, and that are therefore contrary to an investor's values.

>> They combine exclusion screens with a focus on relatively strong ("best-in-class") ESG performers. This can be done by excluding all securities ("worst-in-class") that fall below a cutoff ESG rating.

>> They leverage optimization to maximize a portfolio's weighted-average ESG score while closely tracking the properties of its traditional benchmark index.

In equity markets, the first two approaches described here would lead to a material "tracking error," or a divergence in performance in comparison to the portfolio's benchmark index. However, this isn't as true for bonds because macro risks, such as changes in interest rates, represent the majority of total risk in fixed income. Therefore, over- or underweight allocations in a fixed income portfolio have less impact from a total risk perspective than would be the case for equities. As a result, fixed income investors don't need to sacrifice their yield, diversification, or return targets under such approaches to an ESG bond index benchmark. Therefore, ESG bond indexes have allowed managers to create building blocks that investors can now use to form the core of sustainable multi-asset portfolios. This potentially allows investors to create portfolios that offer an improvement on their main sustainability metrics, including ESG scores, while closely following the fundamental traits of standard bond indexes, such as duration and yield.

Passive ESG funds, which include ESG factors, have seen large inflows since 2019, with overall assets under management doubling. However, the uptake for passive ESG bond funds remains emergent in comparison to equities. Still, in a low-yielding environment with very tight credit spreads, where clients are concerned about the threats of recession and geopolitical risk events, sustainability is quickly becoming a key dimension in the investment model. Therefore, many new bond indexes are being established that incorporate approaches like excluding given issuers from benchmark bond indexes and then re-weighting constituents to tilt the index toward ESG leaders with higher ESG ratings. Alternatively, investors are participating in indexes where a bigger exclusion policy is employed alongside a greater weighting toward the ESG leaders within each sector. This allows investors to have multiple ways in which to express their fixed income ESG views through more passive, index-driven exposures, an approach that is cheaper to deploy than an active management strategy.

Furthermore, ESG bond indexes also underlie exchange-traded funds (ETFs), which act as building blocks for *beta* (the responsiveness of a bond's price relative to changes in the overall bond market), which can in turn reduce the fees associated with some exposure and focus other fees on active funds that can add alpha. In certain sectors or with certain products, investors are also using ETFs to access liquidity, where they can get in and out of exposure quickly. Moreover, trading bonds through ETFs enhances price discovery, where the price of the ETF helps provide input on pricing the fixed income portfolio overall, as an investor immediately has some information on the pricing of related underlying bonds.

TECHNICAL STUFF

Fixed income indexes are available for sustainable bonds as well as ESG-adjusted indexes for regular corporate or sovereign bond issuance. Research shows that in 2019 the Bloomberg Barclays MSCI Euro Green Bond Index returned 7.4 percent, which was higher than the 6 percent for the established Bloomberg Barclays MSCI Euro Aggregate Index of regular Euro-denominated corporate and sovereign bonds. Furthermore, Euro-denominated green bonds outperformed the Euro Aggregate Index for three of the last four years, by an average of 0.7 percent per year. However, the annual volatility of the green bond index was higher for three of those years, which shows that the higher returns were partly due to the higher risk. This can be partially explained by the duration of the Green Bond Index increasing in 2017, when the Republic of France issued its first green government bond with a 22-year maturity, meaning that the overall index became more sensitive to interest rate changes.

Identifying Specific ESG Exposures

REMEMBER

Within fixed income, securities are issued that have specific requirements as to how the proceeds of those bonds are used. These bonds finance projects targeted at generating climate, social, or other environmental benefits. They typically fall into one of five categories:

>> Green bond issuance began in 2007, supported by issuance from the European Investment Bank (EIB) and World Bank. They were designed to back projects that have explicit environmental or climate benefits. The majority of the green bonds issued are green "use of proceeds" or asset-linked bonds. Funds raised from these bonds are reserved for green projects but supported by the issuer's entire balance sheet.

>> Social bonds are use-of-funds bonds that raise finances for new and current projects with positive social outcomes. Social bonds are any type of bond instrument where the funds are entirely related to finance or refinance new or existing qualified social projects. The issuer generally seeks a second-party opinion of their social bond framework to ensure that their bond meets market expectations and industry best practices, while giving investors confidence in the issuance.

>> Social impact bonds pay out to investors, normally from a government; the payout is conditional on the realization of the targeted social program. Funds from these bonds are directed to areas such as education, employment, healthcare, and housing.

>> Sustainable bonds contrast with green bonds by offering issuers a wider mandate of suitable ESG uses for the proceeds from the bonds.

>> Blue bonds are the youngest member of the sustainable bonds family. The first issuance was made in October 2018 with the Seychelles, in partnership with the World Bank, issuing a US$15 million bond. Blue bonds are issues made to finance marine and ocean-based projects that have positive environmental, economic, and climate benefits.

All of these bonds, which are covered in more depth in the following sections, are focused on how the capital raised from issuance is deployed, rather than the performance of the issuer overall, with the exception of sustainability-linked bonds.

For the earth: Green bonds

Green bonds raise funds for climate and environmental programs, and are generally issued by governments, corporations, and financial institutions. Multilateral development banks, including the European Investment Bank and World Bank, originally brought them to market in 2007, but issuance has really picked up in recent years, with new issues topping US$258 billion worldwide in 2019. The green bond market is maturing, with outstanding issuance of green bonds passing US$1 trillion total issuance since inception in September 2020, more than ten times the size of the market in 2015.

The following sections delve into different aspects of green bonds, including the Green Bond Principles, transition bonds, indexes, and working groups.

Green Bond Principles

REMEMBER

The Green Bond Principles (GBP; www.greenbond.org/) are a set of voluntary guidelines that aim to promote transparency and integrity in the market. The four constituents of the GBP establish the minimum requirements for a green bond label:

>> Announcing the qualified project classifications up front

>> Working to determine environmental sustainability objectives

>> Reporting at least annually on the quantified use of proceeds

>> Ensuring funds are ring-fenced for the projects declared

The GBP recognizes ten broad categories, ranging from energy efficiency to renewable energy and sustainable water projects. However, qualifying for green bond status shouldn't be a binary decision; therefore, investment managers are developing rating systems to determine the "greenness" of the bonds under review or the effect of how the proceeds are used. For example:

>> Projects in renewable energy and electric transportation generally receive the highest rating, as they are focused on the long-term objective of a zero-carbon economy.

>> Bonds covering questionable energy efficiency in green building projects would have a lower rating.

>> Improvements to fossil fuel infrastructure, including technologies intended to reduce the environmental impact of coal burning, would be considered ineligible; while such projects could generate environmental benefits, prolonging the useful life of fossil fuel assets isn't consistent with an eligible green project.

>> Nuclear energy projects, despite their zero-carbon benefits, are also excluded due to the prospective environmental impacts of radioactive waste.

The alternative and renewable energy projects tend to dominate the allocation of green proceeds, with green buildings and sustainable transport sectors having a similar share of the market in second and third place, while energy efficiency and sustainable water projects are two other sectors that are worthy of note. With the increasing issuance in this space, it's clear that the material pricing difference between green and non-green bonds has been closing, with no significant differences in bid-offer spreads for government and corporate issuers of U.S. dollar and Euro-denominated green bonds, and the same conditions are true, if not better, for credit risk and liquidity. Furthermore, the performance of green bonds has shown that investment-grade bonds from European issuers have outperformed, but the opposite is currently true for U.S. issuers.

REMEMBER

This confirms that green bonds are no longer a niche strategy for impact investors, and given the current environment with respect to climate agreements, sustainable infrastructure, and water projects, this is set to continue. Another significant milestone was met in September 2020, with the issuance of a 6.5 billion Euro (US$7.7 billion) sovereign bond by the Federal Government of Germany. Moreover, there is also increasing innovation in the market, particularly with respect to transition projects (mentioned in the next section) on pollution prevention and other areas, and bonds linked to explicit targets. In addition, there is a broad array of different debt instruments across a number of different sectors.

Transition bonds

AXA Investment Managers (AXA IM) were the first to advance the idea of "transition bonds," focusing on new instruments for carbon-intensive companies that are actively decarbonizing (for example, fossil fuel companies) but unable to issue green bonds. Such companies lack suitable green assets to issue a green bond; therefore, transition bonds provide an alternative source of funding explicitly aimed at helping them become greener. The idea is that they could depend on the use-of-proceeds approach, which supports green bonds. The funds need to be exclusively used to fully or partly finance or refinance specified projects, and the issuer needs to justify their significance from the standpoint of commercial transformation and climate transition.

However, there are concerns that transition bonds might undermine the credibility of the green bond market where the environmental value of projects being funded is considered questionable, especially where the issuer isn't an entity normally associated with green financing. While the ambition should be that all carbon-intensive sectors will be green industries of the future, it will take time for some companies to convert. However, currently there are no commonly accepted definitions attributed to transition bonds (see www.climatebonds.net/transition-finance/fin-credible-transitions as an example of an initiative to provide a better definition for climate-related bonds). The green bond market has been effectively utilized for transition finance, and some issuers, such as the European Bank for Reconstruction and Development (EBRD), believe the two sectors should be combined. In 2019, the EBRD issued its first "Green transition bond" after creating a portfolio for projects focused on decarbonization and resource efficiency.

Indexes and working groups

The push for greater transparency within the market has promoted the growth of indexes that track the green bond universe. Such indexes provide a way to track market developments, measure performance, and evaluate market risk. Some commonly used benchmarks include the Bloomberg Barclays MSCI Green Bond Index, the S&P Green Bond Select Index, and the Bank of America Merrill Lynch Green Bond Index. In addition, the "climate transition finance" working group is one of the new working groups set up by the executive committee of the GBP, which is supported by the International Capital Market Association (ICMA).

Think big: Social bonds

Social bonds are a separate sector of the sustainable bonds family. They follow a comparable set of values and quality-of-information obligations as green bonds, but the funds are used to support social programs. Some issuance examples include supporting essential services (such as health, education, and financial services), affordable housing, and microfinance.

Increasingly, investors have become more open to investing in social bonds as a means of producing positive impact while making an acceptable return; however, some concerns persist. Until issues surrounding impact reporting standards and liquidity have been settled, issuers and investors may hold back. However, growth in issuance has been strong, with social bonds accounting for approximately 6.5 percent of all issues between 2016 and 2019, during a period when aggregate total social bond issuance has been increasing. The vast majority of instruments issued have been by sovereigns, supranationals, and agencies (SSAs), trailed by financial institution groups and a small percentage by corporates.

The dominance of SSA-led issuance mirrors the early period of green bond issuance (covered earlier in this chapter), with Euro-denominated issuance accounting for roughly two-thirds of the total, contrasted with around one-eighth for U.S. dollar–denominated issuance. Social bond issuance exhibits a similar return and credit risk profile to established fixed income instruments, but the market is still overshadowed by green bonds. The vicious circle of issuance being delayed until an agreed framework for measuring impact is secured, coupled with the lack of supply, and then reducing liquidity, can only be resolved once the industry reaches agreement on impact.

The Social Bond Principles (SBPs) guide, produced by the ICMA, advocates issuers exhibiting impact through qualitative performance indicators, while also advising on the use of quantitative performance measurements in parallel. (Visit www. icmagroup.org/green-social-and-sustainability-bonds/social-bond-principles-sbp/ for details.) Investors need tangible data, but the range of impact metrics and interpretations are still a work in progress. Institutional investors have suggested that they may be willing to agree on "output" type indicators (for example, the number of beneficiaries) as a starting point, stressing the need for "traceability" of project impact. In addition, with more extensive and targeted issuer education, the social bond market should benefit from greater issuance from corporate issuers, in the same way that the green bond market flourished.

Improvements are being seen in calculating the actual "impact" approaches, allowing for more detailed reporting by issuers. The UN SDGs (see Chapter 1) are a valuable source of reference in trying to develop the market beyond green finance. ESG frameworks are also useful, but there appears to be more emphasis on environmental issues than on social or governance issues, with the EU's Action Plan on Sustainable Finance being largely focused on benchmarking environmental actions for corporates rather than their societal impact. The COVID-19 pandemic of 2020 may well act as a catalyst for regulators to increase their focus on societal challenges, particularly as institutional investors are considering allocating more capital to ESG projects, so that social bonds can benefit. Indeed, the EU has recently established the Platform on Sustainable Finance, which has a subgroup considering the possible development of a social taxonomy along similar lines to the environmental taxonomy.

Keep it up: Sustainability and sustainability-linked bonds

Sustainability bonds are a new instrument designed to encourage borrowers to issue bonds linked to broader environmental targets, as opposed to specific projects, following considerable growth in similar deals in the loan market (more than

US$200 billion issued since they were first introduced in 2017). The proceeds from sustainability bonds are wholly applied to finance or refinance a combination of both green and social projects.

TIP

Separately, the ICMA has also published principles for sustainability-linked bonds, which offer guidance to issuers looking to raise environmentally friendly debt with terms linked to specific ESG goals. The guidelines are voluntary, but comparable rules for green and social bonds have been adopted by borrowers and investors. Visit `www.icmagroup.org/green-social-and-sustainability-bonds/sustainability-bond-guidelines-sbg/` for more information.

WARNING

However, a lack of common rules, and the fact that bonds with *step-up coupons* (callable bonds issued with a low coupon rate that gradually increases over the life of the bond) aren't eligible for purchase by the European Central Bank (ECB), have been the main barriers preventing greater issuance of sustainability-linked bonds.

Issuers that could be attracted to sustainability-linked bond structures include companies that produce consumer goods, such as food and beverage firms, as they normally don't have large capital projects that can be paired with green bond issuance. For investors, these new instruments could prove complementary to other sustainable bonds due to the general use-of-proceeds approach. Another new approach, driven by Italian utility Enel SpA, is an ESG-linked bond that increases the coupons payable if the company misses their environmental targets. While the bonds have an environmental theme, they aren't linked to a specific project and the funds are used for general purposes, but Enel pays out a coupon "step-up" of 25 basis points if it doesn't meet the required renewable energy installation and greenhouse gas emission targets (two of the SDGs).

Chapter **10**

Exploring Derivative and Alternative Instruments

R esponsible investment and ESG have traditionally been biased toward liquid assets such as equities (see Chapter 8) and bonds (see Chapter 9). There are several reasons for this, including the weight of assets under management, the availability of information, and the rights and access provided to shareholders. However, more recently, the importance of ensuring that ESG factors are embedded within alternative asset classes has risen in importance. This is primarily due to a reallocation of assets among pension funds toward alternative solutions, and a recognition that more illiquid assets, by definition, have longer-term investment horizons and are thus arguably more exposed to ESG risks. This issue has gained even greater significance with the focus on blended finance (an approach aimed at attracting capital toward projects that benefit society while providing financial returns to investors) as a tool to help deliver the United Nations Sustainable Development Goals (SDGs; see Chapter 1).

In this chapter, I investigate some of the traditional approaches to ESG investing. I then consider the alternative exposures, using listed and over-the-counter (OTC) derivatives to replicate or mitigate risk against underlying assets, and investing in lending or hedge fund strategies, with an ESG twist. After that, I look at investment in real assets from a financial markets perspective, such as real estate, and then at specific sustainable impact investments in the renewable energy space.

Achieving Passive Returns Using ESG Indexes

The combination of increasing demand for index-based investment products (passive investing strategies) and a growing enthusiasm for ESG-based strategies has led to a surge in ESG-focused index products, such as the S&P 500 ESG Index and the STOXX Europe 600 ESG-X index. The number of passive strategies offering a simple and low-cost solution for investors, using ESG measures and exclusions as objective investment criteria, has multiplied in recent years.

WARNING

However, many passive products don't fully disclose how they actually apply ESG strategies, and several of them depend on a single third-party ESG rating contributor (see Chapter 14 for more information) to establish the component stocks in the underlying basket. Therefore, some of these products will exhibit the same restrictions that traditional, passive instruments exhibit, including market capitalization, as well as sector or domicile biases. So, when examining standard indexes or constructing their own index-based ESG strategies, asset managers need to consider the applicable ESG ratings from a handful of data providers to ensure they are comfortable with the resulting components.

Nevertheless, indexes have become essential to investment processes and are entrenched in the investment decisions of institutional and retail investors. Consequently, ESG indexes are now used for similar applications to traditional indexes (such as the S&P 500 and the FTSE 100), including benchmarking for investment policies, asset allocation plans, and performance measurement. Some examples where this has already taken place include when Swiss Re, one of the largest reinsurers in the world, switched its benchmarks to ESG indexes in 2017, and when Japan's Government Pension Investment Fund, with over US$1.5 trillion in assets, changed their Japanese Equity portfolio to an ESG benchmark in the same year.

Historically, sustainable investing has been dominated by active equity managers, given that there was previously a much smaller number of ESG indexes or index funds. More recently, the momentum behind ESG investing, the trend toward passive investment, and investors' uptake of exchange-traded funds (ETFs) have led to a surge in ESG index availability, spreading to other asset classes, such as fixed income. The new ESG-focused indexes have profited from the breadth of data and research in both the established benchmarks and developing efforts to standardize ESG rankings. Investment strategies looking to track indexes' performance provide cost-effective, standardized replacements to reflect higher-cost investments.

Thus, ESG indexes are becoming fundamental building blocks for asset allocation and are used by institutional and retail investors. These indexes help categorize universes that meet explicit ESG criteria for use by asset managers, and offer standards for ESG features to compare with the underlying market. Thousands of different ESG indexes are now offered, but the traditional benchmark contributors are still receiving the lion's share of ESG assets under management as they are connected to their underlying indexes. In turn, this liquidity begets liquidity, as the listed and OTC derivative products tend to employ the most liquid underlying indexes as the foundation for their new products, especially because the major ESG indexes tend to be an ESG variation of the recognized benchmark. While active ESG strategies still correspond to the majority of ESG-related assets under management in total, passive strategies gained the majority of new asset inflows in 2019, principally in the United States.

The following sections outline the alternative products that are linked to ESG indexes, including exchange-traded futures and options, OTC derivatives, and customized, structured products.

The basics of exchange-traded products

The establishment of ESG-focused futures and options contracts on key global, regional, and local indexes from traditional index providers confirms the expansion of a listed derivatives suite to complement the range of other sustainable-themed offerings. Liquid exchange-traded products, such as the Euro STOXX 50 Futures, have long been "the tail that wags the cash market dog," with the benefit of liquidity being funneled into a handful of standardized, benchmark products. Therefore, as the assets under management linked to ESG indexes, or invested in related ETFs, continue to grow, there is an increasing likelihood that volumes in exchange products will grow accordingly. Moreover, with a mounting proportion of investment practitioners regarding ESG as essential to their strategies, these new products provide investors and managers with additional tools to integrate sustainability-driven mandates by replicating or hedging underlying exposures.

Investors are already very familiar with major benchmark indexes, such as the Euro STOXX 50 and S&P 500, in addition to the respective constituent stocks within these indexes. As a result, it's relatively straightforward to switch to an ESG-compliant version, which also helps ensure that new investments aren't divorced from established performance benchmarks that many asset managers use as their yardstick. Exchanges have initially introduced a "screened" family of products, given the current state of ESG awareness and maturity. Negative ESG screening, or exclusions, filter out components from the familiar benchmark, such as controversial weapons companies, tobacco manufacturers, and companies deriving revenues from thermal coal (see Chapter 8 for more information). This offers a transparent and logical approach, with a low tracking error to the respective index. In Europe, this is also in line with the current preference for underlying ESG strategies that focus on negative or positive screening. Some of these futures products, including the S&P 500 ESG futures and the new Euro STOXX 50 ESG futures, also use ESG scores on stocks in the underlying indexes to reweight the constituents by a certain percentage in order to reduce the number of stocks that have the lowest ESG scores within their industry sector.

REMEMBER

An additional benefit is that the exclusion criteria can be standardized for the constituent stocks, irrespective of the rating agency used, which helps eliminate any inconsistencies across index construction methodologies. Furthermore, exclusion-based indexes benefit from the confidence that the UN Global Compact principles (see Chapter 1) have already formed a consensus on which companies should be excluded, so exclusion-based indexes represent a rational entry point to ESG and socially responsible themes. Meanwhile, on the regulatory front, there's increasing activity within the European Union to develop climate benchmarks and a common taxonomy.

These clearer guidelines will help build further momentum in terms of index and product development, while ESG reporting requirements will encourage asset managers to further drive volume in ESG products. In line with this, a broader set of products are likely to appear both in Europe and the United States, ranging from light-screening to best-in-class distinctions, to more focused offerings based on low-carbon and climate impact (including screening for thermal-coal mining and coal-fired power plant stocks).

OTC derivatives

A derivative, simply stated, is a financial instrument whose value is derived from an underlying asset or group of assets. Over-the-counter (OTC) derivatives, as well as exchange-listed products (see the previous section), are widely used to manage or hedge risk in financial markets, but they can also play a very important role in helping firms manage financial risks related to ESG issues. By enabling the exchange of risks, derivatives offer an effective tool to hedge climate risks (either direct physical risks or those related to a required financial transition) by reducing the uncertainty on future prices. In other words, they provide a shield to a portfolio from climate or environmental risk and transform erratic cash flows into predictable sources of return. For instance, ESG derivatives offer a liquid and cost-efficient alternative for managing undesired sustainability risks and integrating ESG into investment decision-making.

Banks can also use derivatives to manage the credit risk of counterparts whose financial results may suffer due to sustainability issues. For example, Credit Default Swaps (CDS) can hedge future potential losses that would be realized following the occurrence of a ruinous event (one that leads to bankruptcies or defaults). In addition, new ESG indexes are being developed to allow market participants to hedge or gain exposure to the most liquid segments of the European CDS market with an ESG focus (for example, ESG-screened corporate or sovereign bond indexes). These indexes also create an effective method to encourage companies to adopt a greener agenda, in line with the European Commission's taxonomy. For example, financial institutions use derivatives to hedge their credit risk exposure to borrowers, and thus potentially increase the supply of credit to firms with sustainable and environmentally friendly investment projects.

REMEMBER

SDG-linked derivatives have been used more recently to support the channeling of capital toward companies focused on ESG issues, thereby enabling risk management. Sustainability-linked derivatives transfer the risk associated with an SDG investment in the form of sustainability-linked bonds (SLBs) and loans (SLLs) to a financial intermediary in exchange for a fixed, recurring payment. These are primarily cross-currency swaps used to hedge against the potential exchange rate volatility and interest rate risk of the investment. In addition, they include a dedicated incentive mechanism that is fully aligned with the sustainable performance indicators outlined in the product's financing solution.

Institutional investors investing directly in taxonomy-compliant companies may use derivatives to hedge their investment against the ESG taxonomy indexes or to reduce transaction costs. To attain such objectives, institutional investors seek to enter into total return swaps (TRSs), which offer to investors the returns corresponding to the agreed-upon ESG underlyings (the underlying of a derivative can be an asset, a basket of assets, or an index). In this regard, synthetic replication through the execution of TRSs by ESG funds, from a passive management perspective, would allow the derivative provider to hedge their position and thus bring more liquidity to the ESG underlyings.

Building blocks: Structured products

Banks see ESG-linked derivatives as one of the highest-potential growth areas in coming years, benefitting from the increasing demand for ESG exposure. As assets under management in sustainable funds have increased, the interest in structured products around those funds has kept pace. For example, one bank sold a new form of structured note to private clients, where they planted a tree for every thousand Euros of their ESG note sold, resulting in more than one million trees being planted! Equity-related products have been the focus for this development, with banks already having notes based on ESG indexes. Meanwhile, more recently, banks have devised similar products to hedge against moves in interest rates and currencies.

REMEMBER

The mainstay investment banking activity of selling structured notes has proven particularly well suited to ESG. These notes are typically sold to retail investors, providing them with an annual payout dependent on the return of a basket of stocks, which is linked to an ESG-friendly index rather than a major benchmark index. Increased interest from the structured products sector is focused on private banks and high-net-worth individuals.

Meanwhile, this theme has been developed further to provide ESG-friendly equity with long-short strategies for institutional clients. The virtuous circle is rounded where, for those banks issuing structured products, having listed derivative instruments that enable them to recycle risk is crucial for maintaining capacity to keep issuing new products. Rather than being stuck with risk and hitting their risk limits, which means they can't issue new products, they can use futures and options to hedge their risk books more accurately, thereby growing their assets in ESG strategies.

Increasing Focus on ESG in Alternative Assets

Alternative asset classes have unique investment considerations and have made significant progress in developing customized ESG strategies, from real estate and infrastructure to structured finance and private corporate debt. The following sections cover alternative lending as well as how hedge funds and private equity are beginning to play a bigger role in the ESG arena.

Sustainable lending

Sustainability Linked Loans (SLLs) represent a structured, practical way for commercial and investment banks to expand their lending portfolios while meeting their sustainability credentials. SLLs (or ESG Linked Loans) are general-purpose loans that are aligned to the Sustainability Linked Loan Principles and incentivize corporate clients to improve their sustainability performance. The use of SLLs grew rapidly in 2019, and they were particular popular in Europe, where around 80 percent of all SLLs were issued. Companies raised US$163 billion of green and sustainability-linked issuance, nearly 2.5 times the levels seen in 2018, with US$137 billion occurring in SLLs.

The advantages of an SLL include the following:

>> Linking the interest rate of the bank loan (cost of capital) to meeting pre-agreed sustainability performance targets

>> Assessing a borrower's sustainability performance against key ESG indicators

>> Offering clients the flexibility to use funds for any aspect of their business

>> Providing a visible indicator of a borrower's sustainability commitment using an ESG rating

TIP

SLLs aren't the same thing as "green loans," which are loans used to finance a specific green purpose (see Chapter 9). SLLs can be applied to any purpose ("green" or not), but a built-in pricing mechanism means that the loan is cheaper if the borrower achieves certain sustainability or ESG-related targets.

REMEMBER

Initially, SLLs were structured simply so that as the ESG targets were met, the pricing decreased; however, there was no penalty if the borrower failed to meet the prescribed targets. This structure has evolved, and more recent deals have used a two-way pricing structure whereby if the targets are met, the pricing decreases, but if the borrower fails to meet their ESG targets, the pricing increases. This two-way structure incentivizes the borrower to meet these targets. However, it has attracted criticism, as ultimately the lender will benefit from the borrower's failure to manage their ESG strategy successfully. One possible solution is that instead of the lender receiving the proceeds of any increased pricing, these funds are transferred to a separate bank account and can only be accessed by the company for expenditure on ESG activities.

In March 2019, the Loan Syndications and Trading Association (LSTA), in conjunction with the Loan Market Association (LMA), published the Sustainability Linked Loan Principles (SLLPs), which set out a list of suggested criteria (see www.lsta.org/content/sustainability-linked-loan-principles-sllp/ for details). The key factor is that the criteria chosen are ambitious and meaningful to the borrower's business. Metrics such as target CO_2 emissions are common, but more specific examples are also prevalent. For example, in real estate finance deals, the sustainability covenants are typically set by reference to outcomes from an environmental report commissioned by the borrower. These often include a minimum capital expenditure per year to reduce the carbon footprint of the building and for all electricity and gas to be obtained from renewable energy sources. The SLLPs state that the need for external review should be negotiated and determined on a case-by-case basis. For public companies, public disclosures may be sufficient to verify performance for the purposes of the loan agreement.

REMEMBER

The potential for lower pricing is a clear incentive to take up SLLs, but the reductions in margin are often fairly modest. Therefore, it's the flexibility of the SLLs that is driving interest, given that a standard corporate revolving credit facility can be linked to sustainability. However, there is no need for the borrower to apply the proceeds toward green activities immediately, which makes SLLs more attractive than more restrictive green loans. A key focus for lenders is developing investment decision-making that incorporates sustainability and ESG factors.

ESG in hedge funds

An ESG hedge fund sounds like a contradiction in terms to some investors, as the goals of absolute returns and the ideals of sustainable investing may at first glance appear to be contradictory. However, a recent study by the Alternative Investment Management Association (AIMA) found that 40 percent of hedge fund managers surveyed were practicing responsible investment, while half reported increased investor interest in ESG. Nonetheless, institutional investors who assess hedge fund managers on their ESG practices believe that responsible investing has two components, which can easily be applied to hedge funds. They should do the following:

>> Incorporate ESG data into their investment process and stock valuation — that is, ESG integration, screening, and thematic investing (see Chapter 8).

>> Engage in active ownership and governance strategies.

Hedge fund managers practice a wide range of strategies covering the full range of asset classes, and managers continue to seek non-directional, absolute returns with an emphasis on alpha (the excess return of an investment relative to the return of a benchmark index) over beta (the volatility of an investment in comparison to the market as a whole). They build concentrated portfolios, use specialist fundamental research to find idiosyncratic exposures, or build sophisticated systematic models to trade markets. These include commodities through equities, credit, currencies, and sovereign debt. They often use derivatives, leverage, and sophisticated instruments to affect their views. They focus on minimizing loss, are performance-driven, and can locate niche, unrecognized opportunities. Importantly, managers prefer to be unconstrained by benchmarks or conventional thinking and base their approach on a longer-term view.

REMEMBER

Therefore, hedge fund managers have the tools to make a telling contribution to ESG investing. Hedge funds can provide an important diversifying complement to institutional portfolios while taking ESG beyond long-only equity management to diversifying strategies and asset classes such as currencies, commodities, global macro investing, long-short credit, relative value, systematic trading, and activist investing. They frequently combine long-term vision with a focus on specifics, are experts at pricing risk and identifying catalysts for change, have experience in actively engaging with companies, and possess the ability and skills to take short positions.

Moreover, hedge funds are at the forefront of developing artificial intelligence as an investment management tool, which could help them overcome some of the data problems in ESG by using techniques such as Natural Language Processing (NLP) to understand a company's current and ongoing sustainability measures. While some hedge fund approaches may be relatively easy to implement in the ESG context, other strategies may be more complex.

REMEMBER

Taking short positions (to profit when a security falls in value by borrowing it and then selling it) is at the heart of the hedge fund ethos. A simple ESG hedge fund strategy could go long on "virtue" and short on "sin." However, some institutional investors may have a policy of prohibiting short as well as long positions in excluded companies (the ethics of shorting the shares of unethical companies is likely to be a topic for debate in the future).

Not owning a stock or sector in an index, the traditional ESG approach, is effectively being short that exposure in the full index composition. Taking a physical short position helps amplify that view while reducing the portfolio's market risk. Investors benefit by taking an active position in line with their long-term ethical view. Hedge fund firms are flexible and sensitive to clients' needs. The use of separate managed accounts can enable the use of custom portfolios. These managers can help define ESG investment practices and develop new strategies using innovative techniques and instruments.

More specifically, some hedge fund strategies are being launched to incorporate exactly this approach, taking long positions in innovative companies that are addressing an assortment of environmental challenges, such as carbon emissions, waste production, and food, water, and energy concerns, and pairing them with short positions on unsustainable firms, or those firms whose business models are vulnerable to transition risk. Hedge funds have a long track record of investing in industries that are subject to disruption and ensuring that capital is allocated to the winners and redirected away from the losers. Stock selection tends to be built around thematic, relative value or catalyst-driven trade ideas, with positions mapped and measured relative to SDGs.

Interestingly, recent studies show that ESG factors now influence the allocation decisions of the majority of hedge fund investors. In addition, governance factors (see Chapter 5) have played an important part in selecting stocks by hedge funds for many years and have contributed to returns in both long and short portfolios. For example, activism and engagement with senior management of companies have been important drivers of returns in event-driven and activist hedge funds as well as many generalist equity long-short funds.

Focusing on Illiquid Assets

In a low-interest-rate environment with high equity valuations, it's increasingly difficult to achieve attractive returns within traditional investments. This, combined with an increasing correlation between the returns of various asset classes, has resulted in investors looking for new investment possibilities with longer-term horizons. This quest for increased returns and better diversification has resulted in institutions allocating substantial portions of their portfolios into alternative asset classes such as property, infrastructure, hedge funds (covered earlier in this chapter), and private equity. Given the parallel focus on responsible investing, institutional investors are increasingly looking at the intersection of these two trends, namely, incorporating ESG into alternative investments.

Around the block: Real estate

The real estate market had already been going through a structural shift before COVID-19 hit in 2020, and the pandemic and its repercussions have just exacerbated some of the trends, such as falling demand for retail property space, and have called into question the future demand for other sectors, such as office space. The property sectors that win will no doubt be those with the resilience to respond to social shocks and stresses, both now and in the future, and investors and managers will be considering how to reposition their property portfolios accordingly. However, this doesn't change the fact that buildings are one of the largest producers of emissions, through waste and electricity, and were due for "a makeover" before the pandemic struck.

Therefore, stakeholders, such as asset owners and investors, were already engaged with ESG as a mainstream issue and were considering how ESG could be integrated into their real estate investment strategies. Given that there are over 60 countries with net-zero carbon neutrality targets, it's likely that more regulations will be enforced that require buildings to be more sustainable, which can help the environment and potentially boost returns from investments.

TECHNICAL STUFF

Buildings account for 36 percent of global energy use through their construction and operation, and they are also responsible for nearly 40 percent of energy-related carbon dioxide emissions. These figures are calculated before you consider how much water and raw materials buildings use. The United Nations estimates that, in order to limit the rise in global temperatures to less than 2 degrees centigrade by 2030, the property industry needs to reduce the average energy intensity of buildings by at least 30 percent.

Research shows that buildings with stronger environmental credentials generate higher rents, lower rates of obsolescence, and improved tenant satisfaction, and they are unoccupied for less time. With the environment becoming a priority for those who construct and manage buildings, the performance gap between green buildings and their less efficient peers should widen further over the coming years. This has important implications for the investors who have poured US$3.4 trillion of capital into real estate in recent years. More than 70 percent of all buildings in the world are 20 or more years old; therefore, progress needs to be made on environmental improvements for existing buildings as well as new ones. As a result, the development of the Internet of Things, facilitated by faster 5G internet connections, will open up even more possibilities to control building environments for optimal efficiency and well-being.

The positive news is that real estate doesn't suffer from the lack of accepted standards for measuring and reporting ESG that other asset classes have. The Building Research Establishment Environmental Assessment Method (BREEAM) certification, created in 1990, is a globally acknowledged way of assessing and certifying the sustainability of the most technically advanced buildings; visit www.breeam.com/ for more information. In addition, the Global Real Estate Sustainability Benchmark (GRESB) is an industry-driven organization that assesses the ESG performance of real assets globally. Find out more at https://gresb.com/.

Laying foundations: Infrastructure

Significant new infrastructure investment is fundamental to the achievement of the United Nations Sustainable Development Goals (SDGs; see Chapter 1), but the sector remains underfunded compared to global sustainable development and economic growth needs. Nonetheless, there has been growing attention on what can be defined as "sustainable infrastructure," where assets and systems may achieve positive real-world outcomes. Many infrastructure investors are already considering the SDGs in their investment approaches, but practices are far from consistent. More standardized approaches are needed to help stakeholders understand how (and which) infrastructure investments shape outcomes in line with the SDGs, and how common interests can be aligned most effectively.

Investors are predominantly taking two approaches to identify SDG outcomes, define targets and policies in relation to the SDGs, and shape SDG outcomes through their investment decisions and asset management. These approaches focus predominantly on existing investments, typically bearing in mind the services provided by different infrastructure assets, or on the way they are managed to achieve certain outcomes, or a combination of the two approaches. Often, these assessments are risk-based, determining the impact of the world on a portfolio or asset. To consider SDG outcomes, the impact of a portfolio or asset on the world must be considered instead. There is no single approach to identifying what type of infrastructure assets are likely to have certain outcomes in line with the SDGs. This is because an asset's context, including its geography, relations with local communities, types of services provided, and wider supply chain, is critical to identifying its different outcomes.

Although infrastructure investors are integrating the SDGs into their investment processes to set targets for elements of asset management or for overall strategy or portfolio construction, significant challenges must be overcome for this integration to become widespread, meaningful, and consistent.

REMEMBER

Some governments are using the SDGs to help shape their infrastructure planning and project design requirements. This should encourage investors to align their own internal processes to position themselves better in government tenders for new infrastructure projects. Also, infrastructure investors are transmitting their work in relation to the SDGs on a more regular basis (see www.unpri.org/sustainable-development-goals/investing-with-sdg-outcomes-a-five-part-framework/5895.article), and service providers are developing metrics and analysis to support these efforts.

However, investors and service providers need to work together to do the following:

>> Create tools and incentives for relevant data gathering.

>> Investigate ways in which reflection on sustainability outcomes can be developed into various stages of the investment process.

>> More closely harmonize asset owners and investment managers to outline SDG outcome objectives.

>> Improve the existing dialogue with governments on infrastructure pipelines and project design to ensure a clearer focus on sustainability factors.

>> Contemplate strategic asset allocation decisions to permit more greenfield investment, where consequences can more often be embedded from the start.

>> Join or continue to support industry initiatives (including those developed by industry associations) to foster greater collaboration between investors.

Hush-hush: Private equity

Private equity has usually stayed "private" and shied away from conveying publicly any non-financial metrics. However, that perspective is changing as over 500 private equity funds have become signatories to the Principles for Responsible

Investment (PRI; www.unpri.org/) to promote responsible investment across several asset classes, including private markets (although the majority of funds haven't signed up). Indeed, there are many similarities between private equity and ESG, given that in many cases, ESG is synonymous with operational best practices, something that private equity funds strive to implement during the period of time they hold a portfolio company. In addition, responsible investment is naturally aligned to private equity through its long-term investment horizon and stewardship-based style.

WARNING

Nonetheless, many have been critical of private equity's lack of engagement with ESG monitoring and reporting, with the task of capturing ESG data from private portfolio companies considered to be too difficult. One of the key challenges for private equity is the inconsistency in how ESG is reflected in investment choices, as well as the absence of an accepted standard on data formats. It's worth noting that the listed space has a multitude of data collection solutions, providers, and indexes, whereas there are few reputable, independent, global ESG providers for the private markets that can offer a service to prescreen and assess current portfolios. Therefore, there are still questions around how to source data in a time-efficient, logical, and accurate manner, and who to measure performance against, such as international standards or sector peers.

Those private equity firms that invest in smaller companies at the earlier stages of their businesses find that they are more ESG conscious of environmental and social factors, so the focus should be on working with the firms to build their governance processes as they grow. The general trend suggests that private equity firms are regarding ESG as increasingly important, with firms based in Europe leading the way while North America continues to lag behind, and with Asia-Pacific seeing an improvement in quality.

Investing in "Traditional" ESG

The renewable energy transition is happening. Wind and solar installations are on the increase due to government programs assisting the industry, and they are now able to produce energy more economically than coal and natural gas. Investment trends in renewables in 2019 varied sharply between sectors and regions, but wind attracted a record US$138.2 billion, helped by a boom in offshore project financing, while solar attracted US$131.1 billion. Overall renewable energy investments, in global aggregate, had their third-highest year on record, with asset financing projects contributing a large majority as in previous years. Moreover, in the ten years after 2010, over US$2.5 trillion was invested in renewable energy projects, with approximately 50 percent of this going into solar projects and 40 percent into wind-related projects.

Even more so than in recent years, it's evident that solar and wind are the real stories from an investment point of view in the sustainable energy space. Hydro-electric energy projects have fallen away from their heights of ten years ago (excluding the amounts invested in a few very large hydroelectric projects), and biomass and waste-to-energy currently occupy a distant third position.

Meanwhile, public support for the environmental movement has continued to soar; for example, in the United States, consumers are now using more renewable energy than coal for the first time. Governmental tax breaks help with the growth of renewable energies; for example, the Investment Tax Credit (ITC) is one of the most important federal policy mechanisms to foster the growth of solar energy in the United States. (The ITC is currently a 26 percent federal tax credit claimed against the tax liability of investors in a solar energy property.) Since 2006, it has helped the U.S. solar industry grow by more than 10,000 percent, with an average annual growth rate of 52 percent over the last decade.

REMEMBER

This type of increased activity has led to an acceleration in the transition to net-zero carbon emissions, which in turn has led to more managers increasing their investment in, and building a diversified portfolio of, renewable energy assets. Managers look to embed ESG considerations into their investment processes, seeking opportunities to implement initiatives that enhance the environment and communities. They then need to measure and track the positive impact their investments have on investors, the environment, and society. Such reports are generally monitored against internal Key Performance Indicators (KPIs), which can be linked to SDGs.

The following sections cover more tangible sustainable assets, such as renewable energy (particularly solar and wind-based assets), rather than the financial instruments and practices more ordinarily associated with alternative assets.

Pull the plug: The basics of renewable energy investment

Investment managers are increasingly offering investors fund opportunities in renewable energy and resource efficiency sectors. The investments made need to have a positive impact on the environment by helping to accelerate the rollout of renewable energy infrastructure and related efficiency technologies. Therefore, rather than investing in exchange-traded funds or similar funds that invest in underlying shares that provide such services, the funds buy green assets, and manage and operate direct assets that generate clean electricity and decarbonize the economy.

Consequently, sustainable practices are built into the investment decision-making process and the ongoing operational processes. A typical approach to this two-step process is summarized here.

Pre-investment involves the following:

>> Pinpointing low-carbon opportunities

>> Screening against investment restrictions

>> Evaluating ESG risks and integrating mitigation plans

>> Requesting investment committee approvals based on a customary process

>> Governing joint venture structures

Ongoing management involves the following:

>> Safeguarding and reporting on health and safety as well as environmental issues

>> Managing impacts and environment enhancements

>> Connecting with and maintaining local community activities

>> Executing due diligence on third parties

>> Determining minimum governance standards

>> Acting in accordance with laws and regulations

>> Safeguarding business integrity

>> Communicating best practices

>> Monitoring and reporting on ESG issues and KPIs in a structured way

Light my fire: Solar power

Solar power is being considered as the energy of the future, given that its cost has dropped in recent years as the technology behind it has developed. This is further driven by the investment in solar energy technologies, which has averaged more than US$140 billion per year for the last ten years. The *levelized cost of energy* (LCOE), the long-term price that a utility needs to charge to cover its costs and satisfy its investors, is commonly viewed as the industry benchmark. Using this measure, the cost of energy from large-scale U.S. solar plants has declined by an average of 13 percent a year for the last five years.

This means that in the United States, solar power is already competitive with other forms of newly built energy generation, and in many states, especially in the southern part of the United States, solar is now the cheapest form of new-build energy production, to the point where solar plants are starting to undercut conventional power plants on price. This cost-competitiveness means that a majority of new solar builds in the United States are now motivated by economics rather than the demands of regulators.

In Britain, solar and onshore wind are also the lowest-cost forms of renewable energy and are very close to grid parity, meaning that plants of the right size in the right location can be profitable in the UK without government subsidies. Solar producers are finding ways to bypass the volatility of electricity prices. One strategy is to agree to a power purchase agreement (PPA) with clients. Under PPA arrangements, companies agree to purchase a certain amount of power generated from a solar plant at a fixed inflation-linked price for between 10 and 15 years. The PPA agreements allow the company receiving the power to either take it directly from the plant or via an electricity company, which in turn buys an equivalent amount of power from the solar plant. This significantly reduces the risk for the producer, and greater certainty lowers overall financing costs.

Some solar income funds have been established, which effectively pay investors for the energy produced by the resulting solar farm panels installed. However, the primary way for investors to benefit from solar energy investments is to invest in stocks that produce solar module products that convert sunlight into electricity or those that build solar power plants. (Some examples can be found here: www. investopedia.com/investing/top-solar-stocks/). In addition, associated mutual funds and ETFs have been developed to benefit from the growth in the number and performance of renewable energy stocks in general (see www.ft. com/content/cad6fcf9-f755-4988-9c75-d41a9b6ff6d8).

There she blows: Wind power

Offshore wind power is due to expand greatly over the next two decades, supporting efforts to decarbonize energy systems and reduce air pollution as it becomes a growing part of the electricity supply. The International Environment Agency (IEA) suggests that global offshore wind capacity may increase 15-fold and attract around US$1 trillion of cumulative investment by 2040. This is driven by falling costs, supportive government policies, and some notable technological progress, such as larger turbines and floating foundations for turbines positioned further offshore.

Moreover, if the European Union reaches its carbon-neutrality goals, offshore wind capacity will jump to around 180 gigawatts by 2040 and become the region's largest single source of electricity. In relation to this, the Sustainable Europe

Investment Plan, the investment pillar of the Green Deal (the European Commission's plan to make the EU's economy sustainable), will aim to mobilize at least one trillion Euros of public and private capital over the next decade.

Offshore wind has also benefitted from a 67 percent reduction in levelized costs achieved since 2012, and from the performance of the latest giant turbines that have been deployed. This background has driven offshore wind financing to US$35 billion in Europe in the first half of 2020, which is up 319 percent year-on-year and a higher total than 2019's record full-year figure of almost US$32 billion (according to research company Bloomberg NEF). Furthermore, onshore wind investment amounted to US$37.5 billion, although this was down by 21 percent.

REMEMBER

These investments are used to fund the construction of new wind farms, refinancing transactions, mergers, and acquisitions at the project and corporate level, carrying out public market transactions, and raising private equity. Given that wind energy projects are currently considered to be attractive investments, there should be plenty of capital available to finance them in the long term.

In addition, there are potential business opportunities for existing oil and gas sector companies to draw on their offshore expertise. An estimated 40 percent of the lifetime costs of an offshore wind project, including construction and maintenance, have significant synergies with the offshore oil and gas sector. That translates into a market opportunity of US$400 billion or more in Europe and China over the next two decades. In particular, China was the largest offshore market again, investing US$41.6 billion in the first six months of 2020, up 42 percent compared with the same period in 2019, due to its offshore wind boom.

Chapter **11**

Highlighting Geographical Differences in ESG Investing

The signing of the Paris Agreement on December 12, 2015, and the adoption of the United Nations (UN) 2030 Agenda for Sustainable Development on September 25, 2015, demonstrated a major shift in the global outlook toward climate change, the environment in general, and social issues. Since then, regulators, central banks, and trade associations have enhanced their efforts to develop the regulatory framework that is required to support a movement toward sustainable investments.

REMEMBER

Today, sustainability strategies and associated ESG policies play a fundamental role in the decision-making processes within companies. The fact that ESG investing is expected to top US$50 trillion in the next 20 years confirms that it has moved from niche to mainstream. As such, these factors are no longer a "nice to have," but are instead an essential part of a company's performance and evaluation. All stakeholders should benefit from the greater transparency and associated disclosure of ESG factors in the investment process; however, disclosure can be required through multiple reporting frameworks. Therefore, there is a strong demand to harmonize reporting standards, which is being supported by efforts from organizations such as the Sustainability Accounting Standards Board (SASB) and the Global Reporting Initiative (GRI; see Chapter 1). Meanwhile, efforts more recently from the World Economic Forum's International Business Council (IBC) are an attempt to produce a baseline set of disclosure metrics, which helps companies report material ESG information (refer to Chapter 15).

The long-term structural trends in favor of ESG investing are expected to continue. Here are some examples:

>> The swing in social and political opinions that has stimulated demand for sustainable investing is accelerating as companies, investors, and public bodies continue to prioritize ESG measures as a key component of their purpose.

>> Companies are under increasing pressure to meet these changing expectations, but the degree can vary depending on the jurisdictions, although reliable ESG data in greater detail and volume is seen as a prerequisite.

>> Growth has been driven by an increasing acceptance that ESG factors should have a material impact on long-term investment returns.

As a result, funds under management with ESG principles continue to attract significant inflows globally as the industry places sustainability at the center of its investment approach and a substantial restructuring of capital is undertaken as awareness increases. This is also true for fixed income, where the variety of bonds related to ESG is growing and green bonds have surpassed US$1 trillion in assets globally.

This chapter highlights the evolution of ESG around the world, including European regulatory developments that continue to keep Europe at the forefront of ESG investment practices; the seesaw commitment of the United States, which is still causing the U.S. to trail behind Europe; and the growing development of ESG investing in emerging markets, particularly in Asia, but from a currently low percentage engagement level.

The Beginning: Europe

In the 1960s, the United States was the center of socially responsible investing (SRI), providing primarily values-based negative and positive screening for investors who wanted to be confident that their funds were sidestepping certain activities or sectors, often linked to issues relating to the Vietnam War. However, the 1992 Earth Summit in Rio de Janeiro and a rising environmental consciousness (triggered by events such as the Chernobyl nuclear power plant accident and the Exxon Valdez oil spill) acted as a catalyst for the emergence of a new breed of European investors. This culminated in the formation of industry organizations such as Eurosif (European Sustainable and Responsible Investment Forum; www.eurosif.org/) in 2002.

Therefore, while the U.S. is the world's largest and deepest market for investors, when it comes to ESG investing, today it lags behind Europe — the subject of this section. The latest data (provided by the Global Sustainable Investment Alliance, or GSIA) confirms that Europe leads the way, with the largest amount of sustainable investing assets (totaling US$14.1 trillion), followed by the U.S. (with US$12 trillion), with sustainable investing making up around 25 percent of total assets under management globally. Investors who focus on Europe, the Middle East, and Africa (EMEA) are seen as integrating governance predominantly in their investment process, with the inclusion of environmental and social factors growing but still being in a relatively early stage. This is also true for corporate bonds and sovereign debt, as well as equity, where governance issues are generally considered before environmental or social factors.

In addition, European funds focused on ESG investing raised a record US$273 billion from clients in 2020, as demand for green and ethical options surged. As such, assets managed by European funds, including ESG, increased by 65 percent to more than US$1.3 trillion, according to the research firm Morningstar. Moreover, an 84 percent quarter-on-quarter surge in the final three months of 2020 was driven primarily by active managers, while the number of sustainable investment funds based in Europe rose to more than 3,000. See Figure 11-1, and check out www.morningstar.com/content/dam/marketing/ shared/pdfs/Research/Global_Sustainable_Fund_Flows_Q4_2020.pdf.

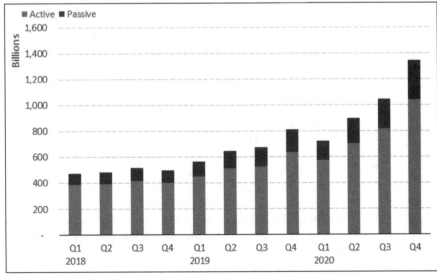

FIGURE 11-1:
European Sustainable Fund Assets (USD billion); data as of December 2020.

Source: Morningstar Research

TIP

For more information on ESG investing trends in Europe, see www.eurosif.org/wp-content/uploads/2018/11/European-SRI-2018-Study.pdf.

Highlighting the regulatory developments

Against this backdrop of leading the way in ESG investing, the European Union (EU) and the European Securities and Markets Authority (ESMA) clarified questions around ESG investments:

» ESMA proposed numerous amendments to current regulations that outlined how financial market participants and advisors must integrate ESG risks and opportunities in their procedures as part of their duty to act in the best interest of their clients. The proposals demand that advisors explain why sustainability factors weren't included in the process. This necessity for ESG integration helps explain why virtually all institutional investors in Europe are engaged or interested in ESG investments.

» EU regulators have taken the lead to introduce a common ESG taxonomy to enable sustainable growth financing and investing. However, in the interim, the fact that stricter standards are being applied also helps explain why the percentage of ESG labeled assets in terms of total assets actually shrank between 2014 and 2018, despite growing interest. This indicates a shift toward providers of investment products being more careful of what they refer to as an ESG product (see Chapter 6 for more information on greenwashing).

The following sections discuss regulatory developments in Europe in more detail.

Regulation on the establishment of a framework to facilitate sustainable investment

A regulation on the establishment of a framework to facilitate sustainable investment was published in the *Official Journal of the European Union* on June 22, 2020, and sets out a pan-European classification system (or "taxonomy") for firms and investors to recognize which economic activities and performance levels are "environmentally sustainable." (You can find a summary of the regulations and links for more information at https://eur-lex.europa.eu/legal-content/EN/TXT/?uri=CELEX%3A52018PC0353.)

To be environmentally sustainable, the activity must make a "substantial contribution" to at least one of the six "environmental objectives." These include the following:

>> **Climate change mitigation:** Does an activity impact greenhouse gas stabilization targets (consistent with the goals of the Paris Agreement), such as through the creation of renewable energy or advancing energy efficiency?

>> **Climate change adaptation:** Does it incorporate solutions that significantly reduce the expected adverse impact on the climate of either a) other people, nature, or assets; or b) the economic activity itself, without escalating the risk of an adverse impact?

>> **Sustainable use and protection of water and marine resources:** Does it significantly contribute to realizing the good status of water bodies or marine resources, or their deterioration, by protecting the environment from adverse wastewater discharges or contaminants?

>> **Transition to a circular economy:** Does it significantly add to waste prevention, reuse, and recycling by, for example, funding the expansion of more efficient recycling centers or products, and preventing the use of waste in landfill sites?

>> **Pollution prevention and control:** Does it significantly add to pollution prevention and control by stopping or cutting pollutant emissions into air, water, or land (other than greenhouse gases)?

>> **Protection and restoration of biodiversity and ecosystems:** Does it significantly contribute to conserving or restoring biodiversity and to realizing the good condition of ecosystems through conservation efforts or the restoration of ecosystems?

This taxonomy works in parallel with the Sustainable Finance Disclosure Regulation (SFDR), published in December 2019, and will be enforced after March 2021; it will only operate once all of the delegated acts and implementing measures have come into effect, with the first two climate-related environmental purposes operating from December 31, 2021, and the four remaining objectives operating from December 31, 2022. (This article provides more information: www.responsible-investor.com/articles/ensuring-the-eu-sustainable-finance-disclosure-regulation-can-deliver-on-its-ambitions.)

The SFDR obliges EU-based asset management firms to disclose the extent of environmental sustainability of funds and pension products that they oversee, or to include disclaimers where they don't, as well as compelling most EU-based firms to give environmental disclosures in their regulatory filings. In all, these regulations allow managers to differentiate themselves from those investing in polluting or unsustainable investments, or not otherwise meeting fundamental environmental standards. This should reduce greenwashing where firms offer ESG products whose ESG credentials are overstated. (Flip to Chapter 6 for more information on greenwashing.)

Other regulations and amendments

The European Commission has also proposed a number of amendments to the EU's existing Benchmark Regulation: the Insurance Distribution Directive, the Markets in Financial Instruments Directive (MiFID) II, the Investment in Transferable Securities (UCITS) Directive, the Alternative Investment Fund Managers Directive (AIFMD), and the Non-Financial Reporting Directive (NFRD). Despite the UK's withdrawal from the EU, both the SFDR and the Taxonomy Regulation, covered in the preceding section, will be executed into UK law, requiring UK-based alternative investment fund managers, UCITS management companies, and MiFID investment firms to also comply. While these legislative changes won't have a direct effect on U.S. firms, they will likely have an indirect effect on U.S. managers where their activities are conducted in Europe (for example, European marketing).

REMEMBER

I just threw a whole bunch of letters at you, and you're probably wondering: What do they all mean? In simpler terms, they mean that the range of these new regulations may force asset managers and investment firms operating in Europe to assess and revise many of their disclosures (to both their regulators and their investors), as well as their policies and procedures. They will have to update their regulatory submissions, annual reports, and other disclosures to confirm that they fulfil the new regulations.

Meanwhile, the UK's Financial Conduct Authority (FCA) published a Policy Statement in December 2020, outlining new climate-related disclosures required in the annual financial reports of companies that are "premium listed" on the London Stock Exchange to apply to accounting periods beginning on or after January 1, 2021. The FCA proposal is to require Task Force on Climate-related Financial Disclosures (TCFD)–aligned reporting by those premium-listed companies. The TCFD is a reporting framework focused on the disclosure of climate-related risks and opportunities that was established by the Financial Stability Board in 2015.

Within the FCA Policy Statement, the TCFD advocates four "overarching recommendations" relating to governance, strategy, risk management, and metrics and targets, which are accompanied by 11 "recommended disclosures." The FCA proposes a "comply or explain" regime where premium-listed companies need to disclose, for example, the board's oversight of climate-related risks and opportunities or explain why they haven't included such a disclosure. The proposal doesn't directly affect asset managers operating in Continental Europe and the UK, but this could have an indirect impact on portfolio composition and risk weightings, and indicates a more rigorous regime for climate-related disclosures.

Enjoying a first mover advantage on ESG investment

The US$14.1 trillion ESG investments in Europe represent close to half of the estimated US$30 trillion in total assets under management in the ESG space, and also close to half of total assets managed in Europe. According to a forecast published by Deutsche Bank in September 2019, ESG investments are expected to grow globally to the point of passing the US$100 trillion mark by 2030. While the forecast may have some constraints, due to different understandings of ESG criteria, if ESG investments in Europe follow that trend, there is still plenty of room for upside!

While passive investment strategies — due to their easier and more instant application — were the first to quickly gain volume, multiple ESG-related investment approaches are now available for selection by asset managers.

There was an initial shift to more intermediate and sophisticated solutions that evaluate how investments promote activities that are globally sustainable (in terms of climate change or water security) or "best-in-class" (companies with the highest ESG scores and performance). These approaches were further included within broader ESG factor integration mandates (an agreement with an investment manager that sets out how funds are to be invested). As ESG sentiment has increased, particularly since 2015 (for example, after the Paris Agreement and UN SDGs were established; see Chapter 1), investors' preferences have started to shift to even more active ESG approaches, such as impact investing or active investing with greater engagement with individual companies, where investments have a direct impact on ESG goals.

However, while investments in pure exclusion and negative screening approaches have declined, they still remain the most common form of ESG strategies and the ones with the largest assets under management. Concerns around fossil fuels and the potential for the value of such assets to become financially "stranded" have contributed to this asset pool.

WARNING

The regulatory developments described earlier in this chapter are also becoming a key factor driving the uptake of ESG strategies, with many investors looking to get ahead of regulation. Mitigating ESG risks, meeting their fiduciary responsibilities, and avoiding reputational risk are also major factors that have been considered. Meanwhile, the lack of reliable data is still a key obstacle to deeper ESG integration, which with the regulatory changes creates a degree of uncertainty and potential barriers to entry. If the common taxonomy is adopted to define minimum requirements for sustainable activities, and the SFDR clarifies the standards for ESG disclosures, then many of the impediments to ESG investing should be removed. Moreover, the NFDR will entail specific disclosure requirements for EU companies. This should go a long way toward addressing the quality and comparability of available ESG data and ratings in Europe but may still leave room for improvement in other jurisdictions and across certain asset classes.

Given that all financial institutions will need to comply with new regulatory requirements, certain participants may choose to modify their business operations more aggressively in order to position themselves as ESG innovators and attract new clients or investors.

Continuing inflows for ESG funds

2020 was a key year for ESG investing strategies and funds targeting retail investors. The sustainable funds universe saw a continuing demand at the outset of the pandemic, recording 30 billion Euros of inflows during the first quarter of 2020, while the broader European funds universe dropped by 148 billion Euros. Furthermore, total assets in sustainable funds fell from the record levels recorded at the end of 2019 to 621 billion Euros; however, this was below the level of the broader market, which declined 16.2 percent (per Morningstar), while ESG-focused versions of funds outperformed their non-ESG equivalents during the market downturn.

The sub-sector funds that saw the most interest were environmental and climate-aware funds, which controlled the "best-seller list." It is felt that such funds will continue to see investor support due to regulatory developments, including the EU Action Plan on Sustainable Finance (for more information on the smorgasbord of activities, visit https://ec.europa.eu/info/business-economy-euro/banking-and-finance/sustainable-finance_en). Data shows that there are over 2,500 open-end funds and exchange-traded funds (ETFs) domiciled in Europe that use ESG criteria (notwithstanding greenwashing!), of which there were 72 new sustainable funds, and a further 24 conventional funds that were repurposed to fit ESG criteria. The strategies offered a range, from broad ESG funds with exclusion policies to thematic funds, impact investing products, and strategies targeting the UN's SDGs. Interestingly, in the first quarter of 2020, active sustainable funds recorded a smaller drop in inflows than passive sustainable funds. Meanwhile, in the fixed income space, there has been growing interest in green bonds, including within sustainable versions of multi-asset funds for retail investors.

REMEMBER

While these are all positive developments, investors need to determine whether these products will meet their sustainability expectations. The vast majority of ESG ETFs can be classified as "ESG focused," where they use ESG analysis as a core feature of security selection and track an index that is weighted based on companies' ESG scores. The index contains more shares of companies that have convincing ESG credentials. In Europe, ETF investors are generally large, knowledgeable institutional investors rather than retail investors. Impact funds attempt to achieve specific environmental or social goals while producing investment returns, and sustainable sector funds focus on industries such as renewable energy and energy efficiency.

In addition, some European providers are trying to apply the new EU Taxonomy Regulation to their portfolios, promoting an early understanding of the changes required for their operations and helping to position themselves as trusted partners with regulators, in order to help influence any future rule changes.

The Middle: North America

While European investors hold the largest amount of ESG-associated assets (as described earlier in this chapter), more of the world's recent growth can be credited to increased demand in the United States. Between 2014 and 2018, assets under management with an ESG mandate, held by retail and institutional investors, grew at a four-year compound annual growth rate (CAGR) of 16 percent in the U.S., compared with 6 percent in Europe. Moreover, flows into ESG funds in the U.S. continued growing in 2020, with equity and bond ESG mutual funds and ETFs achieving record inflows for the fourth straight year.

Morningstar's 2020 Global Sustainable Fund Flows report found that assets in sustainable funds hit a record high of US$1.7 trillion, up 28 percent from the third quarter. While Europe continued well above the US$1 trillion mark, global sustainable fund inflows were up 26 percent in the fourth quarter of 2020 to nearly US$368 billion. The U.S. accounted for 14 percent of the global inflows, or approximately US$53 billion, which was in line with similar inflows for the whole of 2020. Surveys also suggest that more than 60 percent of Americans feel that investment funds should consider ESG factors, but only 15 percent actually invest in sustainably themed investments, so there is plenty of room for upside. See Figure 11-2, and check out www.morningstar.com/content/dam/marketing/shared/pdfs/Research/Global_Sustainable_Fund_Flows_Q4_2020.pdf.

Regardless of greater interest, the different approaches to ESG incorporation by asset management firms, regulators, and investors suggest that full ESG potential has yet to be realized. Consider the following:

>> Asset managers need to consistently reflect ESG metrics in their investment decisions to meet expectations that client demand will drive ESG-mandated assets to consist of half of all managed investments in the U.S. by 2025.

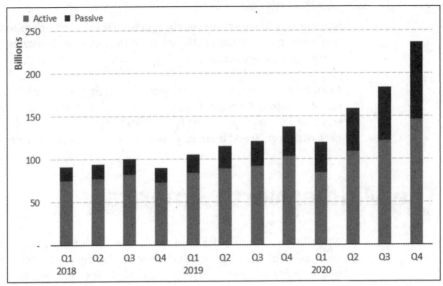

■ Active ■ Passive

FIGURE 11-2:
U.S. Sustainable
Fund Assets (USD
billion); data as of
December 2020.

Source: Morningstar Research

>> Some of the concerns around ESG investing are linked to historical perceptions that accepting ESG comes at a cost to returns and therefore underperformance. Many Americans still believe it primarily covers divestment or screening out of given industries, such as tobacco, alcohol, and firearms.

>> Of the US$16.6 trillion in U.S.-domiciled assets using sustainable strategies at the beginning of 2020, ESG integration is applied to approximately 75 percent of assets. This compares with Europe, where screening is by far the dominant approach, and ESG integration is only the third most common strategy, accounting for around one-third of assets. This new U.S. data is taken from the U.S. SIF Foundation's 2020 *Report on US Sustainable and Impact Investing Trends,* published in November 2020. Visit www.ussif.org/files/US%20SIF% 20Trends%20Report%202020%20Executive%20Summary.pdf for details.

The following sections discuss ESG investing in both the United States and Canada.

Highlighting political and regulatory roadblocks in the United States

In the United States, regulation pertaining to ESG has fluctuated between neutrality and active discouragement over the last few decades. The U.S. Department of Labor (DOL) supported sustainable investing back in 1994, but new guidance in 2008 made some fiduciaries question pursuing ESG investing. A more positive outlook was taken in 2015, when guidance was updated to acknowledge ESG as an important material factor, which promoted ESG investing again. However, the pendulum has swung back to negative, because under the Trump administration, the federal government discouraged sustainable investing and environmental protections, resulting in political and regulatory hurdles. The administration pulled out of the Paris Agreement while pushing back environmental regulations.

Moreover, the DOL in 2020 presented some proposals that will discourage investment managers from considering ESG issues:

>> The proposed rule for private pension plans governed by the Employee Retirement Income Security Act (ERISA) states that private employer-sponsored retirement plans aren't required to promote social goals or policy objectives but should provide retirement security for workers. Approximately US$29 trillion in assets were managed under ERISA rules in the first quarter of 2020.

>> The DOL proposed a further rule that requires plans to only cast shareholder votes for issues that have an economic effect on a retirement plan, inferring that they shouldn't vote on ESG-related issues unless they have a measurable financial impact. Ordinarily, U.S. disclosure requirements on shareholder votes have allowed investors to review information relating to a company's ESG practices, and managers have applied these rules to influence a company's implementation of ESG principles.

>> Investment professionals can follow ESG strategies but need to prove that they produce benefits in line with traditional investments. Public feedback against the proposals highlight that excluding ESG funds from acting as a default investment option in pensions would reduce inflows and limit the growth potential for ESG investing, and so managers wouldn't fully reflect on ESG risks.

In contrast to the DOL's approach, regulation in the EU and UK endorses the integration of sustainability and ESG concepts into financial decision-making, supporting a more formalized consideration for pension fund managers. The European Commission's proposed amendment to Markets in Financial Instruments Directive (MiFID) II rules will also mandate that investment firms should consider the ESG preferences of their retail clients when providing investment advice.

WARNING

Clearly the difference between U.S. and EU/UK regulations concerning sustainable investing is growing. The diverging regulatory paths are unlikely to converge in the near future, given the DOL's historically conservative position during the evolution of ESG investing in the EU/UK. These contradictory attitudes won't immediately affect credit ratings assigned to investment managers, pension funds, or the institutions sponsoring such plans; however, they are likely to translate into opposing investment considerations, risks, and potential returns over the longer term.

Furthermore, the U.S. Securities and Exchange Commission's (SEC) Office of Compliance Inspections and Examinations (OCIE) declared its examination priorities for SEC-registered investment advisers during 2020, with a number of advisers receiving significant document requests concerning their firms' ESG investment activities, including their disclosures, marketing, use of metrics, internal controls, and other policies. While the OCIE's focus is on ensuring that SEC-registered firms aren't greenwashing (covered in Chapter 6), these actions show that ESG is an area of considerable and increasing focus in the United States.

During the first decade of the new millennium, although the rest of the world became more engaged with ESG integration, the U.S. was slower to make the change. The conviction that an SRI form of investing was too negative (because of the use of negative screening) and the belief that it came with reduced returns had prevented U.S. investors from engaging too heavily in ESG investing. That said, the Sustainable Accounting Standards Board (SASB; see Chapter 1) has worked since 2011 to produce common standards for company filings to the SEC to identify key, sector-specific ESG metrics that are likely to be financially material. However, despite pressure from investors seeking information that allows for peer comparisons between companies in the same sector, the SEC hasn't required companies to include specific ESG-relevant data in their reporting requirements.

Investigating Canada's approach

Canada has followed a similar route to that taken by the UK regulators (described earlier in this chapter). Asset managers, owners, and trustees are compelled by regulations to reflect on key risks and opportunities when making investment decisions and hiring managers. For example, the province of Ontario compels pension funds to reveal whether ESG-related factors are part of investment policy statements. Under law, scheme trustees must evaluate how ESG integration will influence their funds' investment returns, if at all, and confirm that statements of investment policies and processes contain ESG-related information.

Importantly, the law doesn't compel funds to make ESG-friendly investments; instead, it encourages the awareness of likely, material ESG-related issues, rather than regulating how to invest. Ontario remains the only province in Canada with this legislation; however, interest from Canadian investors in governance, diversity, and climate change has grown considerably, and most institutional investors consider ESG aspects when voting their proxies. Moreover, asset managers are expected to report regularly to asset owners on ESG matters. This may be in the form of ESG-related engagements with companies and based on positive conclusions from such interactions.

Driving up demand

Research shows that more than half of asset managers in the U.S. are considering the creation of ESG investment solutions, with many active managers looking to gain an advantage over passive products, amidst an increasing focus on wealth transfer between generations, with younger investors believed to consider ESG more favorably. More explicit demand from clients is likely to be the vital driver of more implementation of ESG in this space, suggesting that apart from performance identified through quantitative screening, sponsors are eyeing other value-added services. Flows into ETFs have nearly reached parity with flows into open-end funds, with originally sustainable ETFs focusing on sector funds related to renewable energy, environmental services, and clean technology, and with only two diversified ESG-focused ETFs existing.

Following the trend toward passively managed funds in the industry overall, flows into passive sustainable funds have outstripped flows into actively managed funds for the past three years, with reports suggesting that more than 70 percent of flows went into passive funds. This has highlighted some key messages for the industry to consider:

>> ESG-mandated assets in the U.S. could grow much faster than non-ESG-mandated assets, at a 16 percent compound annual growth rate (CAGR), to cover half of all professionally managed investments by 2025, totaling almost US$35 trillion.

>> Over 200 new funds with an ESG investment mandate are anticipated to launch in the next three years, more than doubling the offerings from the previous three years.

>> The use of artificial intelligence (AI) and alternative data is giving managers greater scope to unearth material ESG data and potentially achieve alpha.

>> Firms that proactively convert from customized ESG product offerings toward more encompassing operations are likely to gain a greater percentage of future ESG asset flows.

WARNING

On a more negative front, in addition to the somewhat unsupportive regulatory environment in the United States, there's a risk of litigation from shareholders given that regulations put the responsibility on trustees to demonstrate that ESG investing generates improved performance. Moreover, there are also problems with ESG terminology, with some investors using the phrase "impact" to represent everything from ESG integration to screening. Unfortunately, this "muddies the water" when investors are trying to find out what a fund delivers.

However, in some cases it may help to increase understanding of the differences between SRI and ESG integration, as investors will already be familiar with associated concepts. In addition, more managers are seeing ESG as a strategic business imperative and believe it's viable to maximize returns while investing sustainably. Moreover, as emerging technologies such as AI facilitate enhanced-quality ESG data, and the regulatory environment becomes clearer, investors are likely to further demand that ESG factors be employed in a larger percentage of their portfolios.

The End: Developed versus Emerging Markets

Nearly 90 percent of global assets under management are held across three regions: North America, Europe, and Asia (excluding Japan and Australia). There-fore, this section's focus on emerging markets has concentrated on Asia, although the general discussion is relevant to all emerging markets. For example, investors tackling emerging markets face distinctions in culture, regulatory environments, and technology, so why add another layer of complication by including ESG? Clearly the pace of economic growth in emerging markets is greater than in more developed markets, and pockets of opportunity can be found, but they can be opaque and challenging to navigate.

WARNING

Investors looking to understand the environmental and social performance of Asian companies have struggled with the lack of robust and appropriate data to enable investors to better appreciate a company's ability to recognize and mitigate ESG risks. As with companies in any region, a cursory adherence to ESG values through some form of "check box" exercise isn't sufficient. Therefore, the value of ESG data can differ, and there is a lack of standardized reporting. Moreover, many companies don't consistently deliver information in English, and there may be issues with common ESG terminology. Add to that the traditional governance issues and lighter regulation, and it's easy to see why emerging markets present additional challenges for ESG investors.

Traditionally, an active approach to investment in emerging markets has paid dividends, as tracking benchmarks is limited by the lack of homogeneity. Asia, in particular, consists of a large group of diverse countries, cultures, economies, and political systems. Benchmark tracking doesn't provide the necessary diversifica-tion, as indexes are largely concentrated on a country level and fast becoming "China-plus" on a regional allocation (which is around 46 percent compared to the previous 30 to 35 percent).

Meanwhile, approximately 26 percent is allocated to the more developed markets of Taiwan and South Korea. This is also true at a stock level, with the top five stocks in a regular emerging market benchmark representing about 20 percent of the entire index. This leaves little space for other, less-known opportunities; therefore, overlaying ESG factors on some of the small to mid-cap stocks should help unearth some gems. This is also true when incorporating greater exposure to countries such as India and Vietnam.

Certainly, the performance of investing in emerging markets through ESG factors has been proven, given that in the last decade, the MSCI Emerging Markets ESG Leaders Index, which tracks companies with high performance in ESG metrics relative to their peers, outshone the broader MSCI Emerging Markets Index, with a 14.5 percent annualized return versus 10.7 percent, respectively. See Figure 11-3, and check out www.morningstar.com/content/dam/marketing/shared/pdfs/Research/Global_Sustainable_Fund_Flows_Q4_2020.pdf.

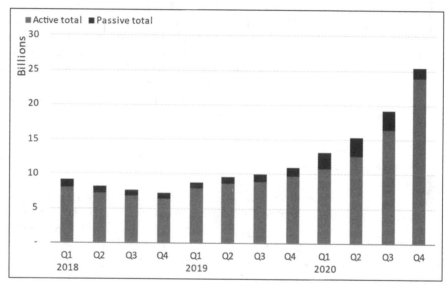

FIGURE 11-3: Asia ex-Japan Sustainable Fund Assets (USD billion); data as of December 2020.

Source: Morningstar Research

Seeing that emerging markets are lagging but disclosure is increasing

Asian companies have been slower than their counterparts in the rest of the world to integrate ESG concepts into their business strategy, to realize the effect on their costs, or to recognize the chance to benefit from broader ESG trends and integration. However, ESG awareness is now building momentum among asset owners and managers, and companies recognize that investors are interested in receiving more non-financial information on their businesses, while corporate social responsibility reports are now more frequently published in English! However, given that companies in many emerging markets aren't legally compelled to disclose so much ESG information, there are still concerns that lower standards and greenwashing (see Chapter 6) are likely if there are no standardized, measurable rules in place.

The alternative view from some managers is that the inconsistency in ESG disclosure and standards of practice across emerging markets present more opportunities to use ESG to differentiate between companies and select potential winners. Meanwhile, governance remains the most followed of the three ESG mainstays in emerging markets, with companies showing effective stewardship and governance being the most likely to outperform and create alpha. (Chapter 5 has more on the governance aspect of ESG.)

Moreover, fund managers are signing up to the United Nations–supported Principles for Responsible Investment (PRI), demonstrating their commitment to ESG principles. In Asia, in 2019, the signatories grew by about 20 percent, to 339, from a year earlier. But there is a requirement for education, followed by company steps to produce better data, with banks also using ESG-related factors to determine whether to lend and how to price loans. In addition, alternative data, particularly in China, consisting of search engine data, job postings, and satellite snapshots, is providing new insights.

Furthermore, carbon footprints, diversity, and human rights are developing as major themes to encourage meeting minimum standards. This should evolve into more detailed analysis as conversations between companies and investors develop, with more engagement persuading companies to supply better transparency. In particular, there are calls for greater transparency around materiality assessment (recognizing financial consequences), which should be tailored given that each company owns its own distinctive set of material risks and opportunities. The better firms recognize, prioritize, and mitigate those risks while capturing opportunities.

Other important sources of information in emerging markets are the local stock exchanges, which have been leaders within the international Sustainable Stock Exchanges Initiative. Emerging market exchanges are quick to recognize better ESG practices and disclosure as a way to develop local and international investor trust in their markets. Allied to this, smaller domestic companies are willing to listen and change their corporate behavior if it means attracting active managers. Investors can also align with their SDG targets, and create greater impact investing, by using investor engagement to improve ESG and sustainability performance. On the other hand, stronger corporate engagement represents a productive strategy as shareholders can share with companies their peer competitor comparisons in terms of performance.

REMEMBER

The COVID-19 pandemic has generated a greater focus on the vital need to develop resilience in healthcare, food, and water security, as well as across supply chains. It's likely that more emerging market governments will transfer funds to the private sector to tackle these urgent needs. On the other hand, more regular opportunities may remain in stocks and debt of technology assets that are linked to ESG. Given that more than one billion people in emerging markets are using mobile technology for healthcare services, by 2025, a large percentage of those people may have access to smartphones, which can drive demand in industries from education to logistics, as well as ESG. Moreover, technology stocks generally make up the biggest weightings in benchmark indexes, such as the MSCI ACWI ESG Leaders Index.

Highlighting political and regulatory developments

In Asia, regulators have accepted that requiring further disclosure obligations around sustainability practices can promote foreign investment. For example, Singapore was an early adopter of ESG-related standards, which had an encouraging effect on the growth of its capital markets. Investor certainty in the value of ESG data was created in Singapore after sustainability reporting was mandated in 2016. In addition, in 2018, the Chinese government, in order to support transparency and investment, announced that listed companies and bond issuers would be compelled to disclose ESG-related risks. Frameworks such as those established by the Global Reporting Initiative (GRI) and the Sustainability Accounting Standards Board (SASB; see Chapter 1) can be used as a "blueprint" by emerging market countries to help companies report material information associated with ESG in a consistent manner.

Therefore, companies have accepted that the enhanced value placed on transparency by investors can benefit them, and they have begun reporting performance on relevant ESG factors in greater detail than is otherwise required by regulators. Another blueprint from that region comes from Australia, which is one of the pioneers of ESG integration. The adoption of ESG analysis was driven over the past decade by the country's superannuation pension funds, known as "super funds." The super funds are now very large and use high-level investment strategies that incorporate advanced levels of ESG integration and active ownership.

REMEMBER

Exchanges should also ensure that listed companies enhance the quality of reporting on ESG-specific issues. The Singapore Exchange (SGX) introduced sustainability reporting for listed companies on a "comply or explain" basis in 2016. In addition, Hong Kong Exchanges and Clearing Ltd. (HKEX) has sought views to strengthen ESG rules through consultation with members. Meanwhile, industry groups, such as the Asian Corporate Governance Association (ACGA), support programs for ESG discussions between stakeholders through regular conferences and events.

Determining whether an ESG approach is better suited to developed economies

Some market participants have suggested that an ESG approach to investing is better suited to developed economies, given that they have gained from the general trend of governance, oversight, and regulation to date. The majority of emerging market economies, including Brazil, Russia, India, and China (BRIC), have copied developed markets by driving their economic growth with carbon-based energies, such as oil and coal. The issue is that this approach is no longer felt to be sustainable because of the damaging effect of fossil fuels on the environment.

Some governments are tackling the problem proactively, including the leaders of the second-largest economy in the world, China:

>> In 2007, they announced a model of "ecological civilization," whereby leaders highlighted public transport and green buildings as a way to cut pollution, and China has become the largest market for electric vehicles.

>> More significantly, China has now committed to aim to reach peak emissions before 2030, which will be followed by a long-term target to become carbon neutral by 2060 (China is responsible for around 28 percent of global emissions), the first time they have committed to a long-term emissions goal.

Not all developing nations can be as progressive as China in setting sustainable policies. Nonetheless, they are responsible for feeding millions of people, delivering energy, and maintaining access to clean water and medical supplies.

India, which is also home to more than one billion people, is a country facing the contradiction that large parts of its population don't have access to power, sanitation, or clean water, so they will use coal to generate power rather than not provide power at all.

Emerging markets are known for having many more state-owned enterprises and numerous family-owned or controlled companies, which some argue has exacerbated the governance issues. Nevertheless, a possible advantage of family-controlled businesses is that managers and leaders tend to stay employed for prolonged periods of time. As such, they take a long-term view of running the company, which can result in more stable or sustainable profits, which investors appreciate. State participation in a company can also be useful to ensure that any red tape can quickly be disregarded or streamlined when a government has ownership of a stake in the company. This helps reduce costs and thus boost profits for companies benefiting from partial government ownership.

However, the general assumption is that corporate governance risk is higher in the developing world, due to an apparent lack of maturity. They have not yet evolved from family ownership to a public company with a broadly distributed share register. Despite this, regulation has been criticized for not being strict enough, and that corporate disclosure standards need to be enhanced. However, the counterargument is that this makes ESG more suited to emerging markets as the inadequate environment generates more opportunities for ESG to guide the insight into company selection. While this sounds reasonable, it relies on the view that emerging market governments and regulators are ensuring that ESG risks are being well managed. After all, Asia has accounted for less than 2 percent of all sustainable investments across the world, with the exception being Japan, where sustainable investing has been growing steadily.

So, how can Asia's economic landscape be more promising for sustainable investments, given that a number of private market participants are keen to be engaged? Many companies have realized that sustainability is the most feasible approach for their business, particularly as current levels of environmental degradation have reached a crisis point. Against this backdrop, businesses have supported initiatives such as the Task Force on Climate-related Financial Disclosures (TCFD), created by the Financial Stability Board in 2015. The TCFD (www.fsb-tcfd.org/) is authorized to create a framework that financial institutions and companies can use to provide information about the financial impact of climate-related risks and opportunities, and is well supported in Asia.

REMEMBER

So, there is an urgent need for governments in Asia to take leadership in the drive for sustainability, which should start with their own government-backed sovereign wealth and pension funds. They should collectively enforce compulsory ESG metrics on investments made by publicly funded investment bodies. By doing so, and directing funds into companies that meet these criteria, sovereign wealth funds and pension funds can establish the framework for private investment markets to follow.

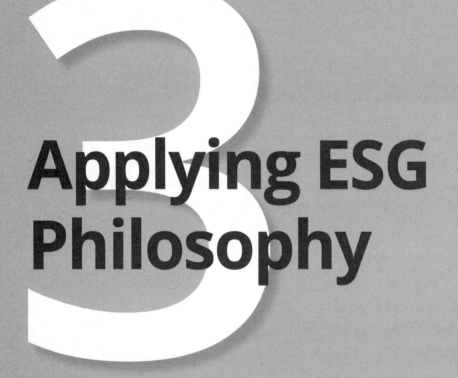

3
Applying ESG Philosophy

IN THIS CHAPTER

» **Looking at corporate disclosure and transparency**

» **Generating greater returns**

» **Getting more customers**

» **Decreasing costs**

» **Boosting productivity and attracting talent**

Chapter **12**

Creating Value through ESG for Corporations

ompanies don't operate in a vacuum. In a global economy that relies on cross-border trade, multifaceted supply chains, and diverse workforces crossing the globe, companies are increasingly challenged by environmental issues, such as climate change, pollution, and water scarcity, as well as social factors including product safety and interactions with regulators and the societies in which they work. In this environment, ESG can directly impact a company's competitive positioning. Therefore, integrating ESG factors is part of maintaining a competitive advantage in today's economy and vital to long-term competitive success.

The benefits of proactively tackling ESG issues go beyond satisfying institutional shareholders and generating a good public relations story. A strong ESG program can help create access to large pools of capital, develop a clearer corporate brand, and endorse sustainable long-term growth that profits companies and investors alike. Major institutional investors realize this and are clearly stating that they require companies to take a preemptive approach to ESG policies and messaging. Therefore, ESG aspects will be a component of investment decisions, and will be factored into the sustainability, valuation, and primary risks that are fundamental to every portfolio position.

Many investors have reduced their focus on fundamental company analysis in favor of passive investing, with less primary research, broad diversification, a liquidity focus, and reacting to short-term catalysts; therefore, many companies may feel that investors are dissuading them from practicing shared value through ESG programs. In this situation, the economic benefit of shared-value approaches is exhibited only in share prices after a long delay; therefore, some companies argue that there is no short-term reward for pursuing improvements in ESG factors.

However, while corporate leaders agree that ESG programs won't inevitably increase shareholder value right away, they suggest that they are willing to pay a premium to buy a company with a positive record on ESG matters rather than one with a negative record. Moreover, increasing amounts of research show that companies focused on material ESG issues outperform their counterparts and are more resilient and less volatile than other companies during times of crisis (such as the COVID-19 pandemic and the 2008 economic crisis).

This chapter focuses on the ESG journey from a company's perspective and on the benefits that a company can achieve in embracing a more holistic approach to ESG factors. You discover how corporations approach the challenges of meeting corporate disclosure and transparency requirements, as well as the benefits of enhanced returns that can be achieved, from generating more business to increased productivity and reduced costs.

Crystal Clear: Corporate Disclosure and Transparency

In reaction to increasing inquiries concerning how sustainability impacts their business, numerous companies have integrated corporate social responsibility and sustainability programs, and they report on ESG specifications. For example, in 2000, the United Nations (UN) launched the Global Compact (see Chapter 1) to address principles of anti-corruption, human rights, labor, and the environment. Now, thousands of companies share their improvements each year, using voluntary reporting frameworks, to deal with the lack of standards in corporate sustainability reporting. In addition, considerable progress has been made to improve the accessibility and quality of intelligence through market forces. These also include the efforts of non-governmental organizations (NGOs) and, in some jurisdictions, regulation — for example, the Non-Financial Reporting Directive (NFRD) in the European Union that requires all companies of a certain size to report non-financial information once a year.

Companies need to realize that investors will focus on their willingness and ability to maintain a competitive advantage over the long term, and analyze the companies' ESG-oriented strengths and weaknesses across many aspects, including the following:

>> **Environment:** Environmental supervision to reduce externalities is vital to efficient operations. Minimizing consumption of energy, water, and resources while reducing emissions, pollution, and waste may alleviate costs and increase profitability. (See Chapter 3 for more information about the environmental sector of ESG.)

>> **Customers:** Companies can protect their reputation by certifying product safety, reacting to customer preferences, and contributing to local communities through charitable efforts.

>> **Employees:** Attracting and retaining talent is crucial, given the shortage of skilled human capital. Appreciating workplace policies with regard to salaries, development, health, and safety of employees is imperative to safeguard good relationships between management and their workforce. (See Chapter 4 for more about social factors — the 'S' in ESG.)

>> **Suppliers:** Continuity of supply chains through efficient management of operations and supplier audits is increasingly important in an interrelated world.

>> **Regulators:** The potential impact of any legislative and regulatory changes that might modify an investment approach merits assessment.

>> **Governance:** Analysis can focus on capital allocation, independent and engaged boards, management incentives, and transparency of accounting. (See Chapter 5 for more about governance.)

Within emerging markets, where the rule of law and corporate governance standards are frequently lower than in developed markets, companies must recognize that additional due diligence steps are required. Risks originating from accounting issues, corruption, governance, and political instability must be thoroughly investigated, and companies should engage to alleviate investor concerns.

The following sections discuss two aspects of corporate disclosure and transparency: company engagement and board communication.

Meet the team: ESG engagement

ESG factors have become an important way for investors to measure the quality of a company and are thus a critical part of any investment process. A target of long-term investors is to comprehensively understand the companies in which they invest. Many investors adopt a "bottom-up" approach to the investment process, requiring months of thorough due diligence on focus companies. As such, they must meet with company management, competitors, and suppliers while performing their "deep dive" into the company's primary fundamentals.

After they have an investment opinion on the merits of the company, they typically look to establish the sustainability of their competitive advantage and how profitable it can be. This could be determined by confirming whether a company is disrupting a market, or whether it's protected from market changes, and whether it has the financial capacity to maintain its position. In today's environment, companies also need to highlight whether there are any environmental or social externalities not created by the company, or governance and accounting risks, all of which could adjust the investment opinion.

Regardless of whether it is active managers, who expect to hold a stock for the long term, or passive managers, who could hold a stock forever if it stays in a benchmark index, all investor types have a reason to see that companies tackle the material ESG issues that will increase their financial performance. Active corporate engagement generates value as it develops information flow and interpretation between companies and investors. For example, it helps companies improve their understanding of investors' expectations with regard to ESG issues and enables them to develop their image during any controversy, or to explain aspects of their business model that aren't fully recognized from the outside. Meanwhile, investors can look for more comprehensive and accurate information about ESG practices and alternatives. In doing so, they also develop their own ESG-related communication and accountability to clients or regulatory authorities.

The approach from investors is something that companies should embrace, and companies should recognize that increased engagement gives them the opportunity to tell their story and explain what they are doing in terms of becoming more ESG compliant and how that makes them a more resilient and less volatile investment. Therefore, companies should identify the benefits to their business and clearly communicate those benefits when engaging with existing and new shareholders. They should ensure that communication is both effective and enlightening.

REMEMBER

For the company, it should always be preferable to engage openly with investors rather than face proxy resolutions and voting concerns, which is a preferred strategy of active ownership for sustainable investing. According to records, the number of environmental and social shareholder resolutions filed in the United States has gone up considerably in recent years. The main topics of these resolutions include climate change and other environmental issues; human rights; human capital management; and diversity in the workforce and on corporate boards. Therefore, companies should also use any investor calls to explain progress on ESG targets, and how the targets are contributing to financial performance.

Thank you for sharing: Communication from the board

The increasingly common way for board members to communicate their company's place in society today is to issue a Statement of Purpose. In this statement, the board communicates the company's reason for being, identifies the stakeholders most relevant to its continued success, and lays out the time frames over which the board's decisions are measured and rewarded. However, the statement could also be part of a larger, integrated report for shareholders. As defined by the International Integrated Reporting Council (IIRC), "An integrated report is a concise communication about how an organization's strategy, governance, performance, and prospects, in the context of its external environment, lead to the creation of value."

Investor communications should also include an explanation of how major societal trends are affecting industry structure and competition, and how a company's response will affect its future growth and profitability, even to the point of changing its business model in response to the pressures of climate change. Appreciating these social and environmental dynamics will help investors foresee changes in industry structure and recognize opportunities to create shared value.

This targeted quantitative and qualitative information needs to be presented in a manner so that investors can use the information effectively. Ultimately, sustainable information should be standardized in the same way that financial accounting standards have been adopted; therefore, it's in the interest of companies to support such efforts wherever possible. Sustainability reporting also enables the investigation, analysis, and perhaps rethinking of an organization's management, strategy, and vision. Therefore, disclosure and reporting, combined with general ESG communication programs, should increase shareholder value and improve financial performance by strengthening the organization's competitive position and meeting society's expectations for good corporate behavior.

Grow the Pie: Generating Enhanced Returns

Companies that integrate ESG factors into their long-term strategic projections, and convey that message to investors, offer a more extensive picture of their potential value. Effective ESG practices can diminish both business and financial risk, resulting in a more profitable business, as well as stronger credit metrics, indicating a lower cost of capital. Moreover, recent reports have shown that operational and stock price performance of companies is positively influenced by strong sustainability and ESG practices. Effective ESG practices tend to generate better operational and stock price performance, thereby reducing the cost of capital for the vast majority of companies; thus, those with strong ESG scores were less of an investment risk.

REMEMBER

For other market observers, ESG activities are seen as a way to safeguard company value. Conventional investors have predominantly used ESG metrics as indicators of risk, emphasizing governance weaknesses or the likely environmental and social disputes that can result from governance failures. Because they weren't intended to quantify financial value, ESG metrics aren't necessarily suited to help investors establish the financial impact of their ESG performance. As such, some firms should spend more time explaining the causal effect between their ESG strategy and their financial performance. Some companies have generated explicit, financially relevant ESG metrics that indicate to investors how much value their ESG approach has created. In addition, they integrate expertise from across the company, and from external advisors and partners, to establish alternative ways to continue to enhance financial performance.

The following sections discuss a few ways that companies can use ESG to generate enhanced returns.

Increasing access to capital

The benefits of proactively addressing ESG issues go beyond satisfying institutional shareholders and establishing a good public relations story. A robust ESG program can open up access to large pools of capital, build a stronger corporate brand, and promote sustainable long-term growth that benefits companies and investors. Investment research and consulting firms have created indexes that measure and rank companies based on ESG criteria relative to their industry peers. The investment funds and exchange-traded funds (ETFs) that benchmark these indexes are raising significant funds to be deployed toward companies that execute sound ESG policies; these are long-term oriented shareholders that can further fuel demand for a company's stock (see Chapter 8 for more information).

Moreover, individual and institutional investors are investing substantial sums of money in companies that proactively govern and operate in an ethical and sustainable manner. Sustainable and impact investing is actively growing at double-digit compound rates, with the U.S. SIF Foundation suggesting that total U.S.-domiciled investments using sustainable, responsible, and impact (SRI) strategies have risen to nearly US$17 trillion, representing about one of every three dollars under management (see `www.ussif.org/files/US%20SIF%20 Trends%20Report%202020%20Executive%20Summary.pdf`).

Corporate adoption and action

The movement toward more corporate transparency will persist as investors across a wide range of asset classes show an increasing interest in ESG issues. The UN Principles for Responsible Investment (PRI) have been signed by approximately 350 asset owners, credit ratings are including ESG considerations, and some of Europe's largest asset managers are promising to fully screen for ESG in all of their investments. Social and human capital issues are also on the rise, with topics such as data privacy, diversity, and the management of labor in supply chains being inspected with a closer lens. Company disclosure obligations on ESG issues will also increase because so many stock exchanges have either issued ESG reporting guidance or mandated ESG disclosure. This could even result in corporations in developed markets, where there are no mandatory disclosure requirements, finding themselves competing for capital with emerging market corporates that have adopted better ESG disclosures.

REMEMBER

Increasingly, ESG adoption is required by stakeholders, including customers, employees, analysts, and investors, to the point where it has to be part of a corporation's culture and values. For example, understanding and mitigating environmental impact is no longer optional in publicly traded companies. If companies don't adjust their corporate strategy to be more sustainable in the long run, then large asset managers may divest their shares, causing stock prices to fall. So, boards of all companies are under pressure to confirm that they are creating a sustainable, long-term corporate strategy and moderating their carbon footprint going forward. In addition, changing employee preferences indicate that people want to work for companies that care about their community and the planet, while consumers increasingly want to understand the sustainability profile of the companies that they are buying from.

REMEMBER

In principle, companies have the ability to respond quickly where some governments can't or won't. Given the size of the largest corporations and asset managers, there is a growing anticipation that these multinational firms are becoming the primary drivers for transformation globally. Their businesses are focused on geopolitical issues, sustainable economic development, and the threats posed by climate change. This creates a responsibility and an ability to address broader ESG issues with a greater sense of urgency than most governments, which they should act upon. They acknowledge that being a "good citizen" produces a more viable and sustainable long-term business. Good governance by the boards of these companies is certifying that appropriate 'E' and 'S' factors are fulfilled for the benefit of their customers, communities, employees, and ultimately shareholders. So, if ESG principles are good for business, the environment, and society, is it just a matter of time before optional measures become mandated? Should we expect new regulation around disclosure and implementation requirements?

Alternatively, many of the operational factors highlighted by the Sustainability Accounting Standard Board (SASB; see Chapter 1) as material are common across entire industries and aren't exclusive to a particular company's competitive positioning. Consequently, incremental enhancements in material ESG factors converge over time into industry-wide best practices. For example, greenhouse gas emissions are a material ESG factor for every logistics company, because they correlate with the cost of fuel usage. Therefore, all major logistics companies need to implement best practices to reduce their fuel consumption as a competitive necessity. This "acclimatization" increases the requirements for operational efficiency across the industry and lowers carbon emissions naturally, without the need to mandate this approach.

Roll Up, Roll Up: Attracting More Customers

Implanting ESG concerns into business strategies is not only good for a company's business, but also crucial for customer loyalty and to guard against the growing number of serious threats to social stability as well as inclusiveness that makes a healthy business possible in the first place. Senior management that take steps to improve labor conditions, increase the diversity of their teams, give back to their communities, and take a position on sustainable environmental policies also strengthen the company's brand. As millennials and Generation Z, in particular, become consumers, employees, and investors, they are constantly watching for the performance of good corporate actions and rewarding those businesses with loyalty.

Companies that appreciate the importance of adjusting to changing socioeconomic and environmental conditions are more able to recognize strategic opportunities and meet competitive challenges. Proactive and amalgamated ESG policies can broaden a company's "competitive moat" in relation to other industry players. For example, Starbucks learned this as they were trying to expand their market share in China. They had struggled to gain momentum on expansion but stumbled upon the answer when they offered healthcare to their employees' parents; suddenly, sales growth boomed, and Starbucks now has over 2,000 stores in one of the fastest-growing markets on the globe!

The following sections talk about methods for attracting more customers via ESG.

Tracking sustainability practices

Corporate research has often failed to distinguish between traditional corporate social responsibility (CSR) efforts, such as philanthropy, and embedded sustainability and ESG practices that are part of the corporate strategy DNA. The financial performance of entrenched sustainability outperforms CSR due to its focus on material ESG factors, and recent research has demonstrated that stock market outperformance depends on companies focusing on ESG factors that have a material impact on their business.

However, some executive leaders find it challenging to comprehend the sustainable management approaches that enhance financial performance. Some of the issues remain difficult and unclear for employees, leaders, and organizations to grasp. It's a challenge for today's organizations to define these concepts and to be able to measure how they improve financial performance. Moreover, this can be further muddied by investors employing different investment strategies that have different requirements to meet their performance profiles. Therefore, companies should continue to focus on ways in which they become more efficient, improve their brand value and reputation, achieve better growth, cut costs, and strengthen stakeholder relations while employing best practice sustainability approaches. It may still be difficult to precisely evaluate the improved financial performance, but companies will be moving in the right direction.

REMEMBER

Consequently, sustainability is seen as an essential component of the next wave of best management practices that can expand business performance. This entails recognition of further factors that can propel improved financial performance, including innovation, increased sales, employee retention, operational efficiency, productivity, and risk mitigation. The relationship between ESG practices and financial results has clear consequences for corporate decision-making, and corporate executives largely share a consensus on what creates material sustainability strategies in their sector, although that can differ per jurisdiction. For example, in the car industry, the key strategies range from waste reduction to product innovation. However, to fully and accurately measure the financial impact of sustainability efforts, investors and managers must examine not only a strategy, but also how that strategy was executed and the benefits that followed.

REMEMBER

To achieve this, companies need to set up accounting systems that track the return on investment (ROI) of sustainability efforts across divisions from the outset. Tangible items, such as increased sales, and intangibles, such as risk mitigation, need to be built into the calculations to permit companies to embed sustainability into the heart of their business strategy and communications. Meanwhile, investors can use this information to appreciate more clearly where sustainability actions are producing an impact and ensure that they evaluate companies on how they apply sustainability strategies within their sector and monitor the financial results.

Measuring intangible value drivers

Companies are self-reporting using diverse ESG metrics, and so there is a lack of uniformity in the resulting reports. They also produce reports without audits to regulate the accuracy of the data, and so verifying or comparing performance is challenging. Moreover, poor-quality and untimely ESG data presents difficulties to investors and corporate managers themselves. ESG ratings completed by external agencies also lack standardization, so these third-party ESG data providers and rating agencies, similar to companies evaluating themselves, use different data and scoring systems, culminating in very different assessments.

WARNING

One of the chief problems for many corporations trying to create an integrated report is that different elements of ESG information are seldom available at the same time and in an equivalent format to financial information. Non-financial ESG metrics like approaches to climate change or governance of supply chain management, as currently reported, are completely removed from financial metrics like standard accounting ratios, such as revenue growth or working capital. Very few businesses are tracing the return on their ESG investments or endeavors in their accounting systems. Thus, there are effectively no associations being made between accounting data and sustainability investments. Furthermore, intangible company estimates aren't properly followed, as accounting itself is an imperfect tool for ESG evaluation, given that it's poor at monetizing intangibles. Intangibles can make up the vast majority of a company's value today and normally include many sustainability benefits, such as brand reputation and risk mitigation.

The Global Reporting Initiative (GRI) and the Sustainability Accounting Standards Board (SASB; see Chapter 1), by providing a mechanism for reporting specific ESG issues, are improving these developments, but business leaders must contribute to accelerating this change. A potential framework for companies to support this approach is to

» Put standards in place in their own external reporting

» Continue to challenge software vendors that produce financial information to extend into ESG metrics

» Push their audit firms to provide assurance on reported ESG performance, as they do for financial performance

» Integrate ESG reports into their IT systems

» Mitigate any increased liabilities resulting from this process

Companies implementing these frameworks should be rewarded for solving these issues by both existing and potential investors through their continued investment and engagement.

Identifying material opportunities

REMEMBER

There is persuasive evidence that preeminence in recognizing and utilizing selected ESG issues can, over time, have a significant economic impact on businesses and even entire sectors. The SASB has taken a notable step in generating industry standards where the relationship between impact and economic performance is well defined. The enhanced availability and reliability of ESG data, combined with further research, has allowed the SASB to partner with industry representatives to distinguish the specific metrics that are material to a particular sector. Research has shown that, when companies concentrate their sustainability efforts principally on material ESG factors, they outperform the market, with more alpha (the excess return of an investment relative to the market return of a benchmark index) created annually, and outperform peer companies that focus sustainability efforts on non-material factors.

Therefore, rather than take ESG rating agencies' data as given, forward-looking companies may use the SASB methodology as a further reference point to identify the key material sustainability issues, defined on an industry-by-industry basis. This allows companies to consider a range of other variables, such as profitability, size, and ownership, in order to make the ESG indication as complete as possible. Companies could then classify a fundamental range of quantifiable ESG criteria that are material to their business, while also being aligned with their corporate strategies. For example, a fracking company, being in the oil and gas sector, should measure water, waste management, and impacts on scarce natural resources. Conversely, if your business is centered on service personnel, then social training on anti-harassment and racial sensitivity could produce a more tangible effect and support the corporate brand. Therefore, the initial reference points mentioned earlier should not be a substitute for compiling company-specific analysis.

TIP

An effective way to benchmark your company's ESG framework relative to your peers is to research industry rankings within a major sustainability-ranking index. These organizations, as well as ESG advisory companies, analyze a broad range of criteria for each industry, including climate change impacts, natural resource scarcity, supply chain management, labor practices, political contributions, board composition, and workplace diversity and inclusion. A number of nonprofit global advocacy organizations act as standard setters for sustainability disclosure and reporting. Here are some of them:

>> Global Reporting Initiative (GRI): www.globalreporting.org/

>> Sustainability Accounting Standards Board (SASB): www.sasb.org/

>> International Integrated Reporting Council (IIRC): www.integratedreporting.org/

» Carbon Disclosure Project (CDP): www.cdp.net/en

» Climate Disclosure Standards Board (CDSB): www.cdsb.net

TIP

In addition, the influence of proxy advisory firms, such as Institutional Shareholder Services (ISS; www.issgovernance.com/) and Glass Lewis (www.glasslewis.com/), over institutional investors has grown in recent years, so reviewing the governance scores they apply to given companies can offer another useful benchmark.

After a company has decided on the most suitable criteria for its ESG framework, the next steps are to determine metrics, evaluate them on a regular basis, and communicate progress publicly (see Chapter 14 for further information). For example, European Union law already requires large companies to disclose certain information on the way they operate and manage social and environmental challenges through the Non-Financial Reporting Directive (NFRD).

Pare It Back: Reducing Costs

The 'G' (governance) element of ESG (covered in Chapter 5) has always been a big part of the credit rating equation, as good corporate governance is a clear gauge of creditworthiness; therefore, credit rating agencies are familiar with evaluating governance characteristics. It's still unclear exactly how the performance of ratings will be affected, now that 'E' and 'S' factors are considered more explicitly (see Chapters 3 and 4), but a greater emphasis on ESG factors may cause an increase in the cost of capital for those firms that are behind on their ESG integration.

As you find out in this section, the favored form of corporate debt has been corporate bonds, particularly in the United States, but also more broadly since the global financial crisis prompted a low-interest-rate environment. However, there has been growing interest in specific forms of debt, such as green financing, particularly where companies can identify allowable, sustainable projects.

Green financing

The green bond market is maturing, with outstanding issuance of green bonds passing US$1 trillion total issuance since its inception. However, the ability of a company to issue such bonds depends on whether they meet the relevant criteria in terms of environmental sustainability objectives and quantifying the use of proceeds for "green" projects. Therefore, such bonds have been dominated by issuers from the alternative and renewable energy, green building, and sustainable transport sectors.

Therefore, transition bonds, which have been issued by carbon-intensive companies that are actively decarbonizing but have more difficulty issuing green bonds, can provide an alternative source of funding explicitly aimed at helping those companies attempting to become greener. However, the funds need to be exclusively used to fully or partly finance or refinance specified projects, and the issuer needs to justify their significance from the standpoint of commercial transformation and climate transition.

Finally, another alternative is sustainability bonds, which are designed to encourage borrowers to issue bonds focused on broader environmental targets, as opposed to specific projects. The proceeds from sustainability bonds are wholly applied to finance or refinance a combination of both green and social projects. Flip to Chapter 9 for more information on bonds and ESG.

How low can you go? Lower interest rates and higher credit ratings

The link between ESG and downside risk is of great relevance to fixed income pricing. Research on the links between credit and fixed income shows that issuers with strong governance performance have experienced less credit downgrades. Companies should ensure they are familiar with the following material in order to consider ways in which they can best improve their own credit ratings and therefore reduce interest rates on their funding requirements.

Given that a credit rating is a forward-looking opinion about a company's creditworthiness, ESG issues should be incorporated into the overall analysis of an entity's credit quality. Corporate rating criteria should include these factors as well as an entity's industry risk, competitive position, and financial forecast and cash flow or leverage assessments. However, rating agencies need a good degree of visibility and certainty about the timing and potential impact of material ESG risks or opportunities in order to incorporate them into any credit analysis. For example, ESG factors led to 225 corporate credit rating changes between 2015 and 2017, and ESG issues were referenced as analytical considerations in 1,325 rating reports, according to S&P.

ESG analysis can also help companies reveal a number of probable long-term financial risks and opportunities, including the likely impact of future carbon regulations and cost savings related to improved use of resources. It's evident that an independent and stable measurement of non-financial metrics should unearth more information on investment and corporate performance in the near to long term, as a way to distinguish between companies. As mentioned in Chapter 9, evidence suggests that ESG factors affect the cost of capital in a positive way (lower interest rates), with issuers showing higher ESG scores and having a lower cost of capital than issuers with lower ESG scores, for the same credit rating. There is also a clear yield-spread difference between best-in-class and worst-in-class corporations, generally being wider for Euro-denominated bonds than U.S. dollar–denominated investment-grade bonds.

The Bottom Line: Increasing Productivity and Attracting Talent

It's encouraging that ESG deliberations are being directed in most companies by the CEO and their board; however, companies must increase their own middle management's contribution to pinpointing and managing the material ESG issues, as they are "on the factory floor" on a day-to-day basis and the ones dedicating their direct reports as resources to realize strategic objectives.

REMEMBER

In short, business units need to concentrate on distinguishing "ESG" and which material issues to emphasis in order to maximize increasing productivity. Investors and the CEO steer the agenda, but middle management and their teams ultimately generate the products and services that serve both shareholders and society.

Therefore, senior management should involve middle managers in discussions with investors and contribute to the materiality determination process in which companies recognize the ESG issues that influence their business. To safeguard that all interests are aligned, senior management should assess and reward middle managers on both financial and ESG performance, and from a longer-term perspective rather than quarterly or annually. This is particularly required, as any drop in short-term productivity should be recognized as a means toward realizing higher, longer-term productivity. Current staffing may need to be reallocated away from existing short-term roles, impacting short-term productivity and potentially profitability, to the longer-term agenda.

In addition, accepting that a company's financial efficiency is strongly associated with the performance of its share price, research has shown that the most financially productive companies also have the lowest carbon footprint. Moreover, the most financially constructive companies also typically have the strongest corporate governance practices. This further indicates that companies embracing strong ESG principles are well-managed companies that also increase productivity and profitability.

In today's job market, the currency for gaining talent is changing as employees, specifically millennials and Generation Z, look for more than a paycheck for their efforts. Many of these workers acknowledge that they are more likely to be impacted in their lifetimes by social and environmental issues, such as climate change. Therefore, they need to feel that they matter and their work makes a difference. However, many organizations are missing this opportunity to increase engagement, retention, and productivity. Some surveys suggest that only a third of employees within U.S. firms are engaged at work, which ultimately costs the U.S. economy over US$500 billion in lost productivity each year.

REMEMBER

In this environment, keeping purpose constant in corporate strategy isn't just an ideal, it's a business opportunity. A proactive approach can pay dividends for organizations that provide ways for employees to bring their passion for impact to the workplace, resulting in dramatic improvements in retention rates. Millennials genuinely care that the companies they work for (and the related businesses that they support) adopt values that are aligned with their own, and environmental and social accountability are important to them. Employees who are passionate about their organization and show loyalty, and who know they are valued, produce an intangible goodwill that reinforces the brand of the company and develops the overall productivity of the workforce.

REMEMBER

Preserving a good company reputation and attracting and retaining talent continue to be mentioned most often as means by which ESG programs improve financial performance. Moreover, ESG programs are seen to expand shareholder value by developing financial performance, which is propelled by strengthening the organization's competitive position, implying that this is a proxy for good management. Also, talented employees and senior management are drawn to corporations that participate in environmental, social, and governance programs, as they feel they make a definite long-term contribution to the company and society.

IN THIS CHAPTER

» **Creating a plan to develop a policy**

» **Participating in a peer review**

» **Reviewing your core investment principles**

» **Getting familiar with ESG-specific standards**

» **Checking out reporting requirements**

» **Starting ESG engagement**

Chapter **13**

Devising an ESG Policy

sset owners are the economic owners of assets and include pension plans, insurance companies, official institutions, banks, foundations, endowments, family offices, and individual investors, each of which has different investment objectives and constraints. Asset owners can invest in an asset either by purchasing that asset directly or by hiring an asset manager to invest on their behalf. When an asset owner utilizes the investment management services of an asset manager, such investments can be structured as separate accounts or commingled investment vehicles (for example, mutual funds).

Asset owners make critical decisions about how their money is invested, including the following:

» Establishing investment policies (for example, investment objectives, asset allocation policies, and approaches to sustainability or ESG matters)

» Whether to manage their assets internally or outsource to an external asset manager

» How to handle their responsibilities as public company shareholders (for example, proxy voting policies, reliance on proxy advisors, and insourcing versus outsourcing of investment stewardship activities)

This chapter looks at devising an ESG approach for an asset owner. Many corporations have adopted a purpose statement, which normally refers to their mission, primary goals, and core beliefs. Even though such statements are often communicated at a high level, the idea that they outline a longer-term horizon that they aspire to is comparable to the longer-term objectives needed for an ESG policy.

Here's a Great Idea: Creating a Plan

Any document that is developed to show the intent of an organization in a given direction should start with a plan that establishes the short-term and long-term objectives of the company that need to be implemented in order to meet the organization's ultimate ESG aspirations. This could begin with an analysis of the organization's current approach and systems, which could be mapped to the overall objectives in order to identify obvious, initial gaps. This approach could be guided by interim targets for review, and tasks and frameworks set to enable implementation in a coordinated fashion.

TIP

Some investors can struggle to communicate their approach, particularly smaller organizations that are new to the process. An initial approach taken by some is to refer to frameworks such as the UN Sustainable Development Goals (SDGs; see Chapter 1) and Principles for Responsible Investment (PRI) to help inform discussions and identify goals that map to the core high-level beliefs central to an organization. (Visit www.un.org/sustainabledevelopment/sustainable-development-goals/ and www.unpri.org/download?ac=4336 for more information.) This can be combined with a statement of priorities that further defines any essential sustainable themes, in ESG terms, and that also enables mapping to potential investment opportunities. Clearly, some priorities may not be immediately investable, but confirmation of these requirements helps ensure that investors proactively investigate potential paths for investment in the future.

Additional approaches to inform the process should include an internal review process, wider stakeholder consultation, and potentially the engagement of an external service provider. It's important that the methodology employed be inclusive to ensure representation of all relevant and material assessments. Furthermore, it's necessary to recognize that without well-defined core principles, the work of the trustee (who is responsible for ensuring that the assets are managed properly and that owners' benefits are secure) and other fiduciary and regulatory requirements will be difficult to forcefully implement.

As the plan begins to unfold, milestones should be present to ensure monitoring and evaluation of progress are in place to observe the organization's development against the originally planned objectives. In addition, ownership of the policy and results should be held by management at the highest level possible to ensure that cultural fit and organizational governance "buy-in" is maintained.

The following sections outline some of the key considerations to develop an ESG framework. It's important to involve all stakeholders and agree on an internal governance structure, some of which can be gleaned from a peer asset owner review, before determining the core investment strategy.

Promoting ESG among key stakeholders

REMEMBER

The stakeholder model is increasingly followed as part of the stated purpose and vision of the asset owner. (Stakeholders in this situation include beneficiaries, employees, internal and external investment managers, trustees, and executive management.) Consequently, ESG metrics should be used to assess and evaluate investment performance and its comparative positioning on a range of topics applicable to the wider set of stakeholders, in a similar fashion to performance metrics being used to assess investment management performance for share-holders. It's vitally important that ESG stakeholder metrics and goals are chosen and established with the same consistency as other performance metrics to safe-guard that the realization of ESG goals will enhance stakeholder value and not serve simply as a "check the box" or "greenwashing" exercise (see Chapter 6).

There is no "one size fits all" approach to ESG metrics, and asset owners invest across a range of asset classes that influence the type of ESG factors that are appropriate to short- and long-term investment performance and sustainability considerations. Implementing ESG metrics is an asset owner–specific design process. For example, some asset owners may choose to implement more qualitative ESG investment goals, even though they have rigorous ESG factor data and reporting, while others will consider quantitative ESG goals that integrate the new data elements (see Chapter 14 for more information on the integration of ESG factors).

Creating an internal governance structure

REMEMBER

Core responsible investment guidelines can look very different from organization to organization, predominantly based on the responsible investment practices that fit with your organization's investment process and philosophy. This may also be driven by differences relating to internally or externally managed assets, and dependent on the jurisdictional requirements and legal aspects that can affect the guidelines.

For example, your organization may set minimum ESG standards that investee companies need to adhere to. Some investors may impose high-level require-ments on ESG, while others may require specific information on how companies manage ESG issues, with minimum standards having to meet a broader industry standard. Similarly, standards can be set relative to different asset classes, which may differ relative to the ESG ratings available for listed equities, bonds, private equity, real estate, hedge funds, or commodities.

Guidelines for working with external managers will tend to be more specific, as internal managers will, of course, be covered by already-set internal guidelines. External investment managers may be required to have their own responsible investment policies in place, or alternatively to adopt the asset owners' policy. Some asset owners may extend this further to include guidelines on manager selection and monitoring, inclusion of ESG issues in Requests for Proposals (RFPs) for investment mandates, and requirements on reporting for ESG issues.

Don't Reinvent the Wheel: Undertaking a Peer Review

Given that the principle of having an ESG or responsible investment policy in place is still relatively new for many asset owners, there is an understandable tendency to be interested in how other owners have approached the process rather than "reinventing the wheel." In addition, understanding what your peers have done can encourage high-level investment policy discussions, which can further help the drafting of any policy. In principle, given the current assets under management, ESG investment practices should follow the same structure and consistency as more traditional items of an investment policy statement.

Peer reviews provide guidance on how investment policies were formulated, and the outcomes they produced may be transparent. When considering how your policy compares to other approaches, it's instructive to see how stakeholders are involved in the establishment of policy. In addition, you need to understand how ESG risks or opportunities are defined and identified, or how issues are weighed and evaluated in investment decisions. Interestingly, rather than just meeting the investment requirements for such a policy, some organizations also monitor the positive real-world influence achieved through their portfolio!

The following sections consider peer reviews and different types of ESG investment strategies, including their identification, assessment, and selection.

Devising ESG investment strategies

There are five primary strategies for ESG investing: exclusionary screening, positive screening, ESG integration, impact investing, and active ownership. (You can find out more about these strategies in Chapter 8.) Such strategies exhibit a wide range of intentions, from avoiding or reducing ESG risks to seeking measurable impact. They also exhibit a wide variety of investment and impact considerations that investors should take into account. Some objectives overlap other ESG strategies to some degree, and multiple ESG strategies are sometimes combined within a single investment vehicle to realize the unique goals of an asset owner. Moreover, these strategies can also be executed across asset classes and investment styles.

It can be argued that much of the value of ESG as an investment framework results from predicting shifts in political and social priorities, which subsequently generate shifts in economic opportunities for investors. These shifts, while clearly significant from an ESG investing perspective, nonetheless introduce problems when developing metrics that anticipate changes in social norms that haven't yet happened, and when estimating the social impact of any related changes in corporate behavior. The fundamental aspect of ESG investing is that a long-term time frame can be required to see how the trend plays out. ESG can be considered as an investment process, which suggests that markets and many companies are too short term in their assessment of value, and that by investing in its structure, people, and community, a company's long-run performance should improve.

Others argue that certain ESG risks are already financially material and should be considered regardless of your investment horizon. In fact, given the rapidly growing assets under management that follow responsible or sustainable investment strategies, some would argue that people shouldn't be talking about ESG investing integration because ESG investment strategies will become the norm rather than the exception in the not-too-distant future.

TIP

Based on this framework, you should publish your comprehensive investment strategy and principles so that the market recognizes that you're committed to responsible investment practices that generally consider a long-term trend. Moreover, this incorporates ESG factors that focus on risk-management mitigation while also looking to uncover potential opportunities. Wherever your policies adhere to best-practice requirements, these requirements should also be highlighted to emphasize your awareness of their importance; such statements should at minimum be displayed on your website if not with other industry-relevant organizations. In addition, you should consider signing the internationally recognized Principles for Responsible Investment, which allows your organization to publicly demonstrate its commitment to responsible investment (see www.unpri. org/signatories for more information).

Identifying, assessing, and selecting ESG investments

Asset owners should fully incorporate ESG analysis into their investment process, incorporating initial screening, issue selection, portfolio construction, and risk management. They should also have transparent and well-implemented programs to actively engage with portfolio holdings on ESG stewardship (for more information, check out www.unpri.org/investment-tools/stewardship).

Many sustainable funds take an integrative approach to creating their portfolio. Their emphasis tends to be on identifying stocks that have "best-in-class" practices when incorporating ESG issues relevant to that company. This tilts the portfolio toward companies that are generally managing ESG issues better than their peers and are thus less likely to face financial risks or controversies such as fines, lawsuits, and reputational damage. Negative (or exclusionary) screening is still used today, particularly by funds investing in line with religious values; however, the fact that this approach rules out established companies for non-financial reasons can lead to underperformance or cause issues when tracking an established benchmark index.

An increasing number of funds state in their *prospectus* (the document that funds need to publish as a guide to their investment strategy, costs, risks, and management) that they make sustainability factors a featured component of their process when building their portfolio and choosing investments (known as ESG Focus funds). Another group, Impact funds, tends to focus on broad sustainability themes and on delivering social or environmental impact alongside financial returns. They tend to focus on specific themes, such as low carbon, gender equality, or green bonds (funding new and existing projects with environmental benefits; see Chapter 9). Lastly, Sustainable Sector funds concentrate on companies that proactively contribute to the transition to a green economy in areas such as energy efficiency, environmental services, renewable energy, water, and green real estate.

Go Over It: Reviewing Your Core Investment Principles

An Investment Beliefs Statement acts as a conduit between high-level goals and practical decision-making. Investment Belief Statements are valuable because they help trustees and fiduciaries clarify their views on the current state of financial markets in which they have to operate and how these markets are currently functioning. They outline the institution's rationales for their selection of investment styles and managers, while considering the core investment principles that they apply in the investment process. Generally, your responsible investment principles should be informed by these beliefs and this strategic investment approach, and reflect your organization's culture and values appropriately, in the ESG policy. Trustees and fiduciaries will be guided by these core principles to ensure that oversight and accountability measures are implemented.

REMEMBER

Some of the guiding thoughts when reviewing your beliefs and principles should include considerations on the value of diversification (and what impact screening may have), which types of risk should be included (and whether ESG factors help mitigate them), what ESG factors are considered material to investment returns, and whether they reflect a risk or an opportunity. Do you adhere to a long-term investment outlook, and are your general principles applicable to your entire asset base, or does it vary for given asset classes? And how do you view impact investing and its potential to benefit people or the planet? Does this lead you to invest thematically, for example, by focusing on low-carbon investing principles?

REMEMBER

Good corporate governance is ensuring appropriate oversight of the company's functioning in pursuit of its corporate objectives for the benefit of its stakeholders. However, fundamentally this should be built on three pillars: economic progress, social development, and environmental improvements. Therefore, good governance ultimately promotes sustainability by generating sustainable values and helping companies adhere to their values. It also helps companies realize long-term benefits, including diminishing risks, attracting new investors, and growing the companies' equity. So, as the pursuit of corporate sustainability continues to enrich and expand the principles of good corporate governance, companies will feel compelled to boost their efforts with greater transparency and public disclosure. In turn, transparency efforts will deliver information to investors on the relationship between corporate governance and improved sustainability.

There is increasing evidence that the support of shareholder preeminence encourages company directors to adopt the same short-time horizon thinking as with the financial markets at large. The suggestion is that pressure to meet the demands of the financial markets drives stock buybacks, excessive dividends, and a failure to invest in productive capabilities. This prompted the European Commission to produce the *Action Plan on Financing Sustainable Growth* (see https://ec.europa. eu/info/business-economy-euro/banking-and-finance/sustainable- finance_en), which sets out a bold agenda to advance integrated reforms in the areas of corporate reporting, directors' duties, and sustainable finance, with a target to address the reorientation of financial flows to more sustainable outcomes. The principle is to correct the failure of companies to manage the financial risks associated with climate change and to encourage a move toward greater sustainability.

Since 2018, the EU Non-Financial Reporting Directive (NFRD) has required large companies, banks, and insurers to disclose non-financial information (see https://ec.europa.eu/info/business-economy-euro/company-reporting-and-auditing/company-reporting/non-financial-reporting_en#review). However, due to a plethora of standards and the flexibility given to reporting entities, this reporting isn't currently comprehensive or sufficiently comparable. The NFRD review of its legislation is aimed at addressing some of these issues, but the amendments have been delayed due to COVID-19. Therefore, the standardization of non-financial reporting will benefit the development of sustainable finance, as it enables comparability of information across investments.

Familiarizing Yourself with ESG-Specific Regulations

In general, local jurisdictional law may compel pension funds to have a statement of investment principles, or their fiduciary duty may require trustees to reflect on any ESG issues that are financially material. In addition, other jurisdictions may explicitly oblige diversity and inclusion to be considered as material ESG factors in their investment analysis and decision-making. Therefore, due to this growing acceptance of responsible investment practices, most pension funds already advocate many forms of ESG investing.

Also, in many countries, the corporate governance and stewardship codes give valuable insight into ESG policies, which should consider the performance of investment portfolios to variable degrees across companies, sectors, regions, and asset classes. Furthermore, many of the points mentioned here for money managers will be comparable for individual companies implementing their own ESG policies.

The following sections compare the regulation in the two major jurisdictions with the largest ESG assets under management, as well as look at the associated sustainability risks and how the issues around "greenwashing" are being addressed.

Comparing Europe and the United States

Europe has been leading the way with a virtual legislative tsunami of regulation, resulting in a range of important rules for asset managers, either as publicly listed companies with new ESG disclosure requirements or explicitly relating to their role in the design, delivery, and sale of financial services and products. This seems to reflect regulators' recognition that certain ESG factors are financially material and should be explicitly considered, as well as a desire to ensure the finance sector reorients capital flows. Depending on the nature of their business, type of client, and activities, asset managers face new requirements at the corporate governance, process, and product levels. In response, by the end of 2020, the number of asset owners, investment managers, and service providers that were signatories to the Principles for Responsible Investment had reached more than 3,000, up more than 50 percent from 2018.

Asset managers are at the center of this challenge, but they face diverse approaches and variable definitions of sustainability concepts set forth by asset owners, business sectors, jurisdictions, and professional and industry standards–setting bodies. Without reliable definitions, it's difficult to establish the data points needed to set equivalent targets, monitor investments, and evaluate and compare performance against peers, let alone across the financial services sector, and national or regional borders. Moreover, asset managers must present this in-depth data analysis to fulfill their own corporate reporting requirements, to manage applicable investment and risk management decisions, and to make disclosures to clients and fund investors. The challenge is compounded by the fact that asset managers typically need to review endless subsets of relevant ESG considerations for multiple, distinct asset classes, industries, and geographies.

In the United States, some accuse the federal government of standing still on ESG, as no blanket mandatory requirements have been imposed. However, certain states are leading the way on substantive regulation designed to encourage sustainable investment. These states are leaning into the market's growing focus on managing capital using ESG factors to further regulate pension systems, trust funds, and board composition. In turn, this is making ESG even more important for those raising and managing funds across the liquidity spectrum. The most proactive state pension systems promoting these activities have been California's Public Employees' Retirement System (CalPERS) and California State Teachers' Retirement System (CalSTRS).

Taking into account sustainability-related risks

Sustainability risks are growing and getting more attention from executives, investors, lenders, and regulators. Examples of where they exist include threats to operating licenses in mining operations, assessments of overconsumption of water, reputational risks linked to investments in projects with potentially damaging environmental consequences, risks to financial performance from volatile energy prices, compliance risks triggered by new carbon regulations, and risks from product substitution as customers switch to more sustainable alternatives.

Executive attitudes toward sustainability are gradually changing. Sustainability has historically been viewed as a cost center, a corporate social responsibility (CSR) issue complete with obligations to meet requirements from climate change goals to charitable donations to local communities. However, more firms are viewing sustainability through the lens of market opportunity and value creation. They now have the financial data to support this assessment with the establishment of new markets and business models associated with sustainability trends. Tangible financial results from such strategic plans will take time to appear, but some of the world's leading brand managers have been converted.

REMEMBER

Therefore, sustainability risk management (SRM) is emerging as a business strategy that affiliates profit goals with internal green strategies and policies. These policies seek to diminish negative environmental impact by shrinking the use of natural resources and cutting carbon emissions, toxic substances, and by-products. The goal of SRM is to make this alignment sufficient to sustain and grow a business while still preserving the environment. SRM is now considered a vital part of enterprise risk management.

Doing effective due diligence on ESG greenwashing

All kinds of businesses and brands are starting to use the word "sustainable" in their marketing. Whether it's a T-shirt made of ethical cotton or an "eco" car, companies are increasingly keen to showcase their green credentials. So, how can you tell the difference between real, positive commitments to change and "greenwashing"? In the current environment, greenwashing (covered in detail in Chapter 6) can take two main forms:

>> One is where a company is trying to hide or cover up their questionable environmental records with an impressive public gesture toward green causes. However, in the age of social media, these big PR campaigns are often criticized and scrutinized pretty quickly.

>> Harder to spot and far more underhanded, the other form is where companies and brands use words like "green," "sustainable," "eco-friendly," or "vegan" simply as a marketing ploy, without any real commitment to the principles and certainly without any accountability for their actions.

WARNING

Investment products aren't immune to greenwashing. Asset managers have seen the opportunity to attract money from investors as the demand for ESG-related products has exponentially increased. They claim to have integrated environmental, social, and governance considerations into their investment processes, but because ESG investing is still somewhat new, the capacity of investment managers and investors to assess the materiality of stated ESG factors is evolving. Therefore, it's vital for asset owners and advisers to question a fund's ESG approach and identify any potential greenwashing by the fund manager.

TECHNICAL STUFF

Certainly, the Markets in Financial Instruments Directive (MiFID) II legislation in Europe obliges advisers to question clients on their ESG preferences when conducting their research, based on a 2020 amendment to MiFID II. In addition, the U.S. Securities and Exchange Commission (SEC) has openly criticized the asset management industry's reliance on a single rating for ESG funds data as "imprecise," due to concerns that overly simple ratings systems are leading to misinformed or even misguided investment decisions. Some may consider this misinformation as an additional consideration in their greenwashing monitoring.

Surveying Reporting Requirements

Broader elements of reporting requirements are covered in Chapter 14, but this section contains a condensed view of the considerations required. A plethora of reporting frameworks, standards, and guidelines are available, to the point that it's difficult to know which one to select:

» Some frameworks, such as the Global Reporting Initiative (GRI), are not industry-specific, while the Sustainability Accounting Standards Board (SASB) is industry-specific.

» However, the GRI and SASB are discussing potential collaboration around reporting requirements. (Chapter 1 has more about the GRI and the SASB.)

» Other standards can be more topic-specific, such as the Task Force on Climate-related Financial Disclosures (TCFD), which focuses on climate change, and the Global ESG Benchmark for Real Assets (GRESB), which is a standard that is more specific to the real estate industry.

REMEMBER

However, there is no one-size-fits-all approach, and it depends on your organization's reporting needs, what you want to report, and whom you are reporting to. It can be a struggle to accurately collect and report quality sustainability and ESG data, but you need to ensure its reliability and accuracy.

Essential characteristics of ESG data

REMEMBER

According to a survey by IHS Markit, a large data provider, seven of the top preferences sought by fund investors on how ESG metrics/data are commonly reported are to

>> Develop consistent and controlled policies for quantifying and reporting purpose-led metrics.

>> Align metrics reported externally with those used by management in running the business.

>> Organize metrics in a systematic way (that is, using technology to make the information interactive and engaging).

>> Offer comparison figures to demonstrate consistency.

>> Determine the appropriate format and frequency of reporting.

>> Implement controls over the preparation and reporting of purpose-led metrics with the same rigor as controls over traditional financial reporting.

>> Provide context (for example, the most relevant metrics consider the entity's industry and markets).

Material factors for investors

While the approaches in the preceding section are being widely employed, and the World Economic Forum (WEF) guidance — to include a full set of metrics in your corporate and financial reporting — represents a well-intentioned route to defining broader ESG metrics, measurement, and quality of ESG data remains an issue.

There are several areas of ESG endeavor that aren't embodied in easily reportable figures and that don't have commonly accepted measurement criteria. Attempts to fill these gaps could include establishing a formal environmental policy and highlighting the management team's competence in observing and tackling the environmental costs of corporate operations. Separately, the capability to estimate carbon emissions, both direct and indirect, including those generated by their wider value chain, would be information that investors would find useful.

WARNING

Where there is a legal requirement for disclosure, such as the gender pay gap in large companies, data is easier to compare but still prone to inconsistencies and limited in scope. Timing is another issue, where without real-time reporting factored in and consequent adjustment of rankings, a company could continue to score highly after a suffering an ESG crisis. Furthermore, the lack of traceability of source material in the current systems throws further doubt on its reliability.

Examining ESG Engagement

REMEMBER

Asset owners should actively use their ownership rights to engage with companies or look for their asset managers to engage on their behalf in a constructive manner. Improvements in sustainable corporate behavior can lead to an enhanced risk/return profile for any investments. Engagement aims to improve a company's ESG approach with the aim of boosting the long-term performance of the investment. The outcomes of engagement efforts need to be communicated to analysts and portfolio managers to ensure they incorporate the information into their investment decisions as part of an integrated sustainability investing framework.

The first criterion is that engagement should be relevant with respect to the investment exposure. Developing a materiality framework can be a starting point to prioritize potential engagements, with materiality insights determining the most relevant sustainability risks and opportunities to be addressed. Sustainability should be viewed as a value driver alongside other components such as company financials and market momentum. The management and board of listed companies that have strong sustainability and governance policies have proven to better manage issues such as non-financial risks and changing regulation. Consequently, they also seem better prepared to cope with long-term trends such as climate change.

The following sections consider approaches with respect to engagement that asset owners should consider and the type of companies that could be candidates for earlier-stage ESG analysis.

Conducting constructive dialogue on managing ESG risks

Engagement should entail a constructive dialogue between asset owners and managers and investee companies to review how they manage ESG risks and grasp business opportunities associated with sustainability challenges. Such conversations can be managed in a reactive manner, to review specific incidents, or in a proactive manner, to improve potential risks and opportunities. The level of commitment involved is generally related to the size of the investment in a company and the situation that the company is dealing with. Where an owner is a major shareholder, engagement should be undertaken directly with the company; however, if the shareholding is smaller, this could be done in cooperation with other investors.

Ordinarily, engagement is on a corporate level, but the World Bank Treasury team has also been proactive in facilitating open and productive dialogues between institutional investors and sovereign bond issuers around ESG issues. Building on experience from the equity market, investors are investigating ways to support and develop their ESG approaches across asset classes, including investments in sovereign bonds, to enrich risk management and returns while achieving a positive impact. Investors that are developing ESG risk assessment and portfolio selection frameworks to evaluate sovereign issuers based on ESG criteria are interested in learning about countries' ESG policies, strategies, and approaches. They also need to analyze data on sovereign ESG performance and assess progress on the SDGs and Paris climate commitments. World Bank Treasury syndication is supporting some of these activities to enhance the access and engagement with sovereign bond issuers.

REMEMBER

Maintaining a dialogue is resource-intensive but has been proven to be effective, so it should continue to be a high priority. ESG and sustainability are increasingly ingrained in institutional thinking, and gradually more in private investments.

Seizing business opportunities associated with sustainability challenges

Change can feel threatening, but applicable strategies and successful management can bring momentum to organizational transformation and, in turn, new business opportunities. Companies that are receptive and start planning now can ensure an early competitive advantage. However, this isn't without challenges, including an ability to reframe the sustainability strategy emphasis from mitigating risks to embracing opportunities by inserting sustainability into the heart of their business model and scrutinizing its future feasibility. Asset owners can contribute to the transition process by engaging with those firms that they believe would benefit most from an improved sustainability approach and share with them some of the best practices employed by their peers. Alternatively, owners should encourage their asset managers to engage further.

The majority of companies agree that sustainability is an important factor for long-term business success, but they aren't identifying developments that will positively inspire current and future development, which should be used to form a clear strategic direction. The current global economic situation means that companies have an opportunity to reframe their strategic perceptions and build effective management structures and systems to rationalize and redirect corporate sustainability responsibility into clear metrics, tangible action, and quantifiable performance. Asset owners could, either directly or indirectly, promote a greater focus on sustainability opportunities.

REMEMBER

Asset owners' fiduciary duties require them to pay attention to ESG issues in their investment processes and to actively engage with companies. Therefore, once the risks and opportunities have been identified, owners need to encourage companies to implement targeted action. This process can start by considering accepted approaches in new ways in order to improve operational and eco-efficiency. This allows corporate sustainability to build on process improvements and investment into effective technologies such as waste avoidance and energy and resource efficiency. The next step is to consider adopting new ways to promote efficiency and achieve conclusive improvements and targets such as carbon neutrality. These measures are increasingly seen in the private sector — for example, with respect to setting carbon targets. In this step, sustainability measures should aim for the decoupling of operations from environmental impacts. Certainly, this process is a continuously evolving circle in which asset owners can work with companies to gradually develop further sustainable transition.

Chapter **14**

Defining and Measuring ESG Performance and Reporting

Reports and studies from a range of sources, from academics to investment banks, continue to reveal that portfolios based on investing in companies with high ESG metrics would have beaten the broader market by impressive amounts every year for the last five to ten years! In response, databases with countless ESG indicators exposing numerous corporate attributes have sprung up, suggesting that a targeted approach to both understanding and utilizing ESG data is necessary. Given the large number of ESG indicators, investors have tended to outsource their requirements in order to improve their assessment.

While many rating agencies provide a single ESG score for an individual security, comprising a composite of different individual factors, using such metrics to assess a single holding or a given portfolio indirectly presumes a shared set of ESG values across investors. However, what is socially responsible to one investor may not be to another. In addition to deciding which ESG factors to converge on, investors need to establish how to calculate the relative value of a given ESG metric. Three primary approaches currently exist:

>> Referencing against peers managing equivalent portfolios

>> Evaluating against a common benchmark index

>> Comparing against the investor's own history

The relevance of any of these approaches is contingent on an investor's specific situation, including, for example, the risk profile of the portfolio, the alignment of stakeholders, and any fiduciary responsibilities.

This chapter elaborates on how to define the criteria and metrics for material ESG factors and how the frameworks for related reporting of the data behind such factors continue to be developed. These elements provide the background to how the market is calculating relative ESG performance and the associated ratings and rankings.

Defining Criteria and Metrics

ESG factors are used in public market portfolios in many different ways, with some active managers using ESG factors as an integrated part of their investing process. Active managers generally look for financially material ways to integrate ESG factors (such as revenue growth, margins, or required capital). Passive investors can accept financially immaterial ways to integrate ESG factors (given that they are normally accepting the constituent stocks of a given index exposure). Examples of financial immaterial methods are those that don't have a significant impact on a company's business model but that may be relevant from a general sustainability perspective.

TIP

However, when analyzing the ESG score of a passive portfolio, an investor can choose to use factors to better align the portfolio with their values by considering indexes that emphasize specific characteristics, such as a higher 'E' score for companies with lower carbon emissions practices (see Chapter 8 for more information).

The following sections look at how corporations have to comply with regulation, what criteria that entails for sustainability reporting, how this is driving corporate social responsibility practices, and how that influences the metrics around associated corporate performance.

Follow the rules: Looking at regulators' work

REMEMBER

As with any investment strategy, investors need to determine their risk-and-return objectives. In an ESG-aware passive portfolio, indications of risk tolerance are important, as higher levels of concentration or tracking error can result from using given ESG metrics to negatively screen (exclude) or proactively bias a portfolio toward a specific 'E,' 'S,' or 'G' direction. With increased data accessibility, technology, and advanced risk management techniques, it's easier for investors to apply ESG factors to enhance alignment of their portfolios with their values, while keeping an eye on increased concentration issues, tracking errors, and risk considerations.

Conversely, the discrepancy among ESG ratings from different providers has motivated regulators on both sides of the pond to create more standardized frameworks and hopefully bring more transparency. The view was that uncertainty around ESG ratings was slowing the progress of determining sustainability market issues. Therefore, in May 2020, the investment committee of the U.S. Securities and Exchange Commission (SEC) proposed an ESG disclosure framework for consistent and comparable information, without the use of a third-party rating agency, to disclose material information that investors can rely on to make investment and voting decisions.

Meanwhile, in Europe, three interconnected regulatory approaches were also introduced recently:

» The Non-Financial Reporting Directive (NFRD), which is currently under review, requires large EU "public interest" corporates to publish data on the impact that their activities have on ESG factors. See `https://ec.europa.eu/info/business-economy-euro/company-reporting-and-auditing/company-reporting/non-financial-reporting_en#review` for details.

» The Taxonomy Regulation introduces a sustainability classification tool aimed at investors, companies, and financial institutions to define the environmental performance of economic activities across a wide range of industries through which investment firms must classify investments based on NFRD data (and other datasets). Visit `https://ec.europa.eu/info/business-economy-euro/banking-and-finance/sustainable-finance/eu-taxonomy-sustainable-activities_en`.

» The Sustainable Finance Disclosure Regulation (SFDR; see `https://ec.europa.eu/info/business-economy-euro/banking-and-finance/sustainable-finance/sustainability-related-disclosure-financial-services-sector_en`), as supplemented by the Taxonomy, requires investment firms to disclose the following:

- The environmental sustainability of an investment and the provenance of any ESG claims made

- The risks that investments present to ESG factors

- The risks that ESG factors present to investments

Not to be outdone, in September 2020, the World Economic Forum (WEF) released a report, "Measuring Stakeholder Capitalism: Towards Common Metrics and Consistent Reporting of Sustainable Value Creation." (Visit `http://www3.weforum.org/docs/WEF_IBC_Measuring_Stakeholder_Capitalism_Report_2020.pdf`). It's aimed at producing a baseline set of corporate disclosures with the objective of driving consistency and standardization of disclosure. Their principles state that benchmarking sustainable business performance will be easier with a universal set of "stakeholder capitalism metrics," including ESG indicators and disclosures for financial markets, investors, and society. The metrics will help companies demonstrate long-term value creation and their contributions to the United Nations Sustainable Development Goals (SDGs; see Chapter 1). According to the WEF, their efforts aren't intended to replace any of the industry-specific ESG metrics that investors already use, and these metrics are complementary, rather than competing, initiatives. In addition, most of the investors that contributed to the consultation would like to see ESG reporting included in a company's annual report.

The devil is in the details: Analyzing corporate sustainability reports

A substantial amount of ESG data on companies is self-reported, which can lead to significant breaks in the aggregate data that is used to generate an ESG score. Moreover, some of the factors aren't sufficiently reported to encompass the universe of investable companies. For example, considering the new WEF disclosures (see the previous section), there is a potential requirement to report on 21 core metrics, or an expanded 35 metrics. Given that many of these metrics may not be deemed material to a given industry, or are too challenging to deliver, there is always a trade-off between complexity, standardization, and relevance.

However, the WEF methodology is being reviewed by many leading disclosure and reporting standard-setters, including the Sustainability Accounting Standards

Board (SASB), the Global Reporting Initiative (GRI), the Carbon Disclosure Project (CDP), the Climate Disclosure Standards Board (CDSB), and the International Integrated Reporting Council (IIRC). Perhaps this is because the approach is intended to build on the existing frameworks from established providers, which in some cases cater to industry sector biases, rather than reinventing the wheel.

REMEMBER

The WEF metrics are built on four pillars, encompassing a number of ESG factors:

>> **People:** Diversity reporting, wage gaps, and health and safety

>> **Planet:** Greenhouse gas emissions, land protection, and water use

>> **Prosperity:** Employment and wealth generation, taxes paid, and research and development expenses

>> **Principles of governance:** Purpose, strategy, and accountability informing risk and ethical behavior

WARNING

So, companies are reporting on the aforementioned ESG metrics, and the WEF move signifies a further initiative toward consistency and standardization, but the measurement and quality of ESG data continues to raise more questions than answers. Self-disclosure reporting, which is supported by the WEF and others, is subject to inconsistency, bias, and opaqueness as it's largely voluntary and still requires agreement on disclosure standards. Several areas within ESG activity aren't characterized by easily reportable numbers, don't have commonly accepted evaluation criteria, or simply don't have accepted definitions. As such, this can still leave an incomplete ESG reporting picture.

In addition, the significance and frequency of given areas of ESG activity differ from sector to sector, if not from company to company. High-level ESG metrics are accepted by investors, as they can be commonly applied across the majority of industry sectors, which allows a broad overview of their impact. Nevertheless, there is a danger of generalizing ESG reporting to a point that can be simply and reliably measured, rather than "digging into the weeds" to highlight more material matters.

Walk the walk: Committing to corporate social responsibility practices

The WEF suggestions around metrics and disclosures were produced in collaboration with the Big Four accountancy firms — Deloitte, EY (Ernst & Young), KPMG, and PwC (PricewaterhouseCoopers) — after consulting with numerous corporations, investors, international organizations, and standard-setters, and with the Impact Management Project (which provides a forum for building global consensus on how to measure, manage, and report impacts on sustainability; see www.impactmanagementproject.com/). The intention is to offer a common set of existing disclosures that produces a more coherent, thorough reporting system and a statement of intent that complements established metrics. The benefit of non-financial reporting is to further highlight issues such as climate change and social inclusion. Therefore, companies can enhance their own corporate social responsibility practices (CSR; see Chapter 7) by demonstrating to shareholders, stakeholders, and society in general that they are committed to measuring and improving their impact on the environment and society.

Interestingly, at the same time, the SEC approved changes to a shareholder proposal rule that substantially increase the ownership thresholds needed to file and resubmit proposals to company boards on ESG issues such as climate change, diversity, and excessive pay for board members. Given the positive moves made in other areas to promote ESG engagement, this amendment seems contradictory and diminishes the ability of smaller investors to highlight unsustainable practices. Shareholder resolutions are an established and effective approach to advocate changes to management, in addition to holding them accountable to make good on their CSR.

Show me the money: Identifying investment performance

ESG performance is a developing consideration in corporate valuations. In an environment where sustainability is increasingly central to business survival, companies are using ESG criteria to evaluate their non-financial performance. The development of ESG investment performance metrics has resulted in the compression of independent ratings systems, voluntary company self-disclosures along with mandatory company disclosures, annual reports, and intermittent media coverage. Even signing up to the UN SDGs places a voluntary commitment on companies to meet explicit ESG criteria, which are incorporated with investment analytics, management data, and ESG factor risks. These are all placed into an ESG "melting pot," and an alphanumeric score is produced as a proxy of ESG performance.

While nobody disputes that an ESG profile is both valued and broadly understood by many organizations, the capacity to link it to material outcomes is often missing due to the discrepancies in measuring it and the absence of a recognized methodology. Of course, the ability to incorporate the multiple aspects that can fall under the broad ESG umbrella into one indicator is challenging, as is the ability of a company to ensure that they are reporting on all of their potential liabilities. Added to this are the different risks that can be attributed to different sectors, if not the risk of failing to report on an ESG element that subsequently proves to be relevant, raising reputational risks for a company.

REMEMBER

For now, performance will have to be viewed against ESG ratings, ranking companies against given ESG criteria and measuring their performance on a sustainability scale. However, no ideal solution exists for ESG scores, which therefore must be considered subjective, if not misleading, given the lack of correlation on certain companies between different rating agencies. Nonetheless, some new services are being offered that incorporate the use of Machine Learning — Natural Language Processing (NLP) technology in particular — blended with informed human oversight, which may resolve some of these issues. In addition, harvesting multiple streams of information, and allowing the machine to learn which ones are relevant, may allow for more real-time understanding and responses to ESG issues.

Calculating Relative ESG Performance

In a constantly evolving landscape, there is still a plethora of different ESG ratings firms trying to more accurately quantify ESG performance (although consolidation has started to happen). ESG ratings grade companies against given ESG standards, evaluating their performance on a sustainability scale. By collating disparate data from annual reports, investment analytics, management data, and media coverage, and allowing for the companies' perceived exposure to ESG risks, an alphanumeric (some ratings agencies use letters and others use numbers) score is generated as a representation of ESG performance.

Unfortunately, no "golden copy" (an official, master version of a record) categorically states the ESG rating for a given company, with the ratings from different ESG scores not even correlating very well with each other. Currently, all ratings are subjective and hostage to the varying methodologies used by different providers, and they vary in consistency between sectors, regions, and the size of the business being analyzed.

WARNING

While the notion of an ESG profile is valued and largely understood by many companies, the capacity to identify tangible results is generally missing. In turn, this exacerbates and challenges a company's ability to report on their sustainability grades and investors' capability to meaningfully measure the output. This is primarily driven by the range of topics that can be considered within an ESG score. No single definition incorporates every environmental, social, and governmental action and resultant impact on a given business. Furthermore, because this is a work in progress, companies are likely to miss reporting on topics that ESG agencies feel are important, and so there is a compounding of the traditional analyst measurement issues with financial statement data, which can also lead to some massaging of available numbers. Multiply this by sector and regional considerations for companies in certain industries, and the ESG liability calculation can become complicated.

Additionally, different stakeholders express diverse priorities with respect to the appropriate relevance of 'E,' 'S,' or 'G' components within the ESG bundle, which leads to different weighting requirements for each component:

>> Shareholders may be focused on companies showing long-term profitability with high ESG ratings to imply reduced risks.

>> Consumers want to ensure that they are using products and services that leave them with a clear conscience.

>> Employees want to work for a company that is aligned with their values.

Therefore, the shareholder is expecting the company to prioritize a reduction in carbon emissions to prevent substantial fines, the consumer expects a reduction in plastic packaging, and the employee wants greater diversity and inclusion in the workforce. The company then needs to determine what prioritization it gives to meeting those requirements when evaluating its overall corporate objectives and whether any impact on its ESG score is relevant.

Moreover, how does an investor appreciate the weighting given to a specific component when the rating agency produces only an aggregated score for all three components? Also, many agencies don't provide a full description of the methodology that they use to arrive at their scores, which makes proper performance attribution difficult. Therefore, enforcing a legal requirement for disclosure at the corporate level should make data easier to compare and contrast, but this approach needs the standards mentioned earlier to ensure it isn't limited by inconsistencies. Near-time (close to real-time) data would greatly assist the process as well, allowing for a potential adjustment of ratings as corporate events occur; otherwise, companies could continue to maintain a given score until periodic updates are publicly available.

Different sectors are subject to different ESG risks and opportunities, and the timeliness of reporting from such sectors may also differ. Given the size of the chips being placed on the sustainable investment table, investors must have accurate ways to evaluate ESG performance and recognize ESG risk to enlighten the investment process. Naturally, they are looking for corporations expected to produce positive financial performance in the long term due to their ESG-driven business models when creating their investment strategy.

The following sections consider how ESG portfolios have performed relative to broader market benchmarks, such as the MSCI Europe, and more specific benchmarks, such as the S&P 500.

Against the broader market

Research from data vendor Morningstar, in June 2020, confirmed that the majority of sustainable strategies, in a sample of 745 Europe-based sustainable funds, outperformed the non-ESG funds in the broader 4,900-fund universe over one, three, five, and ten-year time periods. Previously, there had been incomplete data on sustainable funds' long-term performance due to the comparatively short track records of numerous strategies and significant variation in ESG approaches. Given that the exclusion of non-ESG compliant stocks has been the favored approach in Europe for ESG portfolios, it's fair to say that such funds may have been more concentrated than a broader market universe; however, typically the number of stocks excluded from benchmark indexes is relatively small.

Consequently, although the research doesn't state it explicitly, this may have suited fundamentally managed active strategies, as such portfolios are usually more concentrated. Alternatively, for quantitatively managed passive strategies, any exclusions tend to reduce the power of the model by reducing diversification and thus expected performance. However, historical tests have shown that if the number of excluded stocks is small, the universe is still large enough to retain most or all of its exposure.

When exploring the connection between sustainability and future investment returns, it has been conventional to consider the connection between a company's present sustainability rating and its future investment returns. More recent research has studied the relationship between positive changes in a company's sustainability rating and its future performance. Such research suggests that the best time to invest, for those looking to benefit from upgrades in companies' ESG ratings, is prior to the development being broadly recognized and remunerated by the wider market.

Of course, this raises the question "To what degree is this evidence already assimilated into stock prices?" If positive ESG ratings are already priced into highly rated stocks, an alternative strategy could be to buy the stocks with lower ESG ratings. This would mirror the general approach taken by private equity investment managers who don't ordinarily look to acquire a stake in the best-run firms, but often focus on firms with, for example, operational problems, as they have a larger potential upside when restructured. Similarly, today's ESG "dogs" could be the "rising stars" of tomorrow if they pivot and improve their ESG performance over time.

REMEMBER

Finally, ESG ratings seem to experience greater longevity than other investment factors, which has been confirmed by ESG funds and companies deemed suitable for inclusion in the broader asset allocation discussion and policy benchmarks. Traditional factors such as momentum characteristically persist for a few months at a time, whereas the impact of ESG ratings on systematic and characteristic risks have lasted for several years, according to various studies. Perhaps this suggests that a momentum-driven ESG portfolio is something to consider.

Against specific benchmarks

REMEMBER

Studies verifying positive performance from ESG- or sustainability-focused portfolios tend to highlight stocks with financially material factors. These studies show that investments in stocks with material ESG factors can produce positive returns for shareholders, whereas investing in immaterial ESG factors has little impact on returns.

An example of material factors could be an airline looking to reduce their carbon emissions or to utilize renewable energy where possible. In comparison, an investment bank could aim for similar targets, but reducing their carbon emissions, while noble, would be immaterial, although their use of renewable energy for their offices could be material. Essentially, this would entail extracting the material 'E' rating from their overall ESG rating and applying that accordingly.

Analysis of returns during the first half of 2020 show that many ESG-integrated index strategies have outperformed the broader market, such as returns from the S&P 500 Index. Studies have analyzed the performance of U.S. equity ESG indexes based on the S&P 500 Index, offered by different index providers, that have been created to reproduce broad risk-and-return characteristics while aiming for an enhanced ESG profile. While all of the ESG indexes outperformed the benchmark index, their portfolio construction entailed differences in performance where, for example, some indexes take on more active risk compared to other index strategies. This signifies that some indexes will outperform other indexes during periods when ESG strategies jointly do well; however, this degree of active exposure may not be suitable for all investors. These variances can also be explained by the different weightings given to individual stocks or sectors and the policy on exclusions adopted by each index provider.

TECHNICAL STUFF

When analyzed further, it's noticeable that this market outperformance can be largely attributed to the performance of given sector weightings in the ESG indexes compared to those in the S&P 500 Index. All of the ESG indexes showed that the sector that contributed most to relative outperformance was Information Technology (primarily the FAANG stocks — Facebook, Amazon, Apple, Netflix, and Google). Then, subject to the particular index construction approach, Industrials, Financials, and Consumer Discretionary also contributed to outperformance. However, despite suggestions to the contrary, the energy sector underweight position (due to exclusions) relative to the benchmark index, which is an anticipated theme in ESG index portfolio construction, didn't contribute much added value to the outperformance.

TIP

While many ESG indexes based around benchmark indexes have very similar characteristics and component stocks, each index provider tends to employ factors that differentiate their methodology approach. This can include indexes that prioritize diversification, through a large number of securities with a smaller ESG focus, to those that give a greater weighting to "best-in-class" ESG stocks or sector weightings, or have different exclusion rules than others. Consequently, investors seeking indexes that provide given levels of exposure to ESG should observe any key methodology differences. You can find examples of different types of index exposure here: www.msci.com/documents/1296102/17835852/MSCI-ESG-Indexes-Factsheet.pdf.

It's also worth noting the effect of demand-driven factors on performance. The growing recognition of ESG has led to a convergence of demand-driven factors, including the growth of passive ESG strategies, and the development of active approaches, which has driven "crowding" into some of the higher-rated ESG stocks while avoiding those with lower ESG ratings.

Getting a Handle on Ratings and Rankings

As frequently mentioned throughout this book, not all ESG rating agencies score the same companies' 'E,' 'S,' and 'G' components equally. This is accurate for both agencies that create aggregated ESG ratings and those that generate more granular ratings to specific 'E,' 'S,' and 'G' levels. In large part, this issue is compounded by the contrastingly high level of correlations seen between credit rating agencies in their rating of corporate default probabilities.

However, it's clear that credit ratings have been in business for a much longer period of time, the data available is more timely and standardized, and the output is more closely aligned to financial statement information. Moreover, the determination of ESG risk factors that contribute to the probability of default are easier to determine than the combination of factors that might result in financial outperformance. Nor should we forget that sell-side research analysts typically have considerably different buy, hold, and sell recommendations, despite having access to identical, publicly available financial statement information.

WARNING

As discussed earlier in this chapter, this highlights the lack of standardization, which is changing with the imposition of mandatory requirements for ESG reporting in certain jurisdictions and industry-led initiatives to overcome these problems. However, these initiatives won't answer all of the data problems and lead immediately to a solution on commonly agreed-upon inputs and outputs that everybody will adhere to automatically. The bottom line is that, as with the already more standardized stock and bond research, analysts will have different perspectives on what relevance and weighting to apply to given companies on their 'E,' 'S,' and 'G' data. Opinions drive markets, and some analysts have access to different intelligence or more timely data than other analysts, which creates a market. So, you have to accept that this is still a work in progress for the time being.

The following sections consider how ESG factors can be integrated into securities and portfolio analysis and where smart beta strategies can be incorporated alongside either of these approaches.

Securities

When ESG factors are incorporated into securities analysis, they are analyzed together with other valuation criteria. Historically it was common to integrate ESG factors using qualitative analysis; however, investors are progressively measuring and incorporating ESG factors into financial forecasting and company valuation models, in conjunction with other financial factors.

Forecasted company financials influence valuation models, such as the discounted cash flow (DCF) model, which ultimately drives the estimated value (or fair value) of a company. Investors tend to adjust forecasted financials such as operating cost, revenue, and capital expenditure for the anticipated impact of ESG factors. Given that future revenues and growth rates have a substantial impact on the fair value of a company, investors will usually guesstimate the industry growth and how much market share a specific company may gain or lose. ESG factors can be incorporated into these forecasts by amending the company's sales growth rate by a quantity that indicates the level of ESG opportunities or risks. Investors will also make assumptions about the effect of ESG factors on future operating costs and the resulting operating profit margin.

The valuation models that investors use to value a firm can then be adjusted to reflect ESG factors. Some models entail calculating a *terminal value* for a company (the anticipated value of the company at a point in the future, assuming the company generates a given level of cash flow forever), which is discounted back to the current day. A positive terminal value should increase a company's fair value; however, ESG factors might cause investors to assume that a company won't exist indefinitely. There are a lot of discussions around the possibility that given fossil fuel companies, such as coal mining, oil, and gas companies, may see their assets *stranded* (prior to the end of their economic life, no longer able to earn an economic return as a result of changes associated with the transition to a low-carbon economy), and there is doubt over the sustainability of the business model. In this situation, the terminal value may be amended to zero.

Portfolios

The jury is still out on how best to ensure consistency when integrating ESG factors into a portfolio and what the best practices are to achieve this. As such, it isn't surprising that ESG integration is applied inconsistently and asset owners aren't fully exploiting the potential advantages of ESG integration in their quest for improved risk-adjusted returns. What is clearer, though, is that institutional investors appear to be focused on integrating ESG for predominantly financial reasons in order to find improved risk-adjusted returns without altering the investment strategy and general allocations of their current portfolios. In addition, except for leading asset owners who have integrated ESG across most or all of their assets, the majority of investors haven't integrated ESG across all of their portfolios and don't apply a consistent approach in different types of allocations or mandates.

REMEMBER

Active investors can investigate (and probably have investigated) numerous routes to integrate ESG factors into their fundamental analysis or portfolio construction, but passive, indexed investors have little choice other than to maintain all or most index components. Active engagement is gaining favor as an effective means to support sustainable long-term growth and risk management, but constant engagement can be expensive and challenging to conduct on a different scale. Thus, as with the wider market, many investors are taking a passive approach and looking to integrate ESG directly into the design of customized index investments or established indexes that meet their requirements, offering them access to an approach that systematically integrates ESG ratings. The general advantages of index investing are equally applicable to ESG-focused index investing.

Nonetheless, there is a need for further tracking measures so that investors can understand their own position on ESG. The following list of metrics can act as a checklist to ensure that relevant issues have been considered:

>> **Wide-ranging data,** beyond company disclosures, either voluntary or mandatory

>> **Perceptible data,** which enables scores to be connected to their fundamental drivers

>> **Meticulous scoring,** both for overall ESG performance and material ESG issues

>> **Sector-specific grouping and weighting,** using industry best practices, such as the SASB standard taxonomy

>> **Sector benchmarking,** understanding a company's profile compared to similar firms in the space

>> **Real-time reporting,** to mirror the speed with which ESG issues are developing

>> **Stakeholder specificity,** to reflect the opposing needs and views that different stakeholders have

These elements need to reflect the reality of continuously changing viewpoints and real-time enquiry of multiple content channels to derive an ESG score. To supplement their strength, any scores could be indexed against benchmark indicators. As stated earlier, the use of Machine Learning and NLP technology would improve the effective analysis of such data, with the goal to produce a reliable, objective view of ESG risk and exposure.

Not the sharpest tool: Smart beta

Smart beta strategies are generally defined as a set of investment strategies that stress the use of alternative index construction rules to traditional market capitalization–based indexes. These strategies are increasingly used in investment analysis to determine portfolio selection and optimization, particularly with respect to ESG factors. To validate the impact of integration between ESG and smart beta analysis, investors tend to employ portfolio-rebalancing methodologies based on the ESG scores of selected securities according to different smart beta strategies. It's then possible to apply different smart beta approaches to sustainable portfolios, screened according to the issuers' ESG scores (for example, using a "best-in-class" screening approach).

Studies have shown that both ESG rebalancing and screening approaches can impact both return and risk statistics but with different levels of effectiveness, depending on the smart beta strategy that is employed. For example, ESG rebalancing tends to be more efficient when it's applied to a values-based portfolio. Alternatively, when smart beta is applied to ESG-screened portfolios, growth-based portfolios tend to be the strategies that show the largest increase in risk-adjusted performance, particularly in the U.S. equity markets. These are particularly interesting conclusions when markets are mulling over a rotational shift from growth- to values-based stocks, or vice versa.

Developing Frameworks for Reporting

REMEMBER

Companies considering the potential implementation of an ESG disclosure framework should be aware of the variety of reporting standards that have been developed. Different frameworks can address different cross-sections of ESG issues and have different concepts of what factors are material. A few of the more frequently used frameworks are mentioned here:

- >> **GRI:** The Global Reporting Initiative is the world's most widely used standard for sustainability reporting, helping businesses, governments, and other organizations understand and communicate their impacts on issues such as climate change, human rights, and corruption.

- >> **SASB:** The SASB framework provides sector-specific guidance on a wide range of ESG topics, including greenhouse gas (GHG) emissions, energy and water management, data security, and employee health and safety, while providing sector-specific guidelines emphasizing topics that the SASB believes are material. (By the way, SASB stands for Sustainability Accounting Standards Board.)

- >> **TCFD:** The TCFD framework provides general and sector-specific guidance, but only on climate-related topics, such as physical risks of the effects of climate change and climate-related opportunities, and also includes resource efficiencies and alternative energy sources. The TCFD framework has been endorsed and incorporated into mandatory reporting regimes by regulators in the European Union, United Kingdom, and Hong Kong. (TCFD, if you're wondering, stands for Task Force on Climate-related Financial Disclosures.)

Some frameworks approach the notion of materiality in noticeably differently ways from the SASB and TCFD, which focus on information they believe to be financially material. In contrast, the GRI's framework, which covers issues from labor and human rights issues to effects on biodiversity, measures materiality based on impacts on the economy, the environment, and society.

The following sections consider which ESG objectives are relevant to investors with different perspectives and how they maintain compliance with regulatory requirements.

In your view: ESG objectives

REMEMBER

Many large companies incorporate sustainable objectives in the creation of their global strategies, but in countless cases many of those objectives aren't well expressed or measurable, thus reducing their contribution to the industry's transformation. Moreover, establishing ESG objectives needs to follow a long-term approach, given that short-term objectives encourage a short-term thinking process that restricts growth and real change. Ideally, objectives should be linked to a reference point in order to set improvements and specific dates to enable their achievement.

As stated earlier, an increasing body of research advocates that ESG factors have added to long-term financial performance. ESG factors are used to pinpoint better-managed businesses or identify companies with business models that are likely to face challenges or opportunities propelled by quickly developing demographic, environmental, regulatory, or technological trends. Investors are progressively relying on ESG factors to highlight and control these risks and to contribute toward long-term sustainable financial performance. While most investors will still invest with a specific emphasis on financial performance, they are more mindful of creating wealth within a healthy planet and social ecosystems environment.

Countless investors consider ESG topics to be a way to align investments with ethical, religious, or political beliefs. They generally use ESG research as a way to exclude controversial businesses such as alcohol, gambling, fossil fuels, tobacco, and weapons from their investment universe. Contrary to ESG integration goals based on their potential economic impact, many investors align their beliefs with values-based objectives that are meant to generate an impact that will make a difference to the world around them. Larger investors may look to invest capital directly in companies providing solutions to environmental or social challenges, and observe the degree to which those investments are generating positive social or environmental impacts along with any financial returns.

For example, traditional ESG objectives were meant to reduce the negative impact of companies' activities, but more recent transformational objectives expect to make changes to the entire value chain and to society. Moreover, sustainability rankings promote establishing ambitious sustainable objectives, enabling companies to ensure a better position for ESG-related bond issues, which is an increasingly competitive market. Lest we forget, good governance objectives are important in allowing the incorporation of ESG factors into the investment processes and internal decision-making for companies. Addressing and mitigating potential issues now, and on a long-term basis, is an effective way to minimize future risks and improve their corporate image toward investors and society in general.

REMEMBER

The fundamental objectives for the transformation of the industry are those of good governance, because they drive the evolution process from the start, with new policies and internal procedures facilitating the establishment of strategic action plans. The long-term objectives, as well as the agreed-upon ESG measures, must be quantifiable to allow companies to progressively monitor their achievements, so that they can broadcast the level of compliance of their commitments in an accurate and transparent way. Long-term ESG objectives help companies enhance risk management, improve business profitability, "refurbish" and augment their brand image, and safeguard that these objectives are met. Likewise, these metrics foster an approach toward the notion of positive net value to society, an approach that is starting to be shared among corporates and their stakeholders, as well as with the wider society.

Play by the rules: ESG compliance

Driven by emerging themes like social value and impact investing, and coupled with the highlighted concerns for the climate crisis and net-zero targets, disclosures are becoming common practice among companies across all industries. While such disclosures might originally have been at the behest of investors and stakeholders, current requirements are focused on addressing the regulatory compliance risk associated with non-disclosure or disclosures that aren't accurate, correct, or complete. This has highlighted the vital role that compliance officers need to perform in this process and the fact that ESG issues have risen in the board agenda.

A good example of this is the European Union "taxonomy regulation," introduced in 2020, where all financial products claiming to be "sustainable" will need to have verification that the defined economic activities are assumed to be sustainable (they have currently mapped out climate change mitigation and adaptation, are working on environmental issues, and are determining how to approach social issues). Prior to this, pension funds and intermediaries could sell and label financial products as "sustainable" without any independent review of these claims, and the regulators were concerned about the potential for greenwashing (covered in Chapter 6). In addition, the NFRD requires large EU "public interest" corporations to publish data on the impact their activities have on ESG factors. Meanwhile, all UK companies are expected to disclose against TCFD by 2022.

Furthermore, disclosures are increasingly required by insurers, investors, and lenders due to the growing awareness of the impact that non-financial risks can inflict on the financial stability and sustainability of investments. The United Nations Principles for Responsible Investing (PRI) is an example of the type of framework used to disclose how capital flows. Some of the PRI signatories are incorporating non-financial elements into the investment decision process, including climate change and ESG screening. To meet these conflicting demands, it's important for firms to recognize who is requesting the non-financial disclosures, the particular disclosures they require, and what they are using them for. Disclosure and reporting is time-consuming and resource-intensive, so it's important to identify the most relevant content in an efficient way for the specific stakeholder.

Meet the players: Comparing different frameworks

REMEMBER

Different frameworks focus on different stakeholder groups. Some focus on specific topics, such as climate change, while others require broader disclosure on an array of ESG topics. In addition, some frameworks may focus on guidance for a general stakeholder audience, such as sustainability reports, whereas others are meant to be included alongside financial disclosures, and so are more appropriate to guide investment decisions by security holders. Moreover, there is a growing trend from institutional investors to issue their own guidelines in support of, for example, SASB or TCFD standards. BlackRock requires that their investee companies produce disclosures in line with industry-specific SASB guidelines and climate-related risks in line with the TCFD's recommendations. A failure to comply will be seen as an indication that the company isn't effectively managing ESG risk and could lead to divestment.

It's also important to recognize that corporations with international operations may be subject to jurisdiction-specific ESG disclosure requirements. For example, U.S. firms operating in Europe may be subject to EU regulations on sustainability-related disclosures in the financial services sector, regardless of the jurisdiction or tax domicile of the company. In comparison, the United States currently has no mandatory ESG disclosure requirements. Consequently, it may be even more important for sustainability teams at U.S. corporations to enhance their ESG disclosures if they are competing for capital against economies with more rigorous ESG disclosure obligations.

Of course, following entities such as the SASB voluntary guidelines to report sustainability issues considered financially material to investors is a strong alternative. Currently 195 companies, with US$60 trillion of assets under management, are using their standards for sustainability reporting. Not to be forgotten, over 40 stock exchanges around the world also offer ESG guidance to issuers, this approach being launched under the Sustainable Stock Exchanges banner back in 2015.

ESG reporting requirements may also be enforced under some material legal contracts, for example, where sustainability-linked loans and bonds require borrowers and issuers to measure and report on given ESG performance metrics that establish the interest payable under the loan or bond. In such cases, the metrics may be based on standards developed by credit rating agencies that now incorporate ESG factors in their ratings reports. Therefore, issuers now need to consider ESG issues in their discussions with credit rating agencies. Similarly, companies also pay more attention to whether they are included in benchmark indexes, because if exchange-traded funds (ETFs) and other funds continue to receive the "wall of funds" that has been invested in ESG funds, their stock price may benefit indirectly. However, these ESG-linked indexes have their own criteria and standards for inclusion.

REMEMBER

Given that there are so many issues to comply with, companies should create a cross-functional team, which could include dedicated sustainability resources, investor relations, risk, legal, compliance, finance, and human resources. In many companies, investor relations tend to own the reporting function, but given the alignment with financial reporting, the finance team would seem to be the appropriate place for collation and analysis to take place going forward. Given the growing number of reporting frameworks, it can be difficult for firms to determine how best to report, and solutions will continue to differ depending on the sector they operate in, the size of the company, and the range of stakeholders they need to placate! The following questions generally need to be considered:

>> **Does the data comply with regulatory reporting requirements?**
Companies need to produce coordinated and structured policies for measuring and reporting purpose-led metrics.

>> **How strong are the internal controls, to ensure that data is reliable and accurate, in line with financial reporting?** Companies need to support metrics that are reported externally with those used by management to run the company.

>> **Is there a requirement to obtain (third-party) assurance on any data reported?** Companies need to employ controls over the preparation and reporting with the same attention as was given to controls for traditional financial reporting.

>> **Does the company have a consistent communication message across all stakeholders?** Companies need to offer comparison figures to establish consistency.

Table 14-1 gives you an overview of the frameworks and how they compare and contrast.

TABLE 14-1 **Comparison of the Alternative ESG Reporting Frameworks and What They Cover**

Framework	Disclosures	Industry	Standard or Framework/ Guidelines	Main Audience
CDP (www.cdp.net)	Specific coverage of climate change, supply chain, water, and forests	Selected industries	Framework	Investors and customers
Global ESG Benchmark for Real Assets (GRESB; www.gresb.com)	Multiple indicators across Economic, Environment, and Social	Real estate	Standard (indexes)	Investors
Global Reporting Initiative (GRI; www.globalreporting.org/)	Multiple standards across Economic, Environment, and Social	Industry agnostic	Standard and framework	Multiple stakeholder groups

(continued)

TABLE 14-1 *(continued)*

Framework	Disclosures	Industry	Standard or Framework/ Guidelines	Main Audience
International Integrated Reporting Council (IIRC; www.integratedreporting.org/)	Framework that covers all financial and non-financial issues	Industry agnostic	Framework	Multiple stakeholder groups
International Standards Organization (ISO; www.iso.org)	Topic-specific standards such as greenhouse gases (GHG) and energy management	Industry agnostic	Standard	Multiple stakeholder groups
Sustainability Accounting Standards Board (SASB; www.sasb.org/)	Multiple disclosures across Economic, Environment, and Social	Industry specific	Standard	Investors
Task Force on Climate-related Financial Disclosures (TCFD; www.tcfdhub.org/)	Climate change–specific	Selected industries	Framework	Investors, lenders, and insurers
United Nations Principles of Responsible Investment (PRI; www.unpri.org/)	Topic-specific questions within the questionnaire relating to investment impacts such as climate change	Financial	Framework	Investors
United Nations Sustainable Development Goals (SDGs; https://sdgs.un.org/goals)	SDGs cover all issues	Industry agnostic	Guidelines	Multiple stakeholder groups
World Economic Forum (WEF; http://www3.weforum.org/docs/WEF_IBC_Measuring_Stakeholder_Capitalism_Report_2020.pdf)	Multiple disclosures across Economic, Environment, and Social	Industry agnostic	Framework	Multiple stakeholder groups

Chapter **15**

Elaborating the ESG Endgame

Earlier chapters in this book primarily outline the different aspects of the ESG landscape, from getting started to investing through different instruments, and then to applying the ESG philosophy for corporations and asset owners. The final chapter in this part brings these elements together and summarizes where the market is heading based on which players are looking to collaborate and how they can promote ESG into the Premier League.

Highlighting the Evolution of ESG from Niche to Mainstream Strategy

If you've read earlier chapters (especially Chapter 7), you're aware that responsible investing strategies aren't new, with the term "ESG" actually being devised as far back as 2004, while the idea of socially responsible investing has been around much longer. Nonetheless, while following such strategies was once the exception, it's now very much the norm, with more than 3,000 signatories, representing over US$100 trillion, signed up to the United Nations–backed Principles for Responsible Investment.

REMEMBER

Detecting and managing risks, and discovering and capitalizing on business opportunities, are the two mainstays of capital market–focused, responsible investing, namely ESG investment strategies. The principle that ESG integration doesn't harm portfolio returns — in fact, more recently, it has been outperforming the market — is intuitive because businesses with good ESG practices represent safer investments. On the contrary, businesses with poor ESG practices tend to be riskier.

Traditionally, institutional investors understood that prudent ESG practices such as good governance, strong shareholder rights, and transparency are positives for investors in any company. However, investing sustainably with ESG criteria was, until recently, a new concept; now, it has almost become standard among institutional investors. This is partly due to a growing concern among institutions about realizing competitive financial returns together with a positive social and environmental impact, and partly because governments and regulators have placed ESG much higher on the agenda of institutional investors.

The value of global assets employing ESG data to power investment decisions has doubled over four years, and more than tripled over eight years, to more than US$40 trillion in 2020. If the last decade saw ESG become mainstream, the coming decade will bring a new wave of shareholder-driven accountability from the world's largest companies, as you find out in the following sections.

Achieving competitive financial returns with positive ESG impact

The inflow of funds, predominantly in equities, has grown tremendously in the last two years, with sustainable open-end funds and exchange-traded funds (ETFs) in the third quarter of 2020 hitting a record high of US$1.2 trillion, while Europe exceeded the US$1 trillion mark for the first time. The United States accounted for 12 percent of the global inflows, while Europe continued to dominate the space with approximately 77 percent.

Meanwhile, the total net inflows in ESG ETFs more than tripled to US$32 billion in assets under management (AUM) as of November 30, 2020. To put that into perspective, it took ESG ETFs around 2 years to achieve US$1 billion in assets, 12 more years to reach US$5 billion in assets, and then just 2 years to reach a US$32 billion AUM score! And the general consensus is that ESG strategies don't result in inferior returns versus conventional portfolios. Indeed, in 2020, where you've seen equities make all-time highs while also exhibiting the fastest market slump in history, ESG strategies have mostly outperformed the most popular conventional passive ETFs. (Flip to Chapter 8 for more on equities.)

Also, ESG strategies are benefiting from a new trend away from growth stocks and into values-based investing, prompted by the COVID-19 and oil crises of 2020. Moreover, investors have been able to observe the performance of ESG portfolios through historic bear and bull markets from 2018 to 2020, and the returns over that longer period have also been favorable to ESG strategies relative to conventional passive indexes and ETFs. ESG-orientated strategies' performance experienced a low-volatility rally in 2017, a sharp pullback in the fourth quarter of 2018, one of the greatest years for equity markets in 2019, and the fastest market slump in history in the first quarter of 2020 through the COVID-19 crisis.

REMEMBER

For ESG strategies to grow so much during such a trying time and to show robust returns is a testimony to their durability. The more research that shows there is no material difference between the investment performance of responsible investment funds and traditional investment funds, the more likely it is that ESG integration will continue.

Emphasizing the need for common terminology

However, to enable a change in allocation and strategy, asset owners may still need greater confidence in investors' ability to correctly price potential longer-term risks and opportunities. Market participants, as well as regulators and policy makers, are seeking common terminology and standards to be able to identify sector-specific ESG factors and quantify the capital variance of more sustainable enterprises.

Advancing globally recognized principles and Key Performance Indicators (KPIs), including transparency, governance, and environmental impact, is an important enabler for broader levels of impact investment in areas such as clean energy and other sustainable infrastructure. Allowing investors to speak the same language when evaluating investments enables them to better compare the relative merits of one asset against another. Naturally, the demand for more information is an inherent response to a broad range of issues that have been unearthed in the financial services sector in recent decades. Disclosure and transparency have become mantras in policy and in regulation, with the unintended consequence of vast reams of data, making it less obvious where the important information is buried. This can further result in companies becoming guilty of too much disclosure, or occasionally too little, when the real question is whether they are making the right disclosures that highlight material issues more succinctly. (I cover data, disclosures, and standards in more detail later in this chapter.)

This frequently happens where regulation develops a logic of its own and can be seen as the solution to every problem. Without a doubt, the demand for sustainability information will continue to grow as business models are increasingly exposed to social and environmental issues. Equally, investors need high-quality information that permits them to evaluate how companies are managing ESG issues and the impact they have on a company's long-term prospects. Sustainability frameworks and standards already exist, but investors are demanding their convergence into a single framework that will bring consistency and comparability.

Watching the Growing Use and Acceptance of ESG Standards

As ESG issues have progressively become the focal point for investors and regulators, standards of disclosure produced by intergovernmental and non-governmental organizations (NGOs), as well as market participants, have increased in market prominence, and the number of ESG disclosure standards and frameworks continues to grow. The following sections talk about the future of ESG disclosures as well as data and reporting standards.

Digging into disclosures

While many ESG disclosures are made on a voluntary basis, that's starting to change, particularly in Europe, as regulators are becoming increasingly proactive. As such, investors are gradually demanding disclosures within established ESG frameworks. For example, CDP, a global NGO that helps companies and cities disclose their environmental impact, reported that in 2020, 515 investors with US$106 trillion in assets and over 147 large purchasers with over US$4 trillion in procurement spending have requested companies disclose their environmental data through CDP.

However, the increasing number of reporting standards and rating systems in the ESG disclosure arena generates new challenges for organizations, given that they may have to be evaluated by multiple frameworks. The PRI has also acknowledged that the market is calling for greater reasoning and consistency and that asset owners have requested that the PRI should do more to drive better ESG data, including the convergence of reporting standards. The PRI requested investors to participate in consultations around corporate reporting (www.unpri.org/policy/briefings-and-consultations) and to contemplate how data is used in the investment chain. It also asked whether new reporting standards are needed or whether ESG requirements should be incorporated into existing mainstream financial reporting.

Separately, the market needs to decide whether consistent and comparable standards, serving the purposes of multiple stakeholders, will be generally accepted. Meanwhile, a number of different stakeholders, including asset owners, asset managers, and proxy advisory firms, are intensifying pressure on businesses to disclose more forcefully. Lessons may be learned from reviewing the approaches of the accounting standard-setters and credit rating agencies that have many years' experience of establishing standards with market support and consolidating the results.

REMEMBER

Also, while disclosure of climate-related and other ESG issues is now largely a voluntary undertaking, that will change as political pressures cause regulators to move to more prescriptive measures. For example, market participants in Europe will have the Sustainable Finance Disclosure Regulation (SFDR) reporting obligations beginning in March 2021. The increased focus across many segments of society on ESG themes will mean that ESG topics will feature with increasing importance, and as these trends take hold, you should also anticipate more demand for harmonized disclosure measures. On this note it's encouraging to see some of the predominant disclosure framework providers coming together to address some of the confusion, duplication, and educational issues around reporting sustainable information.

The Global Reporting Initiative (GRI), International Integrated Reporting Council (IIRC), Sustainability Accounting Standards Board (SASB), Carbon Disclosure Project (CDP), and Climate Disclosure Standards Board (CDSB) set the frameworks and standards for sustainability disclosure, including climate-related reporting, for the overwhelming majority of quantitative and qualitative disclosures, alongside recommendations from the Task Force on Climate-related Financial Disclosures (TCFD). These organizations have recently announced that they are working to produce an approach to a comprehensive corporate reporting system. This building-blocks approach will provide market guidance on how to navigate the maze of frameworks and standards so that they can be applied in a complementary way.

Moreover, they are working with the International Organization of Securities Commissions (IOSCO), the International Financial Reporting Standards (IFRS), the European Commission, and the World Economic Forum's International Business Council to determine an approach that complements generally accepted accounting principles (GAAP). In short, having navigated through the alphabet soup of acronyms for all of these eminent bodies, this should lead toward the desired common standards for reporting while integrating material factors into current financial reporting!

WARNING

At the time of this writing, this all sounds extremely positive, but it's a starting point for progress, and although NGOs aren't profit-making organizations, there are sufficient egos at the table and red tape to scuttle sensible collaboration! Furthermore, what seems like progress for some can still lead to confusion and overbearing requirements for others, particularly when all-encompassing mandatory regulation is overlaid on top. Mandatory reporting can be summarized as "more rather than less," with requests for information that seem intent on making it impossible to differentiate material from immaterial values. If integration into accounting principles is to be achieved, isolation of material values will be needed. Then, it's just a case of determining explicit valuations for those values.

Providing data consistency

So, once the reporting requirements are covered, there is just the small matter of gaining a clearer picture of how ESG factors impact a company's long-term performance! When the preparation of comparable, reliable information is achieved, asset managers can more readily consume material data via the growing variety of data aggregators, analytics providers, ratings, and index providers that already exist. In principle, they should better understand how ESG ratings are derived, be able to focus on the ESG data providers for the markets they are targeting, and recognize what in-house research they need to enhance the external data they have received. Simple!

REMEMBER

For sure, ESG ratings have helped mainstream sustainable investing by enabling the integration of ESG issues and perceptions into the investment vocabulary. Ratings have fostered greater recognition of ESG issues while helping to educate the investment community and other stakeholders on where those topics are relevant to business. They have also added credibility by validating ESG assessment and analysis into packaged products, which have allowed more integration of sustainability topics. Therefore, while the naysayers will question their methodology and resilience, ESG ratings have helped drive sustainability forward as a primary investment thesis.

Asset managers and investors have progressively been using ESG ratings to more effectively inform their investment decisions. However, there isn't a single, accepted methodology for calculating ESG ratings — nor should there be, some would argue, as different assessments are what drives a market. Moreover, unlike with the non-profit NGOs, the ESG data providers are fully focused on extracting the economic rent from a growing, fragmented market rather than considering collaboration and standardization of methodology. With the growing consolidation, as outlined further in Chapter 18, there is increasing competition in this space, and many of the established index and credit rating providers are adding more ESG capability to their existing offerings. This doesn't help asset managers or owners when determining a "fair valuation" for the ESG pricing component of a given stock. Therefore, some financial technology (FinTech) firms are looking at ways to aggregate disparate ESG scores for different entities. But will basic aggregation allow more of a clear indication of the spread between values than an understanding of the underlying drivers for the scores themselves?

Further complicating these issues is that most data used in ESG ratings is backward-looking, which makes it difficult to predict how resilient companies are to future risks without the aid of complementary data analysis. Also, many investors are interested in understanding how breaking news around ESG factors can be incorporated into stock price movements, and whether the news is sufficient to require them to exclude a company from the portfolio. Natural Language Processing (NLP) allows companies to ingest unstructured data, such as text or speech, interpret it, measure sentiment, and determine which parts of the data are important. This enables the receipt of alerts in a consistent, unbiased way that allows an investor to be aware of a material event with respect to an underlying investment.

REMEMBER

Therefore, investor expectations of future ratings include the provision of real-time data, which can be integrated into traditional financial reporting and research. They also anticipate that companies will develop their reasoning around ESG to focus on material data factors, which allows investors to assess the impacts of products more easily. For some investors, this can be interpreted as requiring greater comparability between ratings to find a common score or rating. These investors tend to have fewer resources available internally to review the differences between the ratings and to glean their own additional understanding from the disparate scores. However, other investors value the ratings' diversity because they have internal analysts who have conducted more in-depth research on a given company or topic and are using the ratings to challenge their interpretations. This dichotomy isn't new, as similar differences can exist between passive and active managers for more conventional financial reporting today, with some being happy to take the analysts' consensus number while others value the diversity of analysts' views.

Developing national and international financial reporting standards

As mentioned earlier, the independent sustainability standard-setters, together with the integrated reporting framework providers, are now collaborating to deliver a basis for development of a more comprehensive corporate reporting system. The optimal combination of framework and standards should help companies provide, and users accept, more complete information. At the core of this concept is agreement, wherever possible, on a shared set of sustainability topics and associated disclosure requirements. Achieving this goal would ensure that companies can gather information about performance on a given sustainability topic once, and utilize that information to meet the needs of alternative users and their objectives. This would enable reduced misunderstandings and costs for producers and users of information, and encourage companies to invest in the robust controls and systems that are essential to confirm information comparable with financial reporting.

Given that organizations are accountable to multiple stakeholders, disclosure needs to incorporate standards that meet the needs of a broad range of users and should achieve interoperability through related disclosure requirements. Interoperability can be achieved through a formal collaboration model, such as GRI's due process, where a reporting organization identifies its material impacts on the economy, environment, and people, with the SASB's conceptual framework and due-process-filtering disclosure requirements to identify whether they are relevant for enterprise value creation.

The SASB and the CDSB have already communicated to the market their corresponding and interlinking benefits, particularly with the co-branded publications of the *TCFD Implementation Guide* and the *Good Practice Handbook* (see www.cdsb. net/tcfd-good-practice-handbook). These documents unite the CDSB's guiding principles and reporting requirements with the SASB's industry-specific metrics to offer a combined solution for companies seeking to report in line with TCFD recommendations. Moreover, sustainability disclosure that is material for enterprise value should ideally be disclosed with information already reflected in the annual financial accounts. Therefore, connecting this with financial GAAP and allowing integrated reporting as the conceptual framework should be the target. Indeed, work is underway to engage with the IOSCO and the IFRS Foundation to ensure that such enterprise value creation is linked to financial GAAP.

Interestingly, despite its greater longevity, there are still at least three fundamental problems of financial reporting disclosure that are similar to the issues facing sustainability disclosure:

>> **Relevance and materiality of disclosures are subjective judgments,** where there will always be instances where participants disagree over what might be relevant and material to disclose.

>> **In both instances, disclosure reporting has elements of self-reporting bias,** given that you're "marking your own homework"! Even where financial reporting is heavily regulated, a degree of bias can be expected, given that it

reflects a foreseeable degree of managerial optimism about the firm's continuing prospects.

>> **It isn't in a company's interest to be too transparent,** as some disclosures may highlight valuable information to competitors or contractors. Such information may be considered as proprietary, and under financial reporting, the losses or reduced gains caused by its disclosure are often referred to as "proprietary costs."

REMEMBER

It's also important to consider that countries differ in the extent to which third parties provide reporting assurance. Financial statements have historically been accompanied by an audit statement from a third party, supplying certification of the reported financial numbers. Furthermore, in contrast to sustainability reports, financial statements can be audited only by regulated entities that have been verified and allowed to audit and sign financial statements. Consequently, third-party assurance should be an important element of corporate sustainability reporting, and the broader corporate governance field, as it augments the credibility of reported numbers. In turn, improved credibility establishes the level of trust that stakeholders place on managerial disclosure. But currently, there are no universally accepted auditing principles to guide the certification process of a sustainability report. This needs to be addressed so that the gains for users requesting assurance for regulatory disclosures aren't outweighed by the costs.

RECOGNIZING EUROPE'S ESG LEADERSHIP

In any move toward standardization, recognition should be given to Europe's role in leading the charge on mandatory reporting, and lessons should be learned from their experience in 2021. Furthermore, the European Commission has shown significant leadership in proposing a 1 trillion Euro "Green Deal," which is a pledge to transform the 27-country bloc from a high- to a low-carbon economy, without reducing prosperity and while improving people's quality of life, through cleaner air and water, better health, and a thriving natural world. Europe is in a prime position to mandate all building blocks, which achieves the global standards model accompanied by explicit jurisdictional regulatory requirements.

In addition, the EU Taxonomy for sustainable finance provides a further example of how global standards can be supplemented by jurisdictional requirements. Therefore, including Europe to achieve any global solution is a necessary step.

Looking at the Increasing Impact of ESG Ratings and Rankings

The rapid expansion of the ESG ecosystem has been propelled by increased corporate reporting, which has helped generate new sources of ESG data. For example, from 2011 to 2018 the number of S&P 500 companies producing sustainability reports increased from 20 percent to 86 percent. Ratings agencies use a combination of such company disclosures, publicly accessible resources, and their own proprietary research. Some providers will also use NLP technologies to scrape relevant news and development stories from the internet that might affect the company's rating. While there are a significant number of agencies (a number that is falling due to consolidation in the business), not many can currently say that they have global coverage, although this is equally true for conventional research coverage of global stocks. As a result, some new ESG providers are emerging to provide coverage for Greater China stocks.

WARNING

Meanwhile, in the broader market, some investors and managers are struggling to maintain resources on ESG ratings data collection and reporting. Some companies can require hundreds of hours and multiple dedicated staff members, which larger organizations may also struggle to support. Therefore, a growing number of investors may find that small and mid-sized companies aren't able to produce the information they want. Also, investors and asset managers tend to use ESG ratings differently. Some participants have fully embedded ESG, while others are just starting to employ it, in some cases in a relatively ad hoc manner. These differences in approach highlight the differences in how firms use ESG ratings, with smaller firms relying more heavily on provided ratings, and larger firms possibly referring to the ratings to supplement their own in-house research.

Certainly, ESG ratings (covered in detail in Chapter 14) can be used as a launching pad to better comprehend the landscape and to benchmark companies against each other, while poor ratings may signal the need to do further research or exclude such firms from ESG investment products or portfolios. Some managers may use ratings to directly inform investment decisions, which can be driven by a rush to meet a growing demand for ESG investment products. Alternatively, where they are issuing passive, index-based products, managers can benefit from the considerable work already invested by the index provider. However, some of their active management peers may argue that rapidly created, inferior-quality products may weaken overall demand in the long term, or they may even accuse them of "greenwashing" (see Chapter 6). Many active managers may only use the data to inform their own internal research, KPIs, or scoring methodologies, before establishing their own view on a company's rating.

Investors highlight corporate ESG ratings, engagement with companies, in-house research, and corporate sustainability reports as the most valuable sources of ESG information. They frequently use more than one rating agency to access multiple opinions and regularly assess which ratings agency they should use. Some of the factors that they appreciate from providers include the number of companies covered, the quality and disclosure of the rating methodology behind the score, a greater focus on material issues, the reliability of data sources, and the experience and credibility of the research team. Equally, investors want companies to deliver better ESG data disclosure, concentrate on the most material factors for the business, and more fully amalgamate ESG information into financial statements. Regular reporting, real-time information, ESG data in one place, and better observations on how leadership incorporates ESG, and where it fits relative to company strategy, need to be combined to meet investors' needs. On a stand-alone basis, climate is a common concern, with investors looking for guidance on climate exposure in accord with TCFD guidelines.

REMEMBER

Asset managers and owners are generally looking for the "ideal" rating system, but the reality is that no one is there yet, and it can depend on the investment strategy being pursued, the investment process being executed, and the risk/return profile being sought. For example, it's easier to find ESG ratings for predominantly large-cap international companies; however, if you're looking for coverage of companies in emerging markets, then you may need to perform a more localized search, including subscribing to data providers with a broader coverage of data. More broadly, it's unusual to see a reliance on a single source of ESG data, as portfolio managers wouldn't have sufficient confidence in one source to influence their investment decisions. Firms are looking to augment provider-based ESG data sets with material from their engagement/stewardship functions to create a more informed view on stocks and bonds. Active managers have a strong sense of which ESG factors are most important in a sector, and developing their own evaluation of a company is critical.

Despite improvements in ratings, there are still some issues around data errors or use of old or backward-looking data, and no "silver bullet" allows a company to be distilled down into a single ESG score, or one go-to rating agency. Different agencies have different strengths, from broad coverage to climate coverage or governance scoring. The following sections discuss two areas of decision-making in regard to ratings and rankings: qualitative and quantitative.

Qualitative decisions

Qualitative, bottom-up fundamental analysis is still a core approach for many investment firms and asset managers, particularly active managers, and that's no different for fundamental ESG research, where investors have established their own KPIs and ESG ratings are only one data point in a larger body of research. ESG ratings alone don't drive investment decisions, with many managers more interested in the data underlying ESG ratings scores than the scores themselves, as they use ratings as an opening point to help them appreciate the bigger picture. Scores can also be used as a signal for further research or company engagement, or as a catalyst to exclude or identify best-in-class equities for explicit ESG products.

Furthermore, some suggest that the better research and ratings are provided by sell-side analysts at banks who have covered any industry for a number of years and have a very good understanding of the companies within it. ESG ratings analysts need to cover hundreds of companies and therefore can't know them all well. However, by using artificial intelligence (AI), they can pick up given relationships or issues that mainstream analysts can't uncover, either because they can't ingest all of the data or because they are inherently biased to looking at the company from a given perspective.

REMEMBER

Active managers tend to have a sixth sense for which ESG factors are most significant to a sector and develop their own assessment of a company. They rely on their own KPIs, instruments, methods, and ratings to fully calculate corporate ESG performance, and it's principally their in-house investment research that shapes the foundation for any investment decisions, rather than one externally sourced ESG rating. However, they can be used to help benchmark a company against peers, to identify leaders and laggards, or to get a general sense for the ESG arena within a given sector. Understanding the underlying, fundamental issues that determine how to translate ESG issues into investment completion is the qualitative approach to determine investment outcomes.

REMEMBER

Investors want both ratings providers and companies to emphasize material issues and to communicate in a meaningful way how those issues tie to their business strategy. They are looking for rating providers to determine the tangible ESG impact of the products (both positive and negative) that a company produces. What the company does is just as imperative as how it operates. Therefore, there is a desire for ratings to better rationalize how dynamic ESG issues, such as climate change, will affect a company's product mix and business performance.

Quantitative decisions

The core challenge for all investors is that information isn't consistently reported, so you can't use a reliable metric in the same way that financial analysts are used to sourcing their information. The rating agencies try to resolve this issue by combining different ESG factors together into a number for every company, but if you look closer, the underlying data is missing. This is predominantly because primary disclosures for companies aren't reliable and won't be until the disclosure collaboration, mentioned earlier in this chapter, enables consistency and accuracy rather than subjectivity.

REMEMBER

The more robust and reliable reporting can get, the better served investors will be, enabled by better ESG data scores. Some quantitative investors want to use the resultant raw data systematically as an integral part of their proprietary process. Consequently, they need to efficiently gather ESG data to feed these internal scoring and analysis mechanisms.

Moreover, investors want to collect and compile timely ESG data in a way that minimizes time spent by analysts gathering information. They want ESG ratings (especially controversy ratings) to be more frequently updated to help with real-time decision-making. Additionally, they want the data to be more easily accessible with higher-quality summaries and shorter, more digestible reports, combined with greater transparency around rating methodologies. Many managers are buying multiple rating providers' data and discarding the scores, as they aren't considered to be accurate, and creating their own scoring and undertaking their own analysis.

An area in which different investors are torn is whether it's better to push greater comparability and ratings standardization or to keep ratings differentiated. Some argue for harmonization across ratings, expecting them to become more comparable. Others argue that each rating generates a unique perspective on a company, and while they have the capacity to scan across multiple ratings, there is value in dissimilar types of insights. However, at the same time they warn investors to be wary of the caveats with ratings.

Finally, investors want greater incorporation of relevant ESG information into financial reporting and believe that doing so will help advance the quality of ratings. They also want ESG information to be integrated into credit ratings and sell-side analysis to support investment research. By better connecting sustainability to financial impact, both companies and ESG research suppliers will empower stronger investment research.

Improving Education

REMEMBER

In order for responsible investing to continue to flourish, it's important that both investors and companies are educated in how to identify the traits of a well-run, sustainable company, and how ESG data and scores can be used to build that engagement, respectively. These two elements are covered earlier in this chapter; however, further education needs to be considered with respect to other elements mentioned throughout this book, including the following:

>> An understanding of the importance of the UN Sustainable Development Goals (SDGs; see Chapter 1) and how they guide ESG

- An appreciation of the ESG factors (see Chapters 3, 4, and 5) — in particular, net-zero emissions and climate change, inclusion, and diversity, and the ramifications of the COVID-19 pandemic, as well as the role of stewardship, engagement, and the purpose of a company

- Awareness of the tectonic plates of disclosure reporting moving toward collaboration and standardization (see Chapter 14)

- Knowledge of the potential integration of disclosure reporting into financial reporting standards and procedures

- Embracing of the opportunities afforded by the impact of change on the greater accuracy, transparency, and adoption of ESG ratings with a greater focus on material issues

- Monitoring of the ever-growing assets under management, driven by sustainability and ESG investing and benefitting from that awareness

The following sections talk about ESG education for both individual investors and companies.

What do investors believe is important?

REMEMBER

In general, investors want as much information as possible on what's driving ESG ratings for given companies, as well as more clarity around how those ratings are scored. Particularly where the separate elements of 'E,' 'S,' and 'G' are presented as one aggregate score, it's difficult to understand what may be driving that rating. Therefore, it's wise to monitor when a company receives significantly diverse ratings from different rating providers, and use that as a signal to scrutinize the reasons behind the disparate ESG ratings. This is why a number of asset managers suggest that they use ratings as a guide to their analysis but then use their own data and KPIs to understand the position better.

Another approach is to understand how a company's key investors are using ESG ratings and research to recognize which issues they believe are essential for the company and sector, and what data they use to determine this. Asset managers will also monitor how they are approaching their analysis relative to their peers, particularly when this results in significant differences in performance. It's also important to monitor changes in a company's ESG rating and whether that pushes a company further toward the bottom or top of its peer set within a given sector. This is particularly true when it could result in the exclusion of a company from a given index, or due to the rules for a given ESG investment product.

TIP

If a company's position on an issue changes radically or performance is poor, investors should proactively communicate with the company to understand how they plan to address the issue, especially when this involves some form of controversy. You can check ESG ratings that are publicly reported here: www.msci.com/our-solutions/esg-investing/esg-ratings/esg-ratings-corporate-search-tool and www.sustainalytics.com/esg-ratings.

Investors in passive index/ETF products rely on the methodology and practices of the index provider. Understanding what their methodologies are and what causes their ratings to vary widely from their peers allows these investors to align with a process from the beginning. Most major country or sector areas will have ESG products provided by different index providers; for example, the major companies in the U.S. are not only covered by the S&P 500, so it may be useful to look at variants on indexes if a different perspective is required. Otherwise, when following an index benchmark, investors don't have any options other than to follow the provider's methodology or divest from that product.

WARNING

Most of the liquidity in given country or sector benchmarks may be concentrated in certain products, while the underlying performance is likely to be similar to the respective costs; in particular, the bid/offer spread to open/close positions may vary. This is a more significant issue if you're an active investor, frequently changing positions, than if you're a buy-and-hold investor for some time.

What should a company know about its ESG rating?

Companies should understand how and why ratings are useful to their positioning, and then prioritize the issues that are most useful to driving the ratings outlook for their organization. The initial considerations should be what they can do to influence their 'E,' 'S,' and 'G' ratings, and which of those are most material for their particular business:

>> A number of companies feel that they aren't in a position to influence their Environmental score as they are a service company, but a significant portion of emissions are created by large buildings, so there may be more that's achievable by ensuring that their buildings are more eco-friendly.

>> Following the COVID-19 pandemic, all companies will recognize important Social factors that they can improve upon, which may previously not have been as apparent — for example, the mental well-being of their employees.

>> The 'G' factor is generally one that most companies were following but that affects all businesses — for example, better representation of women on corporate boards, and equal compensation and social mobility for women and people of color.

Understanding which ratings companies follow your company and how they apply their methodologies to your rating is important. This can be particularly relevant where a ratings company is also an index provider that determines whether your company will be an index constituent, which can create greater demand for your shares to replicate the index coverage. A recent major example of this was Tesla's inclusion in the S&P 500; however, smaller examples can involve inclusion in specific ESG indexes. In addition, direct disclosure/reporting and engagement with both ratings agencies and direct investors is vital. If your company wants to use ratings to update investors about ESG performance, some providers will have greater coverage of stocks, such as MSCI or Sustainalytics (now part of Morningstar), some will be more focused on governance issues, such as the ISS Quality Score, and others will be specific to emissions reporting, such as CDP.

If a company is new to ESG reporting, the process of responding to the Corporate Sustainability Assessment (CSA), provided by S&P, may help educate internal stakeholders, develop internal processes to collect ESG data, and initiate discussions at the board level around ESG issues. However, it does take significant time and effort to complete; therefore, other companies may devote resources to achieving better ESG performance or investor engagement.

REMEMBER

Companies should also regularly review their own ESG ratings, as mistakes can be caused by missing or old data, and establish whether they agree with the analysis and rating and where there may be differences. This is particularly true for the main ratings that their key investors are using. More explicitly, they could ask key investors how they utilize such tools in their investment approach, as their answers should help to advise the company's ESG data disclosure reporting.

4

The Part of Tens

Find a summary of the key elements of the book, with frequently asked questions that reference key points within individual chapters.

Apply fundamental elements required to construct and maintain an ESG portfolio.

Analyze the main factors influencing the growth of ESG investing.

Chapter **16**

Ten Frequently Asked Questions for an ESG Approach

You'll have many questions as you enter the world of ESG investing, but don't worry! A lot of the acronyms, phrases, and concepts are also new to many of your friends and colleagues as this is still an evolving space. In this chapter, you get ten of the most frequently asked questions (FAQs) about ESG investing, allowing you to reference some of the key issues you need to remember.

What Is ESG Investing?

REMEMBER

The term "ESG investing" (introduced in Chapter 1) is often used interchangeably with sustainability or impact investing, but it isn't a stand-alone investment strategy that provides positive impact. ESG (which stands for environmental, social, and governance) is a framework that uses a rules-based approach to evaluate companies based on their commitment to positive ESG factors and has become a fundamental part of investment analysis.

Investors are increasingly applying these non-financial but material factors to identify and mitigate ESG-related risks. Therefore, ESG integration is consistent with a manager's fiduciary duty and investment due diligence processes to consider all relevant information, beyond traditional financial metrics, in order to better understand their ESG-related risks. The ESG framework is critical in supporting the shift into mainstream ESG investing, while also being a foundation for more specific socially responsible investments (SRIs) and direct impact investments.

Impact investing is more about the type of investments that a manager is targeting, while ESG factors are part of an investment assessment process. Also, impact investing is seeking to make a measurable, positive, environmental/social effect with the investments a fund manager purchases, whereas ESG is a "means to an end," serving to identify non-financial risks that may have a material impact on an asset's value. Therefore, while there is no direct sustainability impact from ESG, the adoption of the principles has continued to evolve, and some specific trends have emerged that are key elements in evaluating a company's position on the virtual sustainability road map:

>> Currently, climate change and the move toward net-zero greenhouse gas (GHG) emissions by 2050 have dominated the agenda for the Environmental aspects.

>> Meanwhile, the coronavirus pandemic has increased consultation around the interconnection between sustainability and the financial system, with particular emphasis on the Social aspects, highlighting which companies are fully engaged with their employees and community, while championing diversity and inclusion.

>> Last but not least, a similar light has shone more brightly on the Governance aspects, particularly board composition, executive compensation, and a willingness to engage in the sustainability reporting process.

WARNING

Be wary of the potential for "greenwashing," as outlined in Chapter 6, where ESG investment products are sold as some form of solution to the world's ills or a quasi-charity donation that produces a sustainable impact while providing the investor with a return. While achieving a good ESG score is a positive indication that a company has a sustainable approach to management, that doesn't in itself suggest that they will achieve a sustainable impact.

Which Sustainability Goals Should Be Followed?

The United Nations Sustainable Development Goals (SDGs; see Chapter 1), which are aimed at ending poverty, protecting the planet, and ensuring that all people enjoy peace and prosperity, can be seen as a stimulus behind the renewed focus on sustainable investing. The COVID-19 pandemic of 2020 was a stark reminder that the world isn't on track to achieve those goals as we head into the final decade before the deadline, and so world leaders must increase their efforts.

However, everyone needs to pull their weight, and who better than business to lead the charge with their know-how, technology, and financial resources? The target is several life-changing "zeros," with the primary focus of responsible investors currently converging on having zero emissions and ending discrimination with respect to color and gender. It's important to remember that these goals are integrated and that action in one area will affect outcomes in others, which should balance social, economic, and environmental sustainability.

The SDGs are targeted to be met by 2030, while more specific targets under the Paris Agreement, such as net-zero emissions, are due to be met by 2050, with some countries pushing more aggressively for earlier target achievement. Major developments in 2020 with respect to emissions targets included the Democratic election success in the United States, with President Joe Biden being receptive to the U.S. remaining among the Paris Agreement signatories. In addition, China's President Xi Jinping pledged to peak greenhouse gas emissions by 2030 and reach net-zero emissions by 2060. As China is currently a major polluting nation, this is a further positive step toward mitigating climate change.

What Are the Characteristics of an ESG Company?

A company needs to exhibit a set of standards within its operations that show it's effectively managing ESG-related risks:

>> **Environmental criteria,** including a company's use of energy, waste, pollution, and natural resource conservation, underline how it performs as a steward of nature.

>> **Social criteria,** comprising how it manages relationships with employees, suppliers, customers, and the communities it operates in, underscore how it interacts with all of its stakeholders.

>> **Governance criteria,** incorporating how a company uses accurate and transparent accounting methods, and giving stockholders an opportunity to vote on important issues, emphasize how the company's leadership operate and can be further investigated through its policies on audits, executive pay, illegal practices, internal controls, and shareholder rights.

REMEMBER

It's fair to say that no company can pass every criterion in each category; however, investors should determine which factors they find most relevant to their values and use any engagement with the company to verify their ESG criteria. On the positive side, the growing recognition and acceptance of ESG standards are obliging companies to adhere to the requirements outlined earlier. How a business manages financial and non-financial risks has become an increasingly important factor in the decisions made by institutional investors. Moreover, countless studies show that companies with convincing ESG practices lead to better corporate financial performance.

The leading ESG principles that institutional investors view as restrictions on investing in companies include doing business in regions with conflict risk or appearing on a sanctions list, and the manufacture of controversial weapons. Meanwhile, surveys show that the vast majority of money managers are responding to client demands, risk and return factors, and a firm's social benefit when considering relevant characteristics for the firms they invest in. Flip to Chapter 2 for more information on the "personality" of an ESG company.

How Is an ESG Company Rated?

Generally, ESG scores are data-driven, reporting on the most material industry metrics, which can differ across sectors, with marginal company size and transparency preconceptions. The scores can be based on the relative performance of ESG factors within the company's sector (for 'E' and 'S') and country of incorporation (for 'G'). However, ESG scores are independent of the industry in which a company operates and potentially have a strong rating where the wider industry rating is low, and vice versa.

Clarity around company disclosures is key as they are an important component of any methodology, with negative weightings potentially applied if disclosure on material factors isn't reported. Company engagement is required to verify a company's activities relative to assurances and to amplify the impact of any significant events on the overall ESG score. Some approaches may also address the market capitalization bias that larger companies experience, given that the severity of any controversy may be exacerbated, depending on a company's size; BP and Volkswagen are two examples. Industry and country benchmarks may also be considered to enable equivalent analysis within peer groups.

REMEMBER

There is no universal approach to measuring and reporting on ESG performance. A company's score is based on its exposure to company-specific and general-industry ESG risk and how it manages those risks. The score can be calculated relative to the sustainability standards and performance of a company's global industry peers, but a company's overall ESG rating is usually calculated by summing the weighted score of each unmanaged ESG risk. See Chapters 2 and 14 for more about ratings.

WARNING

Although there are core similarities in calculating ESG scores, the exact methodologies used to analyze these data points differ across rating providers. This leads to divergences in scores from one rating provider to the next, to the point where they aren't even strongly correlated. Investors should consider this when deciding which rating providers to follow and whether they should compare the scores to their own internal proxy, although not all investors have the resources to maintain internal analysis.

What Investing Principles Should Be Adopted for ESG?

Applying ESG principles should better align investors with the broader objectives of society. Moreover, institutional investors have a duty to act in the best long-term interests of their beneficiaries. To follow the established United Nations Principles for Responsible Investment (PRI), they should include addressing ESG issues in their investment policy statements, while supporting the development of ESG-related tools, metrics, and analyses. They need to be active owners and incorporate ESG issues into their ownership policies and practices, while exercising voting rights or monitoring compliance with voting policies (if outsourced). This should include developing an engagement capability and asking for ESG issues to be integrated into annual financial reports. Alignment of investment mandates, monitoring procedures, performance indicators, and incentive structures should be reviewed accordingly. Last but not least, they should develop or support appropriate collaborative initiatives to further promote these principles.

WARNING

However, socially responsible investors also need to define their own principles, as what constitutes ESG can be interpreted in different ways. One example is nuclear energy. If you consider the potential repercussions of a nuclear accident, such as Chernobyl or Three Mile Island, the social and reputational damage that the operator faces is sizeable, and therefore nuclear energy couldn't be seen as an ESG investment. Alternatively, when seen as an energy provider, generating a more environmentally friendly substitute for fossil fuels, it's perfectly acceptable as a socially responsible investment.

Furthermore, different ESG providers have different principles with respect to different issues. Some funds choose not to invest in a company like Microsoft, not because Microsoft is ethically irresponsible, but because they question Microsoft's "competitive dynamics." This can mean missing out on investing in a stock that has given a huge return to investors. However, others will say that such principles are justified by instances such as Facebook selling millions of users' personal data, without their consent, to Cambridge Analytica, which subsequently used the data primarily for political advertising.

Chapter 7 introduces the topic of investing principles for ESG in more detail.

What Is Stewardship?

REMEMBER

Once the initial due diligence has been managed and the ESG investment completed, the subsequent challenge is to safeguard that the investments made continue to perform in the way that allowed them to establish the anticipated ESG criteria to begin with. *Stewardship* can be defined as the accountable allocation, management, and supervision of capital to establish long-term value for clients and beneficiaries, leading to sustainable benefits for the economy, the environment, and society. More recently, stewardship has focused on exercising voting rights and being vocal at the annual general meeting (AGM) of a company, as well as engaging, through ongoing dialogue with company management, on metrics, standards, and performance.

Asset owners and managers can't delegate their responsibility and are accountable for effective stewardship. Some of the primary activities include investment decision-making, scrutinizing assets and service providers, engaging with issuers and holding them to account on material issues, collaborating with others, and exercising rights and responsibilities. Funds are invested in a variety of asset classes over which investors have diverse terms and investment phases, rights, and levels of control. They should use the resources, rights, and influence accessible to them to implement stewardship, regardless of how capital is invested.

Engagement fulfilled collaboratively or individually is vital to achieving a better understanding of a company and the key risks that it faces. Through frequent company discussions with senior management, larger investors are able to uncover key observations that data providers and smaller investors might overlook. Investors can make senior management accountable for whether ESG themes are being considered and implemented. Moreover, investors can identify ESG risks that may have been overlooked and forewarn senior management. Awareness built up from engagement (and voting) can then be fed back into the investment process and enhance ongoing research. Continuous engagement with companies is part of the ESG corporate governance function, while the AGM is used as a tool to target specific ESG issues that may arise and work with other asset owners. Engagement should be assumed by the investment team, fund managers, and analysts directly, as they have the deepest knowledge on each company and sector. Chapter 13 covers the topic of engagement and stewardship in more detail.

How Is an ESG Approach for Asset Owners Implemented?

REMEMBER

Asset owners that are comparatively new to the concept of ESG investing can struggle with how they can best incorporate an ESG approach without compromising on their financial objectives. The approach should reflect the asset owner's investment beliefs, values, and financial and sustainability goals, and take into account asset class–specific sustainable investment guidelines for internal and external managers. Some of the specific approaches can include integration, looking at a wider perspective than conventional financial analysis, and clearly including analysis of a series of risks and opportunities connected to ESG drivers. Alternatively, negative screening enables the incorporation of an investor's moral principles by excluding companies that participate in given industries, such as alcohol and gambling.

For such approaches, ESG investing via cash equities is by far the most established approach. Given that ESG factors can be more easily applied at a company level and that institutional investor allocation to equities has traditionally been strongest, this is a natural development, and the overall asset allocation mix is unlikely to change anytime soon. However, fixed income investor allocation is traditionally the second-most popular investment choice, and there has been a marked interest in fixed income allocations to ESG. From a corporate bond perspective, very similar considerations on company exposure to ESG factors apply. However, for sovereign bond investments, ESG factors would address country rather than sector risk. Chapters 8 and 9 provide further analysis on the use of equity and fixed income instruments to implement an ESG strategy.

For asset owners following a thematic approach, where they can focus on specific trends and themes such as the environment or demographics, there has been greater issuance of green and sustainable bonds. This approach requires greater due diligence around the appropriate level of sustainability of the bonds, especially the validity of any sustainable projects associated with a bond's issuance.

How Are Benchmarks and Performance Measurement Incorporated in ESG?

Many active investors will continue to "stock pick" with an ESG bias — for example, buying "best-in-class" shares and using positive screening rather than just excluding given shares. Within the bond arena, there has been much greater interest in the larger social impact that is available from green and sustainability bonds, rather than traditional bond allocations. However, there may be issues with ensuring bond allocations, where the bond issuance size is generally smaller, with lower liquidity when subsequently selling the bond. For passive investors, the emergence of ESG-equivalent indexes on major benchmarks has enabled the use of exchange-traded funds (ETFs) to replicate or overlay ESG exposure. Alternatively, there has been an increasing trend in the availability of exchange-listed ESG futures and options contracts, which is a common approach to get passive exposure, particularly for tactical asset allocation. (Flip to Chapters 8, 9, and 10 for more about all of these instruments.)

Most investors have historically benchmarked their performance against established indexes that the markets know well. Given the exponential increase in sustainable assets under management, there seems to be no reason to suggest that ESG indexes won't outstrip their traditional equivalents by 2030. The shift to sustainable investing measurements is already accelerating quickly, and major institutional investors, such as Japan's Government Pension Investment Fund and reinsurance giant Swiss Re, have already jumped ship by switching to the ESG-focused version of benchmark indexes.

There is a relentless move to more precisely quantify ESG performance through a plethora of different ESG ratings firms. ESG scores grade companies against given ESG benchmarks, measuring their performance on a sustainability scale. By collecting contrasting data from numerous sources and allowing for relative weightings, driven by sector or country exposure to ESG risks, a score, individually or collectively for an index, can be generated to serve as a representation of ESG performance.

REMEMBER

Given the number of benchmark-related ESG-equivalent indexes that have been introduced, there should be the ability to switch from the traditional to "new" ESG benchmarks, given the "wall of money" that has led to approximately US$40 trillion of assets under management. For other asset classes, it may not be as relatively straightforward as for equities, but new, standardized frameworks for reporting should help resolve these issues.

What's the Latest on Disclosures and Reporting?

For what some might see as a turgid topic, there has been plenty of action, if not excitement, afoot in the disclosure and reporting arena in recent times (as outlined in more detail in Chapter 14). Clearly, the discrepancies between ESG rating scores from different providers have motivated regulators on both sides of the pond to create more standardized frameworks and hopefully bring more transparency. While standardization can't guarantee more harmonized ESG ratings, at least users of the ratings can refer to more common, underlying inputs. The view is that uncertainty around ESG ratings was slowing the progress of determining material sustainability issues, while the increasing availability of ESG products to retail investors, coupled with insinuations around greenwashing (see Chapter 6), has moved regulators to act. Certainly, the old adage "garbage in, garbage out" may ring true if companies aren't taking their reporting requirements seriously, and this can lead to spurious ESG ratings, which doesn't help anybody.

Currently, in the United States, disclosure and reporting requirement changes are concentrated on encouraging greater conformity in standards for voluntary disclosure from existing standard-setters, rather than mandated Securities and Exchange Commission (SEC) disclosure. Conversely, on the European side of the pond, three interconnected regulatory approaches have been introduced in 2020, made up of the Non-Financial Reporting Directive (NFRD), the Taxonomy Regulation, and the Sustainable Finance Disclosure Regulation (SFDR). Meanwhile, the World Economic Forum has issued a universal set of "stakeholder capitalism metrics," which help companies demonstrate long-term value creation and their contributions to the SDGs, although these aren't intended to replace any of the industry-specific ESG metrics that investors already use, but rather to be complementary.

Confused? A number of firms faced with this tsunami of paperwork and guidance may just give up. Indeed, SEC findings suggested that the variety of disclosure methods leads to uncertainty as to which methods to use, and subsequently makes it difficult for investors to compare ESG performance across companies. There may be light at the end of the tunnel, as the Global Reporting Initiative (GRI) and the Sustainability Accounting Standards Board (SASB) announced a new project to collaborate for the purpose of "promoting clarity and compatibility in the sustainability landscape." Also, some standard-setters are more focused on specific material issues, such as the Task Force on Climate-related Financial Disclosures (TCFD), which is more applicable to industry sectors that are "emissions heavy." The summary is "watch this space," as greater certainty is required.

What's the Future of ESG Investing?

A survey by PwC (that's PricewaterhouseCoopers) predicted that the share of European assets in ESG-related investments is likely to almost quadruple from 15 percent to 57 percent by 2025. Also, more than three-quarters of investors surveyed, including pension funds and insurance companies, suggested they wouldn't buy traditional funds but rather would focus on ESG products by 2022. Investing in ESG seems to be focused on future-proofing returns but also companies protecting their reputation. Moreover, COVID-19 has added further momentum to the trend, with companies and investors recognizing the need to embrace ESG as the norm rather than the exception.

However, there is still a lack of agreement on the material ESG issues that are impacting firms, a lack of uniformity in the regional approaches to ESG, and a lack of standardization of key ESG ratings and data points. Meanwhile, associated with this is the plethora of disclosure and reporting requirements to consider (see the previous section), along with further mandated regulation on the horizon. Furthermore, there are emerging trends around stewardship (covered earlier in this chapter), with varying degrees of engagement and voting participation undertaken by different asset owners and managers.

Of course, in the background are fundamental concerns around environmental, social, and governance issues that face governments of the day. Europe seems to be leading the way, with the European Commission pursuing a major green recovery package that seems to be focused on the rebuilding of coronavirus-affected economies to tackle the even greater threat of global warming. Meanwhile, the new administration in the United States is making positive noises, and China has pledged to target net-zero emissions by 2060.

REMEMBER

In short, there is plenty of stimulus to further fuel the ESG fires that have contributed toward greater enthusiasm from investors toward socially responsible investment under an ESG framework. Perhaps the further development of Machine Learning (ML) and artificial intelligence will enable enhanced analysis of ESG data; however, the old phrase "garbage in, garbage out" should be remembered if the data isn't verified through appropriate disclosure and reporting standards. The year 2020 also saw consolidation in the ESG ratings space and greater collaboration among the reporting standard-setters, with new actors adding further input to the discussion. You won't be short of material to satiate your appetite for sustainability! Whichever direction the market takes, ESG will be the focal point for sustainable investing for at least the next ten years, to the point where universal acceptance will negate the need to say "ESG investing" anymore, as it will be the norm.

Chapter **17**

Ten Issues Surrounding ESG Portfolio Construction

I n this chapter, you find out about ten issues that are frequently raised around ESG portfolio construction. These issues range from understanding where the differences lie between different rating agencies' views of ESG scores to using sustainability indexes to represent your exposure to responsible investment.

Reasons for Varying ESG Scores between Rating Agencies

As awareness of responsible investing has grown, several approaches to assess companies' ESG performance have been developed. The associated rating systems differ by scope, measurement, and weighting of ESG factors, making it challenging to compare methodologies or appreciate why some agencies rate the same company in different ways.

REMEMBER

For an ESG approach to be effective, investors must comprehend the methodology by which managers and allocators evaluate their assets. Recognizing where rating agencies vary in their methodologies is an essential tool to help institutions improve their ESG strategies. It seems that the main variance between agencies' rating processes is affected by how each ESG factor is measured. Therefore, even if two rating agencies concur on what should be measured, their ratings may differ because of how they evaluated.

Research has shown that the factors included in an assessment and how they are evaluated is more significant than how they are weighted when composing an overall ESG score. A substantial divergence between agencies on the ESG factors they use often plays a major role in where overall scores differ, exposing the broad range of views on which issues are important in responsible investing. When analyzing different ratings approaches, correlations on some ratings are seen to be poor, particularly in topics such as human rights and product safety. Interestingly, a relatively small number of indicators are used by all ratings agencies, with similar indicators being used by only a couple of agencies.

WARNING

This suggests that because certain indicators require an element of judgment, rather than a purely numerical assessment, they tend to be based on values and "soft" data, which makes them harder to evaluate and compare. Consequently, there is a chance that the ratings rely on the team assessing them, which is open to bias, and the performance of a company in one ESG category may influence its score in another. Also, agencies may base their underlying data on different sources, which changes the scope of their ESG scores. See Chapter 14 for more about ESG ratings and rankings.

Criteria Used in Creating a Combined ESG Score

Research from MSCI suggests that 'E' (environment) and 'S' (social) issues are more industry-specific and tend to show up in financial measures over a longer time frame when compared with 'G' (governance) issues. Active managers use such data to analyze a company in greater detail. However, many investors are more concerned about combining 'E,' 'S,' and 'G' issues into an aggregate score rather than relying on one lead indicator. As such, some investors want to understand how best to create a combined ESG score.

In principle, there are three established ways to approach this issue — namely, equal weighting, optimization weights based on historical data, or using industry-specific weighting:

>> Equal weighting has the benefit of being simple, transparent, and more comparable across industries. If an investor doesn't have specific views about the relative importance of ESG issues, then this straightforward approach may be appropriate.

>> An optimized weighting based on historical data may also be applicable for investors who don't have a particular view in order to let the data guide their optimal weights based on historical significance. However, results showed that putting the most weight on the 'G' factor and the least weight on the 'S' factor led to the greatest improvement in exposure to financial variables, giving weights of 70 percent for 'G,' 25 percent for 'E,' and 5 percent for 'S.'

>> Selecting and weighting ESG issues for each industry (which is the approach used in creating MSCI ESG Ratings) more precisely reflects industry exposures to ESG risks. The potential drawback is that this introduces greater complexity and less comparability across industry sectors, where ESG weights can vary considerably over time. However, the average weights over the long term showed a 30 percent allocation to 'E,' 39 percent to 'S,' and 31 percent to 'G.'

REMEMBER

As with most things in life, there is a trade-off for investors using an aggregate ESG score, based on whether they should accept higher performance in the short- or longer-term approach. Also, the analysis suggests that 'E' and 'S' issues are more industry-specific, so they influence financial measures more over the longer term than 'G' issues. See Chapter 14 for more about ESG scores.

Trends Driving ESG Materiality

REMEMBER

Because not every ESG factor is material to all businesses and sectors, it's essential for both companies and investors to identify and manage those factors that are material and to remain cognizant of those that may become material in the future. That being said, what's financially material will change over time and with increasing speed. This requires the ability to understand what makes ESG issues become financially material over time and to adapt to the changes. In a new age of materiality, investors must proactively work to understand ESG factors and incorporate these trends into investment decision-making in a more agile way. While the time frame in which individual ESG factors become financially material varies, they all tend to be influenced by given trends — in particular, transparency, stakeholder activism, societal expectations, and investor emphasis on ESG.

The evolution of materiality also comes through the guidance of key decision-makers. Whether they are policy makers shaping legislation, consumers making purchasing choices, or employees deciding to work for given companies, these influencers can have a direct impact on a company's profitability. Equally, investors can prompt the process by which issues become material by evaluating companies from an ESG perspective and using the results to inform portfolio construction. Moreover, an influential investor that increases public awareness on a specific issue can trigger a management team's attention.

Investors need to balance their sustainable investing abilities with the knack for anticipating and responding to changes in materiality more rapidly and flexibly. This requires an ability to predict how the financial materiality of ESG issues will evolve by sector and industry, and to frequently update those predictions by employing new information and data that go beyond company reporting and ESG scores. In turn, those predictions can be used to inform security selection and portfolio construction, drive engagement with management teams on their strategies for future material issues, and contribute to wider attempts to comprehend the dynamism of materiality through transparent reporting and disclosure. Check out Chapter 2 for an introduction to materiality.

Quantitative Approaches to ESG Analysis

The incorporation of ESG factors has historically only been associated with integration into fundamental strategies, but this is changing. As the appetite for ESG products continues to surge, quantitative managers are rising to the challenge in their search for a reliable way to identify stocks with strong or improving ESG characteristics that are likely to generate alpha. As quantitative investment processes are likely the most efficient at incorporating ESG data, a lot of work is going into discovering a systematic way to identify which ESG stocks to invest in.

However, ESG isn't a factor in the traditional sense, as it can't be defined as a set of quantifiable features that explain a stock's risk and returns. Traditional factors are robust, having been tested across different geographies and market conditions for a long period of time. Moreover, they are well documented, and although they are defined differently by different investors, a consensus view exists on basic definitions. This isn't true for ESG, as data doesn't go back far enough to decisively say that it's a factor driving risk and return in a systematic way. While ESG data coverage has improved, it's still sparse when compared to the data that's available on traditional financial factors, and it's only available for a fraction of companies in the investable universe. It's also necessary to consider that conventional ESG scoring methodologies don't fit into traditional factor models.

For example, larger companies tend to have better corporate governance and disclosure policies in comparison to smaller companies, and (due to regulatory requirements) European companies tend to be more transparent than their North American counterparts. This all affects their ultimate ESG scores. If more companies disclosed more ESG data, using similar metrics to those of their peers, and allowed their ESG data to be audited and released on a more regular basis, then investors could better identify alpha opportunities using ESG metrics.

Moreover, research shows that companies with better ESG scores have similar returns to those with poor ESG scores. This suggests that it should be possible to systematically tilt a portfolio toward better-scoring companies without detracting from performance.

The hunt for that elusive ESG factor continues, but in the meantime, it would help to focus less on the effort a company exerts (such as policies and committees) and more on the measurable impact of their behavior. Here, alternative (or big) data could help generate the necessary ESG insights. In fact, given time, quantitative analysis could fundamentally overhaul the way the investment industry views ESG and the ability of an investor to identify stocks that meet more specific ESG requirements. See Chapter 15 for more about quantitative analysis.

TIP

There are great opportunities for the use of "unstructured data" that would transform your ability to glean valuable ESG insights. This unstructured data could include information taken from social media outlets and websites such as Glassdoor — a forum for employees to anonymously review their company and share salary information. The ability to systematically harvest candid insights from employees about the inner workings of their companies could prove to be far more illuminating when it comes to corporate social responsibility programs than what the company is likely to formally disclose.

Qualitative Analysis: Verifying and Supplementing Quantitative Analysis

As with traditional financial market research, quantitative views of how the data on company-specific, sector-based, or general market changes have developed has become an increasingly influential part of market analysis. Therefore, it's no surprise to see that the quantitative analysis of ESG factors has developed as an integral component of most investors' capabilities to prioritize ESG investments.

However, as a steward of client assets, it's also the fiduciary duty of an asset manager to understand all aspects that create an impact on a security's investment returns. Because ESG incorporates so many non-financial issues, using a fundamental research approach to blend qualitative analysis with quantitative evaluation from ESG factors should help investors make a more informed assessment of the inherent value of a security.

Many asset managers use a combination of quantitative analysis and qualitative judgments to assess the ESG profiles of issuers and sovereigns. Many believe that quantitative measures on a stand-alone basis are insufficient to evaluate the true ESG performance of a company, as they are backward-looking and don't inform how the company will perform in the future. Furthermore, they are sometimes not current, subject to selection bias, or not directly comparable to metrics provided by other companies in their peer group.

REMEMBER

The purpose of qualitative research should be to investigate further into understanding insights into the ESG credentials of a given company. As in other fields of research, quantitative research can be considered as determining the "what" behind ESG behavior, while qualitative research uncovers the "why." Engagement with companies, through interviews with corporate social responsibility (CSR) managers and senior executives, should be designed to explore in depth any identified ESG risks and to detect any potential risks that aren't thus far identified during the rating process. See Chapter 15 for more about qualitative analysis.

ESG Regulations

To use an analogy from the Gartner Hype Cycle, which is used to graphically identify where a given technology currently sits with respect to expectations and time, ESG must be at the "peak of inflated expectations," with many suggesting that this should be the cusp of a period of further transformation in the responsible investment landscape. Unlike with technology, there doesn't appear to be any likelihood of a subsequent "trough of disillusionment," but the market recognizes that there is further work to be done to maintain and grow from this current position.

REMEMBER

Participants in the ESG market are strongly supportive of further developments toward common standards, as there are concerns around the interface between different elements of sustainability reporting and the associated legislation, or lack thereof, in different jurisdictions. Asset owners are increasingly analyzing their ESG investments and wanting more reporting, meaningful impact, and alignment with existing ESG standards and market best practices. The ESG landscape is becoming more regulated, and asset managers recognize that they need to be prepared for more than generalized ESG principles.

Conversely, the variance in global regulations is challenging. There are differing standards for voluntary ESG disclosures, whether from the broader reporting requirements of the Sustainability Accounting Standards Board (SASB) or the Global Reporting Initiative (GRI), or the more specific requirements of the Carbon Disclosure Project (CDP) in the United Kingdom. They all have different requirements and principles around the reporting application and understanding of what the standards should be, which causes issues for the asset managers who need to manage their funds and client portfolios against this backdrop. Recently, the International Organization of Securities Commissions (IOSCO) announced a task force to review the commonalities among the various standards to create a more consistent form of ESG disclosures. (Chapter 1 introduces you to standards.) Furthermore, the International Financial Reporting Standards (IFRS) Trustees have published a consultation paper on sustainability reporting to determine whether there is a need for global sustainability standards and what role they should play in bringing those standards together.

Furthermore, the market also has to contend with the varied landscape of ESG ratings and assessments (see Chapter 14). As mentioned throughout this book, there are several ESG rating providers, measuring different factors, so ESG ratings don't necessarily correlate with each other. This also makes it difficult for asset managers to know which ESG factors to consider and, as a result, which ESG ratings to apply. Therefore, they are generally unable to view the performance attribution of ESG investment factors, even though that is the type of information the industry would find most useful. Consequently, the overall push for standardization across various facets of the ESG industry will continue.

Risk and Reward

ESG portfolios can be more complex and opaque than portfolios based purely on financial factors, but ultimately it comes down to the same compromise as with traditional portfolios: There has to be a trade-off between risk and reward. In the ESG sense, this is a mix of "doing no harm" and an expected financial return.

REMEMBER

In addition, portfolio construction will vary, depending on the goals of each ESG investor. Although it may be difficult to achieve social change via investing, at least ESG investors can pursue strategies that are compatible with their objectives. In matching such objectives to a prospective portfolio, the following construction approaches are considered, assuming in all cases that investors will have a given risk appetite for each method:

>> **Exclusion:** This has been the traditional approach of just excluding unacceptable securities from a portfolio, generally based on ethical or pollution-focused ideals, either by a capitalization-weighted exclusion (low-risk aversion) or an optimized exclusion (high-risk aversion).

>> **Exclusion with strings:** This is a variation on the traditional approach and involves taking ESG ratings to determine which securities to exclude based on a maximum ESG score (low-risk aversion) or a minimized risk (high-risk aversion) expectation. This effectively tilts any portfolio in one direction or the other, based on the investor's specific theme.

>> **Exclusion and ESG scoring:** This combination of ESG scoring and exclusion allows the investor to tilt the portfolio toward a theme and exclude unacceptable securities from the portfolio.

Any analysis then needs to focus on a compromise between higher tracking error, against a benchmark index return, and unacceptable exposures. When unacceptable securities are excluded, or underweighted, a by-product of risk minimization generally leads to overweighting securities that are correlated to the excluded securities, which may also conflict with ESG objectives, as close substitutes are included to reduce tracking error or risk targets. Alternatively, if substitutes aren't included in the portfolio, the overall risk can go up as the portfolio is less diversified. However, there will always be some movement away from the benchmark portfolio risk and return, and investors ultimately have to accept what their asset manager can deliver within their stipulated boundaries. See Chapter 7 for more information.

Derivative and Alternative Instruments

One sure indication that there is a lot of interest in a given product area and that the assets under management are increasing proportionately is when a large derivatives exchange decides to list futures and options contracts on the product. Eurex Exchange, the largest derivatives exchange in Europe, listed its first contracts in 2019 based on an exclusions approach, the most established methodology in Europe with the highest assets under management, on the STOXX Europe 600. Following the standardization for exclusions, where asset managers had the most exclusions in their underlying strategies, they introduced the ESG-X index products, providing a broad benchmark for Europe.

Further research around the product showed that asset managers wanted to have risk and performance parameters close to the benchmark index so that there was a low tracking error. This also ensured initial liquidity and price provision by market makers, given that they could easily hedge any exposure against the established, more liquid products. Eurex has subsequently broadened the ESG derivatives segment beyond Europe, with screened versions of key regional and global MSCI benchmarks being introduced in March 2020. Moreover, products with a higher degree of ESG integration were added in November 2020, with an extension to ESG versions of the DAX and EURO STOXX 50 indexes.

Watch this space, as Eurex has also introduced products based on companies' carbon footprint and more regional indexes are likely, and others may be forthcoming once there is further clarity around some of the new regulations being introduced in Europe. Check out Chapter 10 for more about derivative and alternative instruments.

Stranded Assets

This chapter has predominantly focused on how to build a sustainable portfolio based on ESG factors, but this section highlights the reality of one of the potential consequences to your existing portfolio. *Stranded assets* are assets that, at some point prior to the end of their economic life (assuming the lifetime of a coal mine), can no longer earn an economic return (for example, meet the company's internal rate of return requirements). This is commonly associated with companies that suffer as a result of changes related to the transition to a low-carbon economy (creating lower-than-expected demand or prices). These assets effectively become worth less than anticipated due to the changes associated with the transition to a net-zero-emissions environment per the Paris Agreement.

For existing assets, there are already examples of coal mines, coal and gas power plants, and other hydrocarbon reserves that have become stranded by the low-carbon transition. The types of sub-sectors particularly impacted include the following:

>> **Resources:** Where oil and gas companies currently have resources in the ground awaiting production, including reserves, given the support for renewable energy

>> **Exploration and development assets:** The companies that provide the associated drilling rigs or seismic vessels to facilitate resource extraction

>> **Production and processing facilities:** The companies that provide the processing terminals for extracted resources

>> **Distribution infrastructure:** The companies that provide the pipelines and tankers to distribute fossil fuels

REMEMBER

The stranded assets notion has been understood to incorporate a series of different factors, including the following:

>> **Economic stranding:** Brought about by a change in comparative costs or prices for the affected commodity

>> **Physical stranding:** Due to changes that could be attributed to global warming, such as floods or drought, or just due to the asset's physical location

>> **Regulatory stranding:** A result of changes in policy, legislation, or regulation that makes the business uneconomic or a pariah

Research for potential new investments should aim to avoid stranded assets arising by recognizing where capital expenditure could be allocated to other investments as the world decarbonizes. While many asset owners and managers have excluded such stocks from their core portfolios, it will take some time for the full impact of decarbonization to kick in, and affected stocks aren't seeing their share prices plummet to zero at this point. In addition, a number of fossil fuel companies are receiving better ESG scores as they "get their house in order" and transition to renewable energies. Therefore, a focus is required on the ongoing stewardship of capital, with the objective of preventing capital from being wasted. See Chapter 1 for more information.

Sustainable Investing

Whereas stranded assets deal with the negative impact of responsible investing for your portfolio (see the preceding section), sustainable investing should lead to a more tangible positive impact, even though it isn't always explicit when using an ESG investing framework. This can be rectified by placing a greater focus on thematic or impact investing to achieve more sustainable returns, as opposed to not "doing any harm." For many investors, it isn't apparent which investments might be applicable; therefore, as with other investments, they can take a proactive approach with an active manager or a passive approach through a sustainable index fund. This section focuses on the index fund approach.

Sustainable investing is not a one-size-fits-all exercise, as it can mean different things to different investors. One benefit of taking the indexing approach, ordinarily through exchange-traded funds (ETFs), is that there is a broad range of indexes to choose from, which allows you to follow the approach that complements your portfolio. However, it's important to understand exactly what an index covers, so you should thoroughly check the approach outlined because indexes are inherently rules-based, so they should be transparent around the ESG approach taken, and this should be a repeatable exercise, regardless of asset class or exposure. Furthermore, this approach should help ensure that sustainability is expressed in a consistent way across the portfolio, if you're looking to complement your existing approach. Flip to Chapter 9 for more about indexes.

Chapter **18**

Ten Factors Influencing the Growth of ESG Investing

This chapter discusses ten of the major factors that will influence the growth of investing in ESG. These range from understanding the developments in the omnipresent concerns around climate change to some of the political impacts that may influence sustainable investing in general.

REMEMBER

Developments during the previous decade have laid the path for a more informed ESG environment in this new decade, which is expected to promote broader implementation of ESG-related practices. Companies, investors, and governments that fail to develop an ESG framework will face greater risks and could miss significant opportunities when compared to ESG leaders. Displaying leadership in ESG will become a differentiating factor for entities in the private and public sectors, and early adopters will have a competitive advantage over their peers.

Climate Change: The Route to Net Zero

Climate change is a dominant theme in ESG investing as governments across the globe announce more climate-related regulations. As a result, pledges by companies and investors to meet net-zero emissions will become standard practice by the end of the decade. All sectors, including those that are emissions-concentrated, will join in the transition to the low-carbon economy, because companies acknowledge the risks and opportunities connected to proactively tackling climate risks. Numerous firms will look to capture new business opportunities and promote themselves as climate leaders. Meanwhile, investors will intensify engagements around climate change and begin to integrate climate risk into their voting policies, proactively voting against the boards of slower-moving companies.

Governments' climate advisers have started to propose legally binding "carbon budgets," in line with national targets of "net-zero" emissions by 2050. The United Kingdom will host the United Nations Climate Change Conference (COP26) in 2021, where countries will aim to establish themselves as international climate leaders. Generally, data shows that current plans from most countries still fall far short of the Paris Agreement requirements, and so the 2030s need to see a phase of markedly sharp drops in emissions as high-carbon technologies, such as gasoline and diesel cars, are phased out. The target is to reach a completely decarbonized power system by 2035. Countries are also beginning to wake up to the fact that they need to account for their share of international aviation and shipping emissions.

Thirty of the world's largest investors, managing assets worth over US$9 trillion, have also set a goal of achieving net-zero carbon emissions across their investment portfolios by 2050 as part of the fight to restrain the climate crisis. For more on climate change, see Chapter 3.

Environmental and Social Issues Coming to the Fore

While established corporate governance ('G') will continue to be an area of focus, particularly around proposals to improve board quality, shareholder rights, and management incentive structures, the governance of environmental ('E') and social ('S') issues will take center stage for investors and boards. The management of 'E' and 'S' risks has emerged as the new standard of comprehensive corporate governance practices. The corporate social responsibility efforts of companies will move beyond giving back to society and will incorporate sustainability as a means to systematically manage risk and create long-term shareholder value. In addition, recognizing a company's impact on the environment and society will be a necessary expertise at the board level, with sustainability experts being invited to join many boards.

The 'E' of ESG has generally been considered the most important factor in ESG due to climate change effects, and although the COVID-19 pandemic has increased the focus on 'S,' the awareness of the consequences of a global warming event has guaranteed that environmental concerns are still front and center in discussions amid the push for net-zero emissions. Given that impetus, companies recognize that if they overlook their stewardship obligations toward the environment, they may be subjected to considerable financial risk. Companies failing to take applicable action to limit carbon emissions can face governmental or regulatory sanctions as well as reputational damage.

REMEMBER

Therefore, asset managers have ESG high on their agenda as they adapt to the "new normal." While the 'E' and 'G' have controlled the spotlight compared to 'S,' the unparalleled pace of social change brought about by the pandemic has brought the 'S' into sharp focus. However, it's clear that social matters are generally less understood and not as easily quantifiable or measurable as their ESG siblings. Even the UN Principles for Responsible Investment (PRI) body has acknowledged that the social element of ESG issues can be the most difficult for investors to assess. This will also need to change. See Chapters 3, 4, and 5 for an introduction to environmental, social, and governance issues.

Stewardship as a Driver for Change

Many of the governance structures in place today were born out of the corporate scandals and failures in the 1990s. Investment firms began to acknowledge the need to hold company boards accountable on pay and to protect the interests of minority shareholders. As described in the previous section, this has grown to include environmental and social policies. The launch of the PRI in 2006 and the UK Stewardship Code in 2010, in the aftermath of the global financial crisis, led to the worldwide adoption of Stewardship Codes, including by Japan (2014) and the United States (2018). In 2019 the UK Stewardship Code went through a further and substantive update, and given the increasing demands of responsible investing, it's likely that more can be expected.

REMEMBER

Governance can be considered as the rule book (the way norms and actions are structured, regulated, and held accountable), while stewardship is the playbook (the responsible allocation, management, and oversight of capital leading to sustainable benefits for the economy, the environment, and society).

The focus needs to change from corporate governance and disclosure toward impact and positive outcomes for society and the environment. Investment managers need to be more direct about the explicit stewardship actions they are taking. Ultimately, active stewardship is the investment management industry's social license to operate. Moreover, as pressure builds to incorporate ESG factors and engage in positive societal outcomes, the significance of investor engagement with investee companies is vital.

The next stage of stewardship is to cultivate positive outcomes. Investment managers must engage collaboratively with corporate management, explicitly empowering them to take action to deliver sustainable wealth, while urging them to challenge short-term financial pressures that may destroy a company's long-term sustainable value. Many would suggest that the quantity and quality of engagement in markets without active and well-resourced local investors has been poor. While forthcoming regulation and the UN Sustainable Development Goals (SDGs; see Chapter 1) provide additional momentum, more radical changes are needed to release the full potential of stewardship in the 2020s. If changes are to be successful, they must come from the asset management industry with the backing and encouragement of asset owners. For more information on stewardship, see Chapters 5 and 13.

ESG Disclosures

There are too many disclosure and reporting frameworks for most companies to contend with, which may lead to less reporting (unless there is a mandatory requirement) from companies with fewer resources. Disclosures on sustainability and material factors need to be standardized and common, as increased pressure from corporations and investors acts as the main catalyst for change. Increasing regulations will be a significant part of the new comply-or-explain regime, pushing best practices to address growing environmental and social concerns. Such regulatory initiatives on corporate disclosures are currently more prevalent in Europe, but it's surely a matter of time before they become more widespread in other jurisdictions. Corporate governance codes, executive compensation disclosures, and board gender-diversity mandates allied to the demands of the net-zero emissions requirements have unfolded rapidly across the globe as different jurisdictions implement best-practice governance standards.

Existing reporting standards serve as the blueprint for any mandatory reporting, including reporting standards aimed specifically at meeting the needs of the investment community, such as the Sustainability Accounting Standards Board (SASB; see Chapter 1) and the Task Force on Climate-related Financial Disclosures (TCFD). Reporting frameworks addressing wider stakeholder audiences (such as the GRI) also provide a clear roadmap. Furthermore, there are moves to consolidate the plethora of reporting entities, such as the merger between the SASB and the International Integrated Reporting Council (IIRC), with expansion of the SASB and GRI collaboration extending into other reporting entities under the Comprehensive Reporting Initiative.

Perhaps the vision of a single, coherent global set of reporting standards isn't a "pipe dream" as the market seeks assurance on the confirmation and accuracy of disclosures to enable more transparent ESG ratings, although many agencies also rely on their own data collection exercises to develop their ratings, overlaying all of the data collected onto their own methodologies. Therefore, discrepancies in individual ratings will still exist. See Chapter 14 for more on reporting.

Accounting

While sustainability is now a central concern for many managers, investors, and consumers, a major constraint remains for ESG momentum: the lack of universally adopted standards for how companies measure and report on their sustainability performance. Several non-governmental organizations (NGOs) are working independently to develop standards for sustainability reporting, which is creating complexity and confusion for companies and investors, but further changes are required from the accounting community. Therefore, it's positive to hear that the International Financial Reporting Standards (IFRS) Foundation, the body that oversees the work of the International Accounting Standards Board (IASB) in setting financial reporting requirements for most companies in the world, has started an initiative to address this problem and proposed the creation of a parallel Sustainability Standards Board (SSB).

They are well placed to make such a proposal, given their expertise in standard-setting procedures, authority in the corporate and investor community, and support from regulators globally. If their proposal is adopted, investors and other stakeholders should have a clearer view of any company's sustainability performance, similar to how they view financial performance. Several companies already issue sustainability reports, but these are detached from their financial reports, making it difficult to see the relationship between financial performance and sustainability performance. The SSB proposal would allow the community to integrate their reporting and gain further transparency (visit www.ifrs.org/projects/work-plan/sustainability-reporting/). The proposal also has the support of some heavyweights in the investment and corporate communities, among them California's Public Employees' Retirement System (CalPERS), that are making the case for sustainability reporting for IFRS and also at the U.S. Securities and Exchange Commission (SEC).

The effect of sustainability reporting standards should be huge. Companies can factor sustainability issues into strategy and capital-allocation decisions, using the standards to prioritize the relevant issues while ensuring the sustainability of corporate financial performance. Executives will recognize sustainability as a major issue that their board needs to focus on, and companies most effective at managing sustainability will be more appealing to investors. Sustainability performance can be seen as a leading indicator of financial performance; therefore, investors will be better able to analyze a company's sustainability reporting in a similar way to how they currently analyze financial reporting. Such changes will be further supported if compensation is tied to sustainability metrics rather than only the company's financial performance. For example, Deutsche Bank, Germany's biggest bank, announced that it's linking the remuneration of its top-level executives to its sustainability goals beginning in 2021 in order to boost its commitment to business activities that comply with ESG standards.

Regulation and International Standards

Sustainability and responsible investment are becoming mainstream priorities for pension funds, insurers, and other investors. Asset managers are responding with fund products that look to meet these priorities, while preparing for regulations focused on sustainability-related disclosure. For example, two new EU regulatory initiatives are the Sustainable Finance Disclosure Regulation (SFDR), which comes into law in March 2021, and the Taxonomy Regulation, which has already entered into law:

» The SFDR requires fund managers, such as those operating as alternative investment fund managers (AIFMs), to disclose how they have integrated sustainability into their processes, including due diligence, and an assessment of all relevant sustainability risks that might have a material negative impact on the financial return of a fund investment. Managers will need to quantify or describe any primary adverse impacts associated with their investments' impact on sustainability risks. Furthermore, any fund products marketed within the EU after March 2021 should ensure SFDR compliance with the marketing of such products. Effectively, managers have a duty to comply or explain why they don't consider any "principal adverse impacts" (harmful effects of investment decisions on environmental and social criteria) to apply. However, managers with more than 500 employees aren't entitled to rely on the comply-or-explain regime and must disclose principal adverse impacts on their websites and summaries of engagement policies.

In addition, each manager will be required to review its marketing documents and ensure that the documents don't contradict SFDR-mandatory disclosures.

> They will also need to assess each product and, if applicable, provide additional product disclosures with reference to specified SFDR articles.

> » The Taxonomy Regulation is aimed at introducing a benchmark for environmentally sustainable economic activities and to prevent "greenwashing," where investments don't meaningfully address 'E' or 'S' issues.

For more information on regulation and international standards, see Chapter 11.

Impact Investing: Actively Do Good versus "Do No Harm"

Global institutional investors plan to almost double their allocations to renewable energy infrastructure, but according to the International Renewable Energy Agency, annual investment in renewables will need to almost triple to US$800 billion by 2050 to fulfill decarbonization and climate goals across the world. Meanwhile, in the United States, President Joe Biden (who was inaugurated in January 2021) has pledged to invest US$400 billion over ten years in clean energy and innovation and hold polluters accountable. It's critical that the longer-term threat of climate change remains a center of attention, given the recent focus on COVID-19; this renewed focus may act as a catalyst for a more sustainable future if governments, asset managers and owners, and energy companies start working together.

The greatest increase in renewable energy is planned for wind and solar power plants, where costs have declined significantly in recent years. Solar energy will benefit from the increased interest in renewable energy investments, where it's projected to account for 60 percent of new additions to renewable energy globally by 2025. The growth of the solar industry in the United States is principally driven by cost-competitiveness, as solar is the cheapest form of new-build power generation across most of the country. This helps keep electricity costs down even as the country makes a determined move toward clean energy and away from fossil fuels.

Furthermore, Biden has pledged to reenter the Paris Agreement during his presidency, which should open the door for strengthened global cooperation on climate plans and green finance. Cooperation on global green finance standards, through the potential adoption of agreed internationally accepted standards, would provide regulatory certainty to investors and issuers, and help grow the green and sustainable bonds market overall.

REMEMBER

While green bonds have been taking most of the headlines, social and sustainability bonds have been advancing further than green bonds, given the circumstances surrounding COVID-19. While green bonds are used to finance projects on the basis of their positive environmental impacts, social bonds finance activities inherently linked to social sustainability. Due to the economic fallout triggered by the ongoing COVID-19 pandemic, interest in sustainability financing continues to remain strong. The volume of sustainability bonds (which includes green and social bonds) set a new record of issuance in the second quarter of 2020, totaling US\$99.9 billion. This growth was primarily supported by increased issuance of social bonds to address problems caused by the pandemic, alongside some issuers specifically creating social bonds dedicated to COVID-19, with issuers collectively raising US\$33 billion worth of social bonds. See Chapter 7 for an introduction to impact investing and Chapter 9 for more on green, social, and sustainability bonds.

Data and Technology

Data and technology will drive meaningful changes in the ability to measure, calculate, and monitor ESG factors and assess their materiality and impact on long-term value creation. As such, there is a demand for the conception of one global language for ESG. Nevertheless, this task won't be straightforward or quick to achieve. To manage this complex and evolving landscape, agile and flexible tools are required, which can adapt easily to changing data sources, standards, and reporting mechanisms. The solution requires the ability to draw in many and varied forms of data and present them in a single view, rather than the fragmented picture that is available today.

With the growth in sustainable investing, a tsunami of data has been produced on ESG factors in recent years. Furthermore, the demand for ESG data is rising as asset managers look to integrate ESG factors, such as low-carbon emissions and gender diversity on boards, into their investment analysis and decision-making processes. Traditionally, such ESG data has been sourced out of a company's self-provided reporting and then pored over by analysts through their subjective lenses. This has perpetuated the demand for more accurate data and metrics, where smaller financial technology (FinTech) firms are deploying artificial intelligence (AI) to unearth objective ESG issues that could have a material impact on a company's financial performance. The goal is to deliver actionable insights, in a consistent way, to move the industry toward ESG's more standardized future.

What is ideally required is an approach that sources concurrent information, with objective application to all companies using a common disclosure-reporting tool (such as the SASB's materiality framework) that identifies the likely material issues by industry. This approach can use AI generally, and Machine Learning (ML) specifically, to identify sustainability issues that could affect the financial or operating performance of companies within an industry. In addition, improved and standardized disclosures can give investors the ability to further assess the impacts of ESG factors on valuations. AI will play a major role in identifying patterns that connect economic performance to ESG factors while also allowing companies to make better capital allocation decisions.

Gathering and processing big data has become easier and cheaper. Smart algorithms increasingly allow better interpretation of non-traditional financial information (including unstructured data sources on the internet) or non-company-reported regulatory filings, Twitter articles, and reports from NGOs. Natural Language Processing (NLP) software is used to collect positive and negative sentiments, which allows it to produce a number of potential predictive indicators. Combined, all of these factors have allowed the construction of new data sets to analyze investments. See Chapter 15 for more about data and technology in ESG.

Consolidation of the ESG Ratings Companies

Traditional market data and index providers, such as Bloomberg, FTSE Russell, MSCI, and Refinitiv, have become major suppliers of ESG metrics and ratings on public companies. However, over the last ten years or more, a number of innovative FinTech firms have emerged that focused specifically on ESG metrics and have been able to embrace new technologies and data science tools to advance the predictive analytics that are being generated. In the last year, larger organizations have subsumed their smaller, more agile rivals.

Stock exchange groups have benefitted from greater real-time data fees and associated new data products that have significantly enhanced their revenue stream, as market participants have continuously developed their execution capabilities with low-latency algorithms. Some of the exchanges have taken this a step further by diversifying further into the data space with pure-play data company acquisitions.

TIP

You may want to keep an eye out for the new kids on the block that could be the next mergers and acquisitions (M&A) candidates in years to come. Interestingly, Illuminate Financial, a specialist FinTech venture capital firm, bought minority stakes in two different ESG start-ups in the fourth quarter of 2020 (see https://medium.com/illuminate-financial). These are

>> **Yves Blue,** which pulls together a disparate and growing number of ESG and impact data sources to present a detailed and consolidated view of the impact characteristics of the companies in a portfolio (`www.yves.blue`)

>> **Net Purpose,** which uses data to assess the performance of portfolios against the UN Sustainable Development Goals (SDGs) and other impact measurement standards (`www.netpurpose.com`)

Political Impacts: Geopolitics and Public Pressure

Politics will play an ever-growing role in determining the ESG landscape as geopolitical tensions, populism, and trade wars affect corporate behavior. In the energy, industrials, and technology sectors, national security concerns may influence business partnerships and mergers and acquisitions, with some alliances even being blocked by presidential executive orders. Politics at the national level can and does have a direct impact on corporate governance. (At the time of this writing, the Federal Trade Commission in the United States filed a lawsuit against Facebook alleging that the company had engaged in illegal anti-competitive behavior to sustain a social media monopoly!) Moreover, sanctions against individuals and companies of specific countries aren't going away anytime soon.

REMEMBER

Public pressure on a wide range of social and environmental issues can put additional regulatory pressure on companies and their shareholders in relation to ESG issues. Establishing leadership in ESG will become a differentiating factor for entities in the public and private sectors, and market participants can gain from embracing ESG stewardship as part of their competitive advantage.

In 2020 alone, you saw multiple events playing out on all continents that will have an impact on ESG, and that didn't include COVID-19!

>> In Europe, the final days of the UK's exit from the EU has potentially unforeseen implications for sustainability. Some commentators are skeptical about what the future holds for UK environmental policy outside of the EU during an economic downturn. Because the UK will host the UN Climate Change Conference (COP26) in 2021, this may prove a catalyst to maintain its sustainability credentials. In addition, the UK has been leading on the Stewardship Code and should maintain many of the financial regulatory requirements passed under the EU.

>> The EU itself seems to be a shining example of embracing sustainability as it continues to release an array of regulatory requirements that support an ESG agenda, with greater public disclosure and anti-greenwashing approaches at the heart of the agenda. Also, it has ratified a huge stimulus package that the European Commission has said will make fighting climate change central to Europe's economic recovery from the coronavirus pandemic.

>> Meanwhile, the United States under a Joe Biden presidency is already talking about rejoining the Paris Agreement and is making positive noises around budgets being made available for clean energy and innovation and holding polluters accountable. However, he may have to spend as much time unraveling the U.S. from non-ESG activities conducted under the Trump administration as he moves forward. From a financial markets perspective, the U.S. SIF Foundation wanted to see the reversal of policies under the SEC and the Department of Labor. The hope is that the SEC will reverse limitations on shareholder proposals and access to independent proxy advice. Meanwhile, the Department of Labor has removed the terminology that specifically limited the inclusion of ESG factors in retirement plans, stressing that plan fiduciaries have to focus on "pecuniary" factors when evaluating investments, whether they are ESG-related or not.

>> Asia remains an enigma in the sustainability charge. To a large extent, Asia's rapid economic development has encouraged a realization that change is necessary. Moreover, Asia Pacific is subject to worsening typhoons, tsunamis, and other weather events, while the pace of urbanization and increasing air and water pollution are more pronounced than in other regions. Meanwhile, China is pursuing sustainability because a growing number of its citizens want a better environment and a more inclusive society. Given the importance of maintaining stability and progress, President Xi Jinping has made it clear that sustainability is a priority for the country and has pledged to peak greenhouse gas emissions by 2030 and reach net-zero emissions by 2060, emphasizing the need for a "green revolution." Finally, Hong Kong's Securities and Futures Commission has arguably led the way globally, making it compulsory for listed companies to disclose all their sustainability credentials. Mainland China will soon follow suit, requiring all listed companies to report their ESG risks from 2020 onward.

Appendix

Great Resources for ESG Investing

The principles of ESG investing are common for all investors, but the focus of this book has been more tilted toward institutional investors, so this appendix concentrates on retail investors. It emphasizes the fundamentals of building a portfolio, how investors can find resources to confirm whether ESG products meet their values, and what products they can use to achieve their goals.

The Basics of Building a Retail ESG Portfolio

REMEMBER

In many ways, building an ESG portfolio is no different than building a regular portfolio. Before you start investing, be sure to do the following:

» Think about your goals and determine what you're investing for, whether for retirement or funding your children's education. Your investment objective tends to influence your risk tolerance and whether you want to consider an aggressive, moderate, or conservative portfolio.

>> Consider what asset allocation you want, including whether it incorporates equities, bonds, and other assets. For example, you may want to focus on equities but also to consider large-, mid-, and small-cap stocks, or to include stocks from different geographical jurisdictions.

>> Decide whether your portfolio will be actively or passively managed, or a combination of the two; this may be achieved through mutual funds, exchange-traded funds (ETFs), or personal stock picks.

The following sections provide details on all of these considerations (and more) as they relate to ESG investing.

Making informed decisions

Before determining what type of responsible investment you may consider, it's important to educate yourself on some of the key issues that could influence your ESG framework.

TIP

The following links should be useful in expanding your understanding of specific responsible investment criteria:

>> www.unpri.org/pri/about-the-pri

>> www.unglobalcompact.org/sdgs

For more in-depth training and education, consider the following resources:

>> www.cfauk.org/about-the-esg-certificate-in-investing

>> https://priacademy.org/pages/academy-syllabus

Choosing responsible investment products

REMEMBER

After you've brushed up on the basics using the resources in the previous section, your next step in building an ESG-focused portfolio is to decide how responsible or sustainable your portfolio should be. Investors who decide to put their money where their values are have a smaller but fast-growing array of mutual funds and exchange-traded funds to choose from. However, ESG investing isn't right for everyone, and you should consider whether the index or fund's objectives are aligned with your own values, while understanding any specific risks these products represent.

The following links should be useful in expanding your awareness of the range of ETFs or mutual funds that meet specific responsible investment or ESG criteria:

>> www.etf.com/etfanalytics/etf-comparison-tool

>> www.etfdb.com/tool/etf-comparison/

>> www.justetf.com/uk/tutorial/etf-search/compare-etfs-in-etf-screener.html

>> www.morningstar.com/start-investing

>> https://charts.ussif.org/mfpc/

>> https://mutualfunds.com/geography-categories/europe-funds-and-etfs/

Ethics are personal, and responsible products can invest in a variety of different ways. Therefore, it's important to check the individual stock constituents and the overall objective of each product to ensure it meets your values; otherwise, you could invest in a regular investment product elsewhere. Still, building a portfolio with responsible products isn't easy. It can take time to understand the approach each product is taking — including that some products will accept particular risks, whether sector bets or greater weights for individual stock positions, in the interest of having a more ESG-friendly portfolio. This may include exclusions: for example, where you don't want to own any companies that are producing fossil fuels, which might give the portfolio a very divergent sector positioning relative to the broader market benchmark, such as the S&P 500 or FTSE 100 indexes.

Investment in sustainable fund products saw a global increase in the third quarter of 2020, according to data from Morningstar, with inflows in all major markets contributing to a new high of US$1.2 trillion in total ESG fund assets, with US$800 billion alone in Europe.

Understanding passive versus active exposure

Many products, particularly those focused on a specific underlying index, aim to reduce the tracking error relative to an established market benchmark. So, a product aims for the "best of both worlds" by keeping performance in line with the market benchmark and delivering index-like performance while incorporating ESG characteristics at the same time. Most ETF or index tracker portfolios use this method, taking a more passive approach to ESG investing, while also tending to be more returns-focused with an ESG tilt, rather than values-focused with a returns tilt. In addition, passively managed products tend to have lower costs, due to their standardized approach.

REMEMBER

Nevertheless, some passive products may have a more specific ESG bias than others, so it's worth finding those that fit better with your values, while also considering aspects such as the total assets under management or daily trading volumes to gauge how easy it may be to buy or sell your holdings over time.

On the other hand, mutual fund portfolios tend to have a more actively managed bias. These products can have a more values-based focus, depending on the fund; however, by their nature, they will also have a higher tracking error relative to the benchmark. Again, you should analyze the respective funds to find those that most closely match your ESG and investment goals.

TIP

Investors who have more time available to consider their own bottom-up research may consider comparing the main holdings of different mutual funds, reconciling the differences, and then buying the individual stocks that meet their criteria. But, of course, they will also subsequently need to keep a close eye on those stocks, as they won't have a portfolio manager monitoring any changes for them. In addition, some brokerage accounts provide free transactions, so that would keep costs to a minimum while negating any mutual fund fees, but this is only suitable for proactive investors.

Applying ESG metrics

TIP

Whether you take a passive or active approach (see the previous section), you should consider the rating, or score, given to each company to determine how ESG friendly a company is considered to be. The following links allow you to view the ratings supplied by two of the major rating providers that openly display them, whereas for other providers, you need to subscribe to their data feeds:

>> www.sustainalytics.com/esg-ratings/

>> www.msci.com/our-solutions/esg-investing/esg-ratings

You should recognize that, contrary to credit ratings — where bond issuers request a credit rating and relevant information is collated through a number of interviews with the company before a rating is published — ESG ratings are in most cases unsolicited. ESG rating agencies usually make their assessments based on publicly available information, including corporate sustainability reports and information from corporate websites. Some agencies may also send questionnaires to firms and allow them to review and comment on ratings before finalizing them.

REMEMBER

Investors can monitor how a company scores on the three ESG categories (environmental, social, and governance), as one of these themes may be more relevant for a company in a given industry sector — for example, environmental for oil and gas companies. Investors can then compare the company rating relative to those of their peers. More generally, a high governance score suggests that a company is run well and in a sustainable manner, while a high social score suggests a safe work environment in the broadest definition for all employees. Companies that score highly usually respond better to broader issues, such as the COVID-19 pandemic, and therefore perform better financially than their non-ESG counterparts, which is what happened in the first quarter of 2020 and beyond.

Looking at ESG metrics related to performance

For your information, *index trackers,* or ETFs following specific indexes, tend to overweight investments in companies that score well on a variety of ESG criteria, whether it be the level of carbon emissions, the number of women on the company board, or the quality of disclosure on executive pay. Likewise, they also tend to overweight companies that score poorly on these measures. This helps these providers track the established benchmark index they are replicating, while potentially providing outperformance in given market conditions. For example, many of these funds were rewarded during the market crash in the first quarter of 2020 as oil prices fell and they had limited exposure to fossil fuel energy stocks.

Some of the mutual funds would have gone a step further as they actively exclude investment in sectors such as pure coal producers, makers of controversial weapons, tobacco companies, or persistent violators of the UN Global Compact Principles, including human rights, labor, the environment, and anti-corruption. However, while there was a focus on not buying fossil fuel companies, the 'S' and 'G' factors shouldn't be forgotten, because they continue to have greater prominence as funds focus on healthcare, due to the coronavirus pandemic, social issues highlighted by the Black Lives Matter protests, and governance issues in relation to board diversity and executive pay.

WARNING

It should be noted that technology stocks generally score highly on ESG factors. Where passive or mutual funds overweighted such companies in 2020, because they represented "best-in-class" companies based on their higher ESG scores, investors will have benefitted from the outperformance of the FAANG stocks (Facebook, Amazon, Apple, Netflix, and Google). However, as with any other investments, it's important to remember not to chase "performance for performance's sake." Some commentators have associated the "ESG bubble" with the "tech bubble" in terms of potential inflated valuations, and ESG has certainly benefitted from the technology valuation momentum.

Disclosure, Reporting, and Engagement

The ESG landscape has already changed fundamentally as further principles and standards have been drawn up to help bring ESG thinking into the mainstream, and many ESG-supporting organizations offer guidance and practical support to businesses and investors.

Investors often want to understand some of the disclosure and reporting requirements that many companies follow. Given that in many jurisdictions there are no mandatory requirements to provide such information, which also provides guidance for the rating agencies' scores, the following entities are prominent organizations:

>> www.globalreporting.org/public-policy-partnerships/the-reporting-landscape/

>> www.sasb.org/standards-overview/materiality-map/

>> www.cdp.net/en/companies-discloser

Direct engagement with companies is a key approach to further understanding a company's ESG credentials. Moreover, those investors interested in criticizing a company themselves should also consider how they can actively vote on proposals submitted by management or other investors in advance of company annual meetings, or ensure that their proxy vote will be submitted by a delegate. Similar to exercising your democratic right to vote, you should carefully review any annual proxy materials to consider how you should vote on given proposals. For example, many investors are now cooperating on shareholder resolutions around issues such as climate change.

This approach is openly available to direct investors, while those investing via ETFs or mutual funds can monitor your fund manager's response to such voting requirements, as you should ensure that they represent your values, in line with the values suggested by the purpose of the fund itself. Central to ESG integration is engagement with the asset managers to confirm that they are determined to improve their ESG integration practices over time, and also to ensure that they are engaging with underlying company management teams to influence their behavior in a way that is supportive of good corporate governance, environmental policies, and social practices. For further information, visit https://partners-cap.com/publications/a-framework-for-responsible-investing.

Further Asset Class Information

The information I provide earlier in this appendix focuses on managers' approaches to identifying and understanding the key ESG risks and opportunities of each company, industry, and sector for equity-focused investments. There are fewer funds to choose from that focus on corporate bonds, but ESG ratings can be applied equally to fixed income exposure. In addition, there can be questions around the ESG credentials of certain countries' government bonds.

WARNING

There are also funds that invest based on specific sustainable investment themes, including resource efficiency, sustainable transport, education, and well-being. Although, you should note that any approach where a fund's focus moves toward small and medium-sized companies, this approach can add some risks that investors should be comfortable with, and fewer fund choices will be available.

TIP

However, most investors who are considering putting their own ESG portfolios together should think about getting some professional guidance or working with a financial advisor. Some finance investment professionals are enhancing their understanding of ESG investing, so retail investors shouldn't be concerned about seeking assistance.

Index

About the Author

Brendan Bradley has most recently co-authored *FinTech for Dummies,* published in August 2020. He is associated with a number of FinTech firms, acting as non-executive chairman for Fregnan and iPushPull while being on the advisory board of FinTech Circle, Limeglass, RISE Financial Technologies, and Waymark Tech. He is also a co-founder of Seismic Foundry, a seed-stage venture capital group. With all of these firms, he is focused on developing new ideas around changing market structure, regulation, and technology as an investor, entrepreneur, and consultant.

Prior to this, Brendan was an executive board member and Chief Innovation Officer at Eurex, the largest European derivatives exchange, where he was responsible for championing and "brokering" new ideas, both internally and externally, and looking for new opportunities within the changing market environment, having previously run product development. He has worked in the financial services industry for more than 30 years, leading the product/business development for most of the current high volume/revenue contracts traded on Eurex and the London International Financial Futures and Options (LIFFE) (now operating under the Intercontinental Exchange, or ICE), and playing a major role in the development of the European futures and options industry.

Dedication

I dedicate this book to my beautiful girls — my wife Marilu, and daughters Sinead, Daniella, and Jessica — for their love and support during my self-imposed lockdown and isolation during parts of this book!

Author's Acknowledgments

I would like to acknowledge the support and patience of the Wiley team, from Tracy Boggier for backing the initial outline, to Georgette Beatty and Marylouise Wiack for making it more reader-friendly, and Siobhan Cleary for ensuring the accuracy of the content. Last but not least, thanks to Michelle Hacker for her patience in guiding me through the process, keeping me on track, and pushing me over the line. Thanks also to Will Oulton for supporting the initial outline and highlighting emerging topics.

Publisher's Acknowledgments

Senior Acquisitions Editor: Tracy Boggier

Project Manager: Michelle Hacker

Development Editor: Georgette Beatty

Copy Editor: Marylouise Wiack

Technical Editor: Siobhan Cleary

Proofreader: Debbye Butler

Production Editor: Tamilmani Varadharaj

Cover Photo: © adempercem/Getty Images

Take dummies with you everywhere you go!

Whether you are excited about e-books, want more from the web, must have your mobile apps, or are swept up in social media, dummies makes everything easier.

Find us online!

dummies
A Wiley Brand

Leverage the power

Dummies is the global leader in the reference category and one of the most trusted and highly regarded brands in the world. No longer just focused on books, customers now have access to the dummies content they need in the format they want. Together we'll craft a solution that engages your customers, stands out from the competition, and helps you meet your goals.

Advertising & Sponsorships

Connect with an engaged audience on a powerful multimedia site, and position your message alongside expert how-to content. Dummies.com is a one-stop shop for free, online information and know-how curated by a team of experts.

- Targeted ads
- Video
- Email Marketing
- Microsites
- Sweepstakes sponsorship

20 MILLION PAGE VIEWS EVERY SINGLE MONTH

15 MILLION UNIQUE VISITORS PER MONTH

43% OF ALL VISITORS ACCESS THE SITE VIA THEIR MOBILE DEVICES

700,000 NEWSLETTER SUBSCRIPTIONS TO THE INBOXES OF *300,000* UNIQUE INDIVIDUALS EVERY WEEK

# of dummies

Custom Publishing

Reach a global audience in any language by creating a solution that will differentiate you from competitors, amplify your message, and encourage customers to make a buying decision.

- Apps
- Books
- eBooks
- Video
- Audio
- Webinars

Brand Licensing & Content

Leverage the strength of the world's most popular reference brand to reach new audiences and channels of distribution.

For more information, visit **dummies.com/biz**

PERSONAL ENRICHMENT

Staying Sharp	Facebook	Guitar	Investing	Beekeeping	Digital Photography
9781119187790	9781119179030	9781119293354	9781119293347	9781119310068	9781119235606
USA $26.00	USA $21.99	USA $24.99	USA $22.99	USA $22.99	USA $24.99
CAN $31.99	CAN $25.99	CAN $29.99	CAN $27.99	CAN $27.99	CAN $29.99
UK £19.99	UK £16.99	UK £17.99	UK £16.99	UK £16.99	UK £17.99

Meditation	Pregnancy	Samsung Galaxy S7	iPhone	Crocheting	Nutrition
9781119251163	9781119235491	9781119279952	9781119283133	9781119287117	9781119130246
USA $24.99	USA $26.99	USA $24.99	USA $24.99	USA $24.99	USA $22.99
CAN $29.99	CAN $31.99	CAN $29.99	CAN $29.99	CAN $29.99	CAN $27.99
UK £17.99	UK £19.99	UK £17.99	UK £17.99	UK £16.99	UK £16.99

PROFESSIONAL DEVELOPMENT

 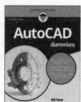   

Windows 10	AutoCAD	Excel 2016	QuickBooks 2017	macOS Sierra	LinkedIn	Windows 10 All-in-One
9781119311041	9781119255796	9781119293439	9781119281467	9781119280651	9781119251132	9781119310563
USA $24.99	USA $39.99	USA $26.99	USA $26.99	USA $29.99	USA $24.99	USA $34.00
CAN $29.99	CAN $47.99	CAN $31.99	CAN $31.99	CAN $35.99	CAN $29.99	CAN $41.99
UK £17.99	UK £27.99	UK £19.99	UK £19.99	UK £21.99	UK £17.99	UK £24.99

SharePoint 2016	Fundamental Analysis	Networking	Office 2016	Office 365	Salesforce.com	Coding
9781119181705	9781119263593	9781119257769	9781119293477	9781119265313	9781119239314	9781119293323
USA $29.99	USA $26.99	USA $29.99	USA $26.99	USA $24.99	USA $29.99	USA $29.99
CAN $35.99	CAN $31.99	CAN $35.99	CAN $31.99	CAN $29.99	CAN $35.99	CAN $35.99
UK £21.99	UK £19.99	UK £21.99	UK £19.99	UK £17.99	UK £21.99	UK £21.99

dummies.com

dummies
A Wiley Brand

Learning Made Easy

ACADEMIC

9781119293576
USA $19.99
CAN $23.99
UK £15.99

9781119293637
USA $19.99
CAN $23.99
UK £15.99

9781119293491
USA $19.99
CAN $23.99
UK £15.99

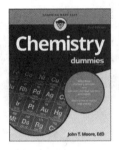

9781119293460
USA $19.99
CAN $23.99
UK £15.99

9781119293590
USA $19.99
CAN $23.99
UK £15.99

9781119215844
USA $26.99
CAN $31.99
UK £19.99

9781119293378
USA $22.99
CAN $27.99
UK £16.99

9781119293521
USA $19.99
CAN $23.99
UK £15.99

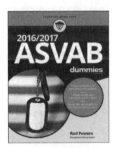

9781119239178
USA $18.99
CAN $22.99
UK £14.99

9781119263883
USA $26.99
CAN $31.99
UK £19.99

Available Everywhere Books Are Sold

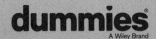

Small books for big imaginations

9781119177173
USA $9.99
CAN $9.99
UK £8.99

9781119177272
USA $9.99
CAN $9.99
UK £8.99

9781119177241
USA $9.99
CAN $9.99
UK £8.99

9781119177210
USA $9.99
CAN $9.99
UK £8.99

9781119262657
USA $9.99
CAN $9.99
UK £6.99

9781119291336
USA $9.99
CAN $9.99
UK £6.99

9781119233527
USA $9.99
CAN $9.99
UK £6.99

9781119291220
USA $9.99
CAN $9.99
UK £6.99

9781119177302
USA $9.99
CAN $9.99
UK £8.99

Unleash Their Creativity

dummies.com

dummies®
A Wiley Brand